Ma[...]

DEAR K ♡

We hope you enjoy this
special bilingual (English +
Spanish) Bible!

All our love,
     Kathleen + José

Mi nombre es
My Name is

_____.

Por favor, ¿podrías leerme esto? Gracias.

Please, could you read me this? Thank you.

La misión de Editorial Vida es ser la compañía líder en satisfacer las necesidades de las personas con recursos cuyo contenido glorifique al Señor Jesucristo y promueva principios bíblicos.

La Biblia para principiantes - Bilingüe
The Beginner's Bible - Bilingual
Edición bilingüe publicada por
Editorial Vida – 2016
Nashville, Tennessee
© **2005, 2016 por Vida**

Originally published in the U.S.A. under the title:
The Beginner's Bible
Copyright © 2005 by Zondervan
Illustrations © 2005, 2016 by Zondervan
Published by permission of Zondervan, Grand Rapids, Michigan 49530
All rights reserved.
Further reproduction or distribution is prohibited.

Editora en Jefe /Editor in Chief: *Graciela Lelli*
Traducción /Translation: *Marcela Robaina*
Adaptación del diseño al español /Design adaptation in Spanish: *Mauricio Diaz*

A menos que se indique lo contrario, todos los textos bíblicos han sido tomados de La Santa Biblia, Nueva Versión Internacional® NVI® © 1999 por Biblica, Inc.® Usados con permiso. Todos los derechos reservados mundialmente. Añadir párrafo: el símbolo ® debe ser pequeño y elevado como el TM

Unless otherwise noted Scripture quotations are from the New International Version®, NIV®. Copyright © 1973, 1978, 1984, 2011 by Biblica, Inc.™ Used by permission of Zondervan. All rights reserved worldwide. www.zondervan.com

ISBN: 978-0-8297-6743-8

CATEGORÍA: JUVENIL NO FICCIÓN/Religión/Historias bíblicas/General
CATEGORY (BISSAC): JUVENIL NO FICTION/Religion/Bible Stories/General

IMPRESO EN CHINA
PRINTED IN CHINA

19 20 DSC 8 7

La Biblia para principiantes Bilingüe

Historias bíblicas para niños

The Beginner's Bible - Bilingual®

Timeless Children's Stories

Vidaniños

Contenido

ANTIGUO TESTAMENTO

NUEVO TESTAMENTO

THE OLD TESTAMENT

THE NEW TESTAMENT

El Antiguo Testamento
The Old Testament

Historias bíblicas para niños
Timeless Bible Stories

El principio

Génesis 1

En el principio, la tierra
estaba vacía.
La oscuridad lo cubría todo.
Pero Dios tenía un plan.

The Beginning

Genesis 1

In the beginning, the world
was empty.
Darkness was everywhere.
But God had a plan.

Dios separó la luz de la oscuridad.
Dijo: «¡Que haya luz!».
Y se prendió la luz.
A la luz la llamó «día» y a la oscuridad la llamó «noche».
Así terminó el primer día.

God separated the light from the darkness.
"Let there be light!" he said.
And the light turned on.
He called the light "day."
And he called the darkness "night."
This was the end of the very first day.

Entonces, Dios dijo: «Voy a separar las aguas». Y así fue que dejó arriba el agua de las nubes y puso abajo el agua del océano. Al espacio que se formó entre ellos lo llamó «cielo». Y así terminó el segundo día.

Then God said, "I will divide the waters."
He separated the waters in the clouds above from the waters in the ocean below.
He called the space between them "sky."
This was the end of the second day.

Luego, Dios amontonó las aguas por un lado para que apareciera la tierra seca. Hizo brotar plantas de muchas formas y colores. Formó las montañas, las colinas y los valles. Y así terminó el tercer día.

Next, God rolled back the waters and some dry ground appeared.
He made plants of many shapes and colors.
He made mountains, hills, and valleys.
This was the end of the third day.

Dios puso al sol brillante en el cielo para que alumbrara durante el día. Puso una luna radiante y estrellas centelleantes en el cielo para la noche. Y así terminó el cuarto día.

God put a shining sun in the sky for daytime.
He put a glowing moon and twinkling stars in the sky for nighttime.
This was the end of the fourth day.

El quinto día, Dios creó los peces sinuosos y las criaturas nadadoras que viven en el océano. Luego, hizo a los pájaros para que volaran por el cielo.

On the fifth day, God made swishy fish and squiggly creatures to live in the ocean. Then God made birds to fly across the sky.

El sexto día, Dios creó los animales que trepan, se arrastran, saltan y galopan.

Entonces, del polvo formó a la criatura más maravillosa de todas: una persona.

Dios lo llamó Adán.

El séptimo día, Dios descansó.

On the sixth day, God made animals to creep, crawl, hop, and gallop.

Then from the dust, God made the most wonderful creature of all—a person.

God named him Adam.

On the seventh day, God rested.

Adán y Eva

Génesis 2

Dios había plantado un hermoso jardín para Adán en un lugar llamado Edén.
Un río cruzó el jardín.

Adam and Eve

Genesis 2

God had planted a beautiful garden for Adam in a place called Eden.
A river flowed through the garden.

Adán estaba encantado con su nuevo hogar. Su tarea fue poner nombre a los animales y cuidar el jardín. Adán quería mucho a los animales, pero no podía encontrar a ningún amigo ideal para él. Entonces, Dios creó a la mujer.

Adam loved his new home. His job was to name all the animals and care for the garden.
Adam loved all the animals, but he could not find a friend that was just right for him. So God created a woman.

Adán la llamó Eva. Era justo la compañera que Adán necesitaba. Adán y Eva se amaban. Juntos cuidaban el jardín de Dios.

Adam named her Eve. She was just right for Adam. Adam and Eve loved each other. Together they took care of God's garden.

La serpiente engañosa

Génesis 3

The Sneaky Snake

Genesis 3

En el jardín de Edén había muchos árboles. Dios les dijo a Adán y Eva: «Pueden comer el fruto de todos los árboles excepto de uno. No coman nunca el fruto del árbol del conocimiento del bien y del mal».

Many trees grew in the Garden of Eden.
God told Adam and Eve, "You may eat the fruit from any tree except for one. Never eat the fruit from the tree of the knowledge of good and evil."

Pero en el jardín también había una serpiente engañosa. Un día, la serpiente vio que Eva estaba cerca de ese árbol especial. Le susurró: «¿Así que Dios de veras les dijo que no comieran el fruto de este árbol?».

Now, there was a sneaky snake in the garden.
One day, the snake saw Eve near the special tree.
It hissed, "Did God really tell you not to eat the fruit from this tree?"

La serpiente quería que Eva desobedeciera a Dios. Le dijo: «Tendrías que probar un poco de ese fruto sabroso. Si lo pruebas, serás como Dios. Podrás conocer la diferencia entre el bien y el mal».

The snake wanted Eve to disobey God.
It said, "You should try some of this tasty fruit. If you eat it, you will be like God. You will be able to tell the difference between good and evil."

El fruto se veía sabroso. Eva recordó lo que Dios había dicho, pero igual comió del fruto. Después, le dio a probar un poco a Adán y él también lo comió.

The fruit looked tasty. Eve remembered what God had said, but she ate the fruit anyway.
Then Eve gave some to Adam. He took a bite too.

Mientras el sol se ponía, Adán y Eva escucharon a Dios que estaba caminando por el jardín, buscándolos. Adán y Eva se escondieron entre los árboles. Tenían miedo.

As the sun was going down, Adam and Eve heard God walking through the garden. He was looking for them. Adam and Eve hid among the trees. They were afraid.

«¿Qué han hecho?», preguntó Dios. «¿Comieron del fruto del árbol prohibido?».
«Sí, pero fue Eva la que me lo dio», dijo Adán.
«Sí, pero porque la serpiente me engañó», dijo Eva.

"What have you done?" God asked.
"Did you eat the fruit from the forbidden tree?"
Adam said, "Yes, but Eve gave it to me."
Eve said, "Yes, but the snake tricked me."

«Por causa de lo que has hecho, siempre te arrastrarás sobre tu vientre», dijo Dios a la serpiente. Y a Adán y Eva les dijo: «Y ustedes, como me desobedecieron, ya no vivirán más en el jardín».

God told the snake, "Because of what you did, you will always crawl on your belly." Then he told Adam and Eve, "Because you disobeyed me, you can no longer live in the garden."

Adán y Eva salieron del jardín. Dios puso ángeles y una espada ardiente para custodiar la entrada. Adán y Eva nunca más podrían entrar en el jardín.

Adam and Eve left the garden. God placed angels and a flaming sword to guard the entrance. Adam and Eve would not be allowed in the garden again.

El arca de Noé

Génesis 6—9

Noah's Ark

Genesis 6–9

Después de que Adán y Eva se fueron del jardín, nacieron muchas personas.
La gente vivía haciendo cosas malas y se olvidaron de Dios.

After Adam and Eve left the garden, many people were born.
The people kept doing bad things, and they forgot about God.

Todos, excepto Noé.
Noé amaba a Dios.

Except Noah.
Noah loved God.

Dios estaba triste porque todos, excepto Noé, se habían olvidado de él. Le contó a Noé su plan de comenzar de nuevo. «Constrúyete un arca», le dijo Dios. «Aquí te muestro cómo hacerla». Entonces, Noé y su familia comenzaron a construir el arca.

God was sad that everyone but Noah forgot about him.
He told Noah about his plan to start over.
"Make yourself an ark," God said.
"Here's how." So Noah and his family began working on the ark.

Cuando la terminaron, Dios le dijo: «Toma a tu familia y a una pareja de cada animal y suban al arca». Los animales entraron al enorme barco de Noé arrastrándose, trepando, saltando y galopando.

When it was done, God said, "Take your family and two of every animal into the ark." Animals creeped, crawled, hopped, and galloped onto Noah's new boat.

Cuando todos habían entrado, comenzó a llover. Y llovió. Y llovió. Las olas mecían el arca para un lado y para el otro, y el agua subía y subía.

After everyone was inside, the rain began to fall. And fall. And fall. The ark rocked this way and that way on the rising water.

Por fin, paró de llover. ¡Había agua por todos lados! La gente dentro del arca estaba a salvo. Noé y su familia estaban muy contentos.

Finally, the rain stopped. Water covered everything! Everyone inside the ark was safe. Noah and his family were very happy.

Un día, Noé envió una paloma a buscar tierra firme. La paloma voló y voló, pero, como no pudo encontrar nada, al final regresó. A la semana, Noé la envió de nuevo. Esta vez regresó con una rama de olivo. Noé estaba feliz: «¡Tiene que haber encontrado tierra!».

One day, Noah sent a dove to find land.
It flew and flew but never found any.
So it came back. One week later, Noah sent the dove out again.
This time it brought him an olive leaf. Noah cheered, "It must have found land!"

El arca al final se encalló sobre la cima de una montaña.
Dios le dijo a Noé que saliera el arca. Noé y su familia alabaron a Dios. Dios puso un hermoso arco iris en el cielo. Era la señal de su promesa de que nunca más inundaría toda la tierra.

The ark finally came to rest on the top of a mountain.
God told Noah to leave the ark. Noah and his family praised God.
God put a beautiful rainbow in the sky. It was a sign of his promise to never flood the whole earth again.

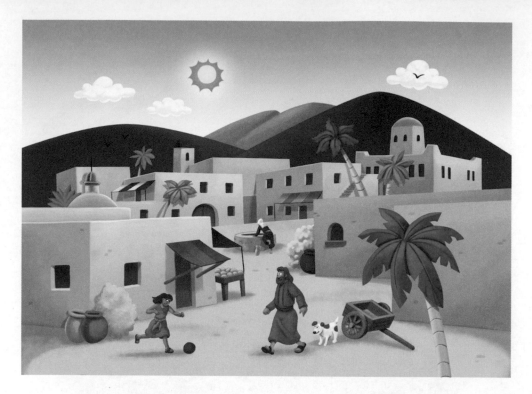

Una torre alta

Génesis 11

Después de ese diluvio, toda la gente hablaba el mismo idioma. Había una palabra para decir «hola». Había otra palabra para decir «mamá» y otra para «papá».

The Tall Tower

Genesis 11

After the flood, everyone spoke the same language. One word meant "hello." One word meant "Mom," and one word meant "Dad."

La gente dijo: «Si nos ponemos a trabajar juntos, podremos lograr cualquier cosa. Vamos a construir una torre que llegue hasta el cielo. ¡Entonces todos verán qué grandes que somos!».

The people said, "If we work together, we can do anything. Let's build a tower that goes all the way up to heaven. Then everyone will see how great we are!"

La gente se puso a construir la torre.

Trabajaban y la torre crecía y crecía. Empezaban a fanfarronear.

A Dios no le gustó lo que hacían. Era como si ya no necesitaran a Dios.

The people worked on their tower.

They built it taller and taller.

They began to brag.

God did not like the way they were acting.

It was as if they no longer needed him.

Así que Dios confundió su lenguaje. Cuando intentaban hablar el uno con el otro, sonaba nada más como «ba-ba-babel». ¡Estaban todos confundidos!

So God mixed up their language.
When they tried to talk to each other, it sounded like "babble."
Everyone was confused!

Entonces, Dios esparció a la gente por toda la tierra. Tuvieron que dejar de construir su torre. A partir de entonces, esa torre se llamó «la torre de Babel».

Then God scattered the people all over the earth.
They had to stop building their tower.
From then on, the tower was called "Babel."

Un nuevo hogar

Génesis 12—17

Abraham amaba a Dios. Su esposa Sara también amaba a Dios.

A New Home

Genesis 12–17

Abraham loved God. So did his wife Sarah.

Un día, Dios le dijo a Abraham
que se fuera a una tierra nueva.
Entonces, junto con sus
sirvientes, Abraham y Sara
empacaron sus cosas y partieron.

One day, God told Abraham to
move to a new land.
So, along with their helpers,
Abraham and Sarah packed up
and went.

Abraham tenía un sobrino llamado Lot. Lot y todos sus sirvientes también se fueron con Abraham.

Abraham's nephew was Lot. Lot and all his helpers went with them too.

Los sirvientes comenzaron a pelearse porque no había suficiente pasto para los muchos animales. Entonces, Abraham le sugirió a Lot: «Elige la tierra donde quieras vivir».

The helpers began to fight. There was not enough grass for all the animals. So Abraham said to Lot, "You pick your own land to live on."

Lot eligió la mejor tierra, la
que tenía el pasto más verde
y más agua para sus animales.
Lot se fue a su nuevo hogar.

Lot chose the best land.
It had the most green grass and
the most water for his animals.
Lot moved to his new home.

Luego, Dios bendijo a Abraham. Dijo: «Toda la tierra que ves aquí será tuya para siempre. Además, tú y Sara tendrán la bendición de tener muchos hijos».

Then God gave Abraham a blessing.
God said, "All the land you see here will be yours forever. Also, you and Sarah will be blessed with many children."

Dios condujo a Abraham y
a Sara a un lugar llamado
Hebrón. Era hermoso.

God led Abraham and Sarah
to a place called Hebron.
It was beautiful.

Las visitas

Génesis 18; 21

Un día de mucho calor, Abraham se encontraba descansando cerca de su carpa cuando escuchó unas pisadas.

The Visitors

Genesis 18; 21

One hot day, Abraham was resting near his tent. He heard footsteps.

Había tres hombres parados
muy cerca. Abraham salió a
saludarlos. «¿Quisieran descansar a la sombra? Tenemos
mucha agua fresca si desean
tomar. ¿Les puedo traer algo
para comer?».

Three men were standing
nearby.
Abraham went out to greet them.
"Would you like to rest in the
shade? We have plenty of cool
water to drink. Can I get you
something to eat?"

Abraham le dijo a Sara que
tenían visitas.
Le pidió que hiciera algo rico
para comer.

Abraham told Sarah about the
visitors.
He asked her to make a tasty
meal.

Mientras comían, las tres visitas anunciaron unas noticias emocionantes. Dijeron: «Tu esposa va a tener un hijo».

While they were eating, the three visitors shared some exciting news. They said, "Your wife is going to have a son."

Sara estaba escuchando lo que hablaban y se rio. *Ya estoy muy vieja,* pensó.

Dios preguntó a Abraham: «¿Por qué se rio Sara? Todo es posible para el SEÑOR».

Sarah heard what they said. She laughed, thinking, *I am too old.*

God asked Abraham, "Why did Sarah laugh? Anything is possible with the LORD."

Efectivamente, al año
siguiente, Sara tuvo un bebé.
Lo llamaron Isaac.

Sure enough, the next year,
Sarah had a baby boy.
They named him Isaac.

Una novia para Isaac

Génesis 24—25

A Bride for Isaac

Genesis 24–25

Cuando Isaac creció, su padre, Abraham, quería que se casara. Abraham le pidió a uno de sus siervos: «Ve a mi país de origen. Allí encontrarás la novia perfecta para Isaac».

When Isaac grew up, his father, Abraham, wanted him to get married.
Abraham told one of his servants, "Go to my homeland. There you will find the perfect bride for Isaac."

Abraham despidió a su siervo y lo envió con diez camellos y muchas joyas y ropa.
Eran regalos para la novia de Isaac.

So Abraham sent the servant on his way with ten camels and a lot of jewelry and clothes.
They were gifts for Isaac's new bride.

El siervo llegó al país de origen de Abraham. Se detuvo en un pozo y oró:
«Querido Dios, muéstrame a la mujer que has elegido para Isaac. Sabré quién es si me ofrece agua y da de beber a mis camellos».

The servant reached Abraham's homeland.
He stopped by a well and prayed, "Dear God, please show me the woman you have chosen for Isaac. I will know she is the one if she offers water to me and my camels."

Ni bien terminó de orar,
una joven con un cántaro
venía caminando hacia el pozo.
Después de que ella
llenara su cántaro, el siervo le
pidió agua.
Ella se la dio. Luego,
les dio de beber a los camellos.
¡Era la respuesta a su oración!
La joven se llamaba Rebeca.

Before he finished praying,
a young woman with a jar
walked toward the well.
After she filled her jar, the
servant asked her for a drink.
She gave him a drink.
Then she gave water to his
camels. She was the answer to
his prayer!
Her name was Rebekah.

El siervo le dio los regalos y, luego, fue a conocer a su padre.

El siervo le pidió permiso para llevarla a Isaac. Rebeca le dijo al siervo que ella estaría encantada de ir.

The servant gave her the gifts, and they went to meet her father.

The servant asked for his permission to take Rebekah to Isaac. Rebekah told the servant she would be happy to go.

Cuando Isaac vio a Rebeca, se enamoró de ella. Poco tiempo después se casaron. Isaac y Rebeca tuvieron dos varones mellizos: Esaú y Jacob.

When Isaac saw Rebekah, he fell in love with her. Soon, they got married. Isaac and Rebekah had twin boys named Esau and Jacob.

La bendición de Isaac

Génesis 27

Cuando Isaac ya era viejo, no podía ver muy bien. Llamó a su hijo mayor, a Esaú: «Prepárame mi comida favorita. Entonces, te daré la bendición de Dios».

Isaac's Blessing

Genesis 27

When Isaac was an old man, he could not see very well. He called for his firstborn son, Esau.
"Bring me my favorite dinner. Then I will give you God's blessing."

«Te prepararé un plato especial», dijo Esaú.
Y se fue a cazar algo que pudiera cocinar.

"I will make a special meal for you," said Esau.
Then he hunted for some meat to cook.

Rebeca, la esposa de Isaac, quería que Jacob recibiera la bendición de Dios. Entonces, mientras Esaú estaba de caza, le dijo a Jacob cuál era su plan. Ella preparó la comida favorita de Isaac. Luego, cubrió los brazos de Jacob con pieles de cabra.

Isaac's wife Rebekah wanted Jacob to get God's blessing. So, while Esau was hunting, she told Jacob her plan. She made Isaac's dinner. Then she tied goatskins around Jacob's arms.

Jacob le llevó la cena a su
padre. Después de comer, Isaac
extendió su mano para bendecir a su hijo. Isaac creyó que
Jacob era Esaú y le dio su
bendición.

Jacob took the meal to his
father.
After dinner, Isaac reached out
to bless his son.
Isaac thought Jacob was Esau.
So he gave Jacob his blessing.

Cuando Esaú regresó, descubrió lo que había sucedido.
Esaú estaba furioso.
Quería lastimar a Jacob.
Rebeca le pidió a Isaac que enviara a Jacob a la casa de su tío Labán.

When Esau returned, he found out what had happened.
Esau was very angry.
He wanted to hurt Jacob.
Rebekah asked Isaac to send Jacob to his uncle Laban's house.

El sueño de Jacob

Génesis 28

Jacob hizo el largo viaje.
Su tío Labán vivía muy lejos.
Una noche, se recostó en el
suelo y usó una piedra como
almohada.
Jacob se quedó dormido.

Jacob's Dream

Genesis 28

Jacob traveled for many miles.
His uncle Laban lived far
away.
One night, he lay on the
ground, using a stone for his
pillow.
Jacob fell fast asleep.

Jacob soñó con una escalera que llegaba hasta el cielo. Ángeles subían y bajaban. Dios dijo: «Yo te cuido, Jacob. Un día, toda esta tierra será tuya y de tu familia».

Jacob dreamed of a stairway to heaven. Angels walked up and down. God said, "I am watching over you, Jacob. Someday, all of this land will belong to you and your family."

A la mañana siguiente, cuando Jacob se despertó, dijo: «¡El Señor está en este lugar!». Tomó la piedra que había usado de almohada y la puso como recuerdo de su sueño. Jacob alabó a Dios y continuó su viaje.

The next morning, when Jacob woke up, he said, "The Lord is in this place!"
He took his stone pillow and set it up as a reminder of his dream.
Jacob praised God. Then he continued on his way.

Jacob y Esaú se reencuentran

Génesis 29

Mientras Jacob vivía con su tío Labán, se hizo pastor. Se enamoró y se casó.

Jacob and Esau Meet Again

Genesis 29

While Jacob lived with his uncle Laban, he became a shepherd. He fell in love and got married.

Dios bendijo a Jacob con muchos hijos.
Jacob también tenía muchas ovejas, burros y camellos.
Un día, Dios le dijo que regresara a su tierra de origen.

God blessed Jacob with many sons.
Jacob also had many sheep, donkeys, and camels.
One day, God told Jacob to go back to his homeland.

Jacob deseaba regresar, pero tenía miedo de su hermano Esaú.
Pensaba que Esaú todavía estaría enojado con él.

Jacob wanted to go back, but he was afraid of his brother, Esau.
He thought Esau would still be angry with him.

Pero Jacob obedeció a Dios.
Él y su familia empacaron
todo lo que tenían. Jacob envió
unos siervos para que, adelan-
tándose, le dieran unos regalos
a Esaú.

But Jacob obeyed God.
He and his family packed up
everything they owned.
Jacob sent servants ahead to
offer gifts to Esau.

Para sorpresa de Jacob,
Esaú corrió a recibirlo
con un abrazo bien grande.
Estaban muy contentos
de volverse a ver.

Much to Jacob's surprise,
Esau ran to meet him.
And he gave Jacob a big hug.
They were so happy to see
each other again.

La túnica colorida de José

Génesis 37

Joseph's Colorful Robe

Genesis 37

Jacob tuvo doce hijos. Uno de sus hijos fue José.
Jacob lo amaba más que a todos los otros hijos.

Joseph was one of Jacob's twelve sons.
Jacob loved him more than all of his other sons.

Jacob le hizo una túnica de muchos colores. Sus hermanos estaban celosos. Ellos también querían tener túnicas lindas. Y también querían que su padre los amara tanto como amaba a José.

Jacob made Joseph a colorful robe.
His brothers were jealous.
They wanted nice robes too.
And they wanted to be loved as much as Joseph was loved.

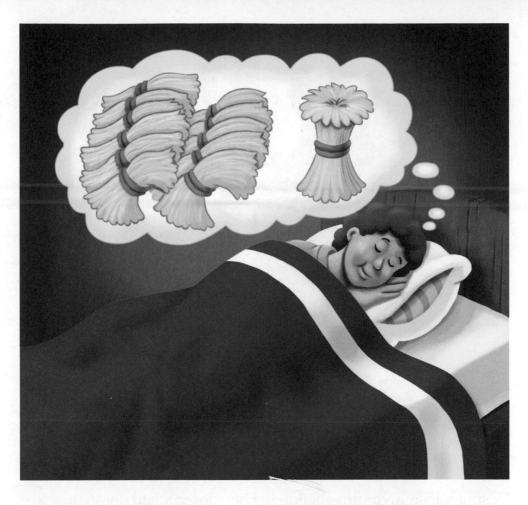

José tuvo un sueño. Se lo contó a su familia: «Estábamos atando gavillas de trigo en el campo. Las gavillas de ustedes le hacían reverencias a la mía».

Joseph had a dream. He told his family, "We were bundling grain from the field. Your bundles of grain bowed down to mine."

Después José tuvo otro sueño.
Les dijo: «Esta vez, el sol y la
luna y once estrellas me hacían
reverencias».
Su padre preguntó: «¿Se
supone que nuestra familia un
día te hará reverencias?».

Then Joseph had another
dream.
He said, "This time, the sun
and moon and eleven stars
were bowing down to me."
His father asked, "Does this
mean our family will bow
down to you someday?"

Los hermanos le tuvieron aún más rabia.

Lo metieron dentro de un pozo seco.

The brothers were even more angry.

They threw Joseph into a dry well.

Pasaron unos mercaderes.
Los hermanos les vendieron
a José como esclavo.

Along came some traders.
The brothers sold Joseph to
them as a slave.

A su padre le mintieron y le
dijeron que un animal salvaje
había matado a José.
Pero Dios estaba con José.

They lied to their father and
said Joseph had been killed by
a wild animal.
But God was with Joseph.

Los sueños del faraón

Génesis 39—41

Pharaoh's Dreams

Genesis 39–41

Los mercaderes llevaron a José a Egipto.
Allí lo metieron en la cárcel aunque José no había hecho nada malo.
José confió en que Dios lo ayudaría.
Se hizo amigo de otros presos.

The traders took Joseph to Egypt.
He was thrown into jail.
But he did nothing wrong.
Joseph trusted God to help him.
He made friends with some of the prisoners.

Uno de ellos había sido el copero del faraón. Probaba el vino antes de que lo bebiera el faraón. El faraón era el rey de Egipto. El copero dijo: «Anoche tuve un sueño. Estaba recogiendo uvas y exprimiéndolas en la copa del faraón. Y, luego, puse la copa en manos de faraón. ¿Qué significa esto, José?».

One of them had been a wine taster for Pharaoh.
Pharaoh was the leader of Egypt.
The wine taster said, "Last night, I had a dream. I was picking grapes and squeezing them into Pharaoh's cup.
Then I put the cup in his hand. What does this mean, Joseph?"

José respondió: «Volverás a ser el copero del faraón. Cuando estés libre, no te olvides de mí. Ayúdame a salir de la cárcel».

Joseph answered, "You will be Pharaoh's wine taster again. Once you are free, please don't forget about me. Help me get out of jail too."

A los pocos días, el sueño del copero se hizo realidad. Salió de la cárcel y volvió a probar el vino para el faraón. Pero se olvidó de José.

A few days later, the wine taster's dream came true. He got out of jail and became Pharaoh's wine taster once again. But he forgot about Joseph.

Después, el faraón tuvo dos sueños extraños.
En un sueño, vio siete vacas gordas y siete vacas flacas. Las flacas se comieron todas las vacas gordas.

Later, Pharaoh had two strange dreams.
In one dream, he saw seven heavy cows and seven skinny cows. The skinny cows ate up all the heavy cows.

En otro sueño, el faraón vio
siete plantas sanas y fuertes.
Luego, vio siete plantas secas.
Las secas se comieron todas
las plantas lindas.
El faraón estaba confundido.

In another dream, Pharaoh saw
seven healthy plants.
Then he saw seven dried-up
plants.
The dried-up plants ate all the
healthy plants.
Pharaoh was confused.

Los sabios de la corte del faraón también estaban confundidos. Entonces, el copero se acordó de José. Le dijo al faraón que José podría explicarle sus sueños. Con la ayuda de Dios, José le explicó al faraón lo que significaba su sueño.

Pharaoh's wise men were confused too.
Then the wine taster remembered Joseph.
He told Pharaoh that Joseph could explain his dreams.
With God's help, Joseph told Pharaoh what his dream meant.

«Durante los próximos siete años, habrá alimento en abundancia. Pero después, en los siete años siguientes, no habrá alimento suficiente porque no lloverá».

El faraón dijo: «José, tú eres un hombre muy sabio. Te haré gobernador de Egipto».

"For the next seven years, plenty of food will grow. For seven years after that, not enough food will grow because there will be no rain."

Pharaoh said, "Joseph, you are a very wise man. I will make you a ruler over Egypt."

José salva
a su familia

Génesis 42—46

Joseph Saves
His Family

Genesis 42–46

Durante los primeros siete años, José se encargó que almacenar alimento adicional para la gente de Egipto. De esa manera, cuando se perdieran las cosechas, todavía habría alimento suficiente para el pueblo.

For the first seven years, Joseph was in charge of gathering extra food for the people of Egypt. That way, when hardly any crops grew, there would still be plenty to eat.

Cuando llegaron los siete años de hambruna, la gente de otros países no tenía nada de alimento. Ni siquiera la familia de José tenía suficiente para comer. Entonces, el padre de José envió a sus hijos a Egipto para que compraran alimento.

The seven bad years began, and people in other countries had no food at all.
Even Joseph's family did not have enough to eat. So Joseph's father sent his sons to Egypt to buy some food.

Cuando los hermanos llegaron a Egipto, se presentaron ante José y le hicieron reverencias. No reconocieron a su hermano. Pero José sabía quiénes eran. José les vendió alimento y los hermanos emprendieron el viaje de regreso.

When the brothers arrived in Egypt, they went to Joseph and bowed down to him. They did not know he was their brother. But Joseph knew. Joseph sold them some food. Then the brothers left to go home.

Un tiempo después, volvieron
a Egipto para comprar más alimento. Igual que en el sueño que
había tenido José, se inclinaron
ante él, otra vez. Por fin, José les
dijo: «¡Soy su hermano!». ¡Qué
miedo tenían sus hermanos!

Sometime later, they returned
to buy more food. Just as
Joseph had dreamed, they
bowed down to him—again.
Finally, Joseph told them,
"I am your brother!"
His brothers were afraid!

Pero José les dijo que no tuvieran miedo.
«Dios transformó el mal en bien.
Tenía un plan especial para mí»,
dijo. Todos se abrazaron.

But Joseph told them not to be
afraid.
"God meant it for good.
He had a special plan for me,"
he said. They all hugged.

Los hermanos de José regresaron de prisa a su hogar. Le contaron a su padre lo que había sucedido. Jacob se puso muy feliz cuando supo que José estaba vivo. Toda la familia se fue a vivir a Egipto.

Joseph's brothers rushed home. They told their father what had happened.
Jacob was so happy to hear that Joseph was alive.
The whole family moved to Egypt.

Un bebé en una cesta

Éxodo 1—2.10

A Baby in a Basket

Exodus 1–2:10

Pasaron muchos años. Ahora otro faraón gobernaba Egipto. No sabía nada de las cosas buenas que había hecho José. Mientras, la familia de Jacob había aumentado mucho. Se llamaban los *israelitas*.

Many years passed. A new pharaoh ruled over Egypt. He did not know about the good things Joseph had done. By now there were many people in Jacob's family. They were called *Israelites*.

Al faraón no le agradaban los israelitas. Los obligó a trabajar duro.
Un día, el faraón decidió deshacerse de todos los bebés varones israelitas.

Pharaoh did not like the Israelites. He made them work hard.
One day, Pharaoh decided to get rid of all the Israelite baby boys.

Una mujer llamada Jocabed
tuvo un bebé varón. Ella
quería salvarlo.

Entonces, con mucho cuidado
lo puso dentro de una cesta
que dejó flotando en el río.

El bebé comenzó a llorar.

A woman named Jochebed had
a baby boy. She wanted to save
him.

So she gently laid her baby
inside a basket and placed him
in the river.

The baby started to cry.

La hija del faraón vio la cesta
y la abrió. Levantó al bebé con
dulzura y lo abrazó: «Quiero
que te quedes conmigo»,
le susurró la princesa.
Lo llamó Moisés porque
lo había sacado del río.

Pharaoh's daughter saw the
basket and opened it. She
gently picked up the baby and
hugged him. "I want to keep
you," the princess whispered.
She named him Moses because
she pulled him out of the water.

Miriam, la hermana mayor del bebé, había estado vigilándolo desde cierta distancia. Le dijo a la princesa: «Yo conozco a una mujer que podría ayudarla a cuidar del bebé». Miriam corrió a buscar a su mamá. ¡Qué contenta estaba Jocabed!

Miriam, the baby's big sister, had been watching nearby. She said to the princess, "I know a woman who can help you take care of the baby." So Miriam ran to get her mother. Jochebed was so happy!

Cuando el niño creció,
Jocabed se lo entregó a la
princesa.
Moisés se crio en el palacio.

When Moses was a young boy,
Jochebed returned him to the
princess.
He grew up in the palace.

La zarza ardiente

Éxodo 3

The Burning Bush

Exodus 3

Cuando Moisés ya era hombre, dejó el palacio.
El faraón todavía trataba muy mal a los israelitas.
Moisés quiso protegerlos, entonces, el faraón trató de matar a Moisés.

When Moses was a man, he left the palace.
Pharaoh was still being mean to the Israelites.
Moses tried to protect them, so Pharaoh tried to kill Moses.

Moisés se escapó de Egipto.
Se fue a un lugar llamado
Madián y se hizo pastor de
ovejas.

Moses escaped from Egypt.
He went to a place called
Midian and became a
shepherd.

Un día, mientras Moisés cuidaba las ovejas, vio algo muy extraño.

Una zarza estaba en llamas, pero no se consumía. Desde dentro de la zarza, Dios habló: «Moisés, saca a mi pueblo de Egipto. Llévalos a una tierra nueva que te mostraré. Esa tierra nueva se llama Canaán».

One day, while Moses was watching his sheep, he saw something strange.

A bush was on fire, but it wasn't burning up. From inside the bush, God spoke, "Moses, bring my people out of Egypt. Take them to a new land that I will show you. This new land is called Canaan."

Moisés estaba preocupado. ¿Qué si el faraón no le hiciera caso? Dios le ordenó a Moisés que echara su vara al suelo. Cuando lo hizo, ¡la vara se convirtió en una serpiente! Dios le mandó que agarrara la serpiente. ¡Se convirtió de nuevo en una vara! Dios dijo: «Usaré señales como esta para mostrar al faraón que yo te envié».

Moses was worried that Pharaoh would not listen. God told Moses to throw his staff on the ground. When he did, the staff became a snake!
God told Moses to reach down and grab the snake. It became a staff again!
God said, "I will use signs like this to show Pharaoh I have sent you."

«Pero yo no sé hablar muy bien», se quejó Moisés. «No te preocupes. Tu hermano Aarón sabe hablar muy bien. Él te acompañará».

"But I cannot speak very well," complained Moses. God said, "Do not worry. Your brother Aaron is a good speaker. I will send him with you."

Entonces, Moisés regresó con Aarón a Egipto.
Cuando llegaron, Moisés les dijo a los israelitas lo que Dios había dicho.

So Moses returned with Aaron to Egypt.
When they arrived, Moses told the Israelites what God had said.

Las diez plagas

Éxodo 7—12

Ten Plagues

Exodus 7–12

Moisés y Aarón fueron al palacio del faraón y le dijeron: «Debes liberar a los israelitas. Si no lo haces, Dios te castigará».

Moses and Aaron went to Pharaoh's palace. They said, "You must let the Israelites go free. If you do not, God will punish you."

El faraón dijo: «¡No! ¡No sé quién es ese Dios de ustedes!». Y obligó a los israelitas a trabajar aún más duro.

Pharaoh said, "No! I do not know your God!"
Then he made the Israelites work even harder.

Dios se disgustó. Así que convirtió el agua del río principal
en sangre. Al faraón no le
importó. «Jamás dejaré que se
vayan los israelitas», dijo.

God was not pleased.
So he changed the main river
to blood. Pharaoh did not care.
"I will never let the Israelites
go," he said.

Entonces, Dios envió ranas a Egipto. Había ranas en las sillas, subían y bajaban por las escaleras y saltaban en las camas. El faraón dijo: «Sáquenme de encima todas estas ranas y dejaré ir a su pueblo». Así que Dios se llevó las ranas.

Then God sent frogs to Egypt. They were sitting in chairs, hopping up stairs, and jumping all over the beds. Pharaoh said, "Take the frogs away, and I will let your people go." So God took the frogs away.

Pero el faraón cambió de idea y dijo: «No».	But Pharaoh changed his mind and said, "No."
Dios envió más plagas sobre Egipto.	God sent more plagues on Egypt.
Primero mandó unos mosquitos molestos. Luego, envió montones de tábanos.	First were the pesky gnats. Then came a frenzy of flies.
Después todos los animales se enfermaron.	Next, all the animals got sick.
Y después a los egipcios les aparecieron úlceras en la piel.	Then the Egyptians' skin broke out in sores.

Llegó una horrible tormenta de granizo, seguida de una plaga de langostas que se comieron todas las cosechas. Después todo el país quedó a oscuras. A veces el faraón decía que dejaría ir al pueblo.

Pero cuando Dios los libraba de las plagas, el faraón cambiaba de idea y decía: «No».

Damaging hailstorms came, and then swarms of locusts ate the crops.

Then darkness covered everything.

Sometimes Pharaoh said he would let the people go.

But after God took away each plague, Pharaoh changed his mind and said, "No."

Moisés tenía un último mensaje de Dios para el faraón: «Si no dejas ir a mi pueblo, el hijo mayor de todas las familias egipcias morirá». De todos modos el faraón no quiso hacerle caso. Así que Dios cumplió su promesa. Por fin, el faraón dijo: «¡Váyanse ya!».

Moses had one last message from God for Pharaoh: "If you do not let my people go, the firstborn son in each Egyptian family will die."
Pharaoh refused to listen.
So God kept his promise.
Pharaoh finally said, "Go now!"

El Mar Rojo

Éxodo 14

The Red Sea

Exodus 14

Moisés sacó a los israelitas de Egipto. Durante el día, Dios iba delante de ellos en una columna de nube. Durante la noche, Dios iba delante de ellos en una columna de fuego.

Moses led the Israelites out of Egypt. During the day, God went ahead of them in a pillar of cloud. During the night, God went ahead of them in a pillar of fire.

Dios condujo a los israelitas hasta las orillas del Mar Rojo. El faraón y su *ejército* les pisaban los talones. Los israelitas no sabían qué hacer.

God led the Israelites to the edge of the Red Sea. Pharaoh and his *army* were close behind. The Israelites did not know what to do.

Gritaban: «¡Estamos atrapados! ¿Qué nos has hecho, Moisés?». Moisés les dijo: «No tengan miedo. Dios nos protegerá». La nube de Dios se puso entre los israelitas y el ejército de faraón. ¡Los egipcios no podían ver nada!

They screamed, "We are trapped! What have you done to us, Moses?" Moses said, "Do not be afraid. God will protect us." God's cloud came between the Israelites and Pharaoh's army. They could not see anything!

Dios dijo a Moisés: «Extiende tu vara sobre el mar». Entonces, el Señor hizo retroceder el mar y les abrió un sendero. Moisés y los israelitas atravesaron el mar por el sendero y llegaron al otro lado. Pero el ejército de faraón ya casi les había dado alcance.

God told Moses, "Raise your staff over the sea." Then the Lord pushed back the sea to make a path. Moses and the Israelites followed the path through the sea and to the other side. But Pharaoh's army followed close behind.

Moisés volvió a levantar su vara y el mar se tragó a Faraón y a su ejército.
Moisés y todos los israelitas cantaron alabanzas a Dios.
¡Estaban libres!
¡Ya no eran esclavos!

Moses raised his staff again, and the sea swept away Pharaoh and his army.
Moses and all the Israelites sang praises to God. They were free!
They weren't slaves anymore!

Alimento del cielo

Éxodo 16

Los israelitas caminaron durante muchos días. Estaban cansados y con hambre. Se quejaron a Moisés: «No hay nada para comer en el desierto. ¡En Egipto al menos teníamos comida! ¡Ahora nos estamos muriendo de hambre!».

Food From Heaven

Exodus 16

The Israelites traveled for many days. They were tired and hungry. They complained to Moses, "There is nothing to eat in the desert.
At least we had food in Egypt! Now we are starving!"

Dios los escuchó. Esa tarde, Dios envió unos pajaritos llamados *codornices* para que los israelitas comieran.

God heard them. That evening, God sent birds called *quail* for the Israelites to eat.

A la mañana siguiente,
Dios envió pan del cielo.
Se llamaba *maná* y sabía a
miel.
Los israelitas encontraron
el maná en el suelo.
Pero volvieron a quejarse:
«¡Nos morimos de sed!».

The next morning, God sent
bread from heaven. It was
called *manna* and tasted like
honey.
The Israelites found the manna
on the ground.
But they complained again:
"We are thirsty!"

Moisés le preguntó a Dios qué debía hacer. Dios dijo: «Golpea la roca con tu vara». Cuando Moisés golpeó la roca, brotó agua fresca y clara para que todos pudieran beber. Mientras estuvieran en el desierto, los israelitas no pasarían más hambre ni sed.

Moses asked God what to do. God said, "Hit the rock with your staff." When Moses hit it, cool, fresh water gushed out for everyone to drink. While they were in the desert, the Israelites would not go hungry or thirsty again.

Los Diez Mandamientos

Éxodo 19—20

Ten Commandments

Exodus 19–20

Dios condujo a los israelitas a una montaña. Entre los truenos y relámpagos, el pueblo escuchó un fuerte sonido de trompeta.

God led the Israelites to a mountain. Thunder roared and lightning flashed. The people heard a loud trumpet blast.

Entonces, Dios llamó a Moisés para que subiera a la cumbre del monte y le dijo: «Yo soy el Señor tu Dios. Yo te saqué de Egipto». Dios escribió los Diez Mandamientos sobre dos tablas de piedra para que todo su pueblo los obedeciera.

Then God called Moses to the top of the mountain and said, "I am the Lord your God who brought you out of Egypt." God wrote the Ten Commandments on two stone tablets for all his people to obey.

1. DIOS ES EL ÚNICO VERDADERO DIOS.
1. GOD IS THE ONLY TRUE GOD.

2. NUNCA TENGAS ÍDOLOS.
2. NEVER MAKE IDOLS.

3. NUNCA EMPLEES A LA LIGERA
EL NOMBRE DE DIOS.
3. NEVER MISUSE THE LORD'S NAME.

4. DESCANSA EN EL DÍA DE REPOSO,
CONSIDÉRALO SAGRADO.
4. REST ON THE SABBATH DAY.
KEEP IT HOLY.

5. HONRA A TU PADRE Y A TU MADRE.
5. HONOR YOUR FATHER AND
YOUR MOTHER.

6. NO MATES.
6. DO NOT MURDER

7. LOS ESPOSOS NO
COMETAN ADULTERIO.
7. HUSBANDS AND WIVES MUST
NOT COMMIT ADULTERY.

8. NO ROBES.
8. DO NOT STEAL.

9. NO MIENTAS.
9. DO NOT TELL LIES.

10. NUNCA DESEES LO QUE
PERTENECE A OTROS.
10. NEVER WANT WHAT
BELONGS TO OTHERS.

Los israelitas necesitaban un lugar para adorar. Dios les mostró exactamente cómo debían construir una carpa especial. Se llamaba el *tabernáculo*. Dios puso una nube sobre la carpa. Cuando la nube se marchaba, los israelitas empacaban sus cosas y la seguían.

The Israelites needed a place to worship. God showed them exactly how to build a special tent. It was called a *tabernacle*. God placed a cloud over the tent. Whenever the cloud moved, the Israelites packed up and followed it.

Los doce espías

Números 13

Por fin los israelitas llegaron cerca de la tierra prometida. Dios le dijo a Moisés que enviara espías. Moisés eligió a doce hombres. Les dijo: «Fíjense cómo son los habitantes de esa tierra. Averigüen si la tierra es buena».

Twelve Spies

Numbers 13

Finally, the Israelites arrived near the promised land. God told Moses to send spies there. Moses picked 12 men.
He told them, "Find out what the people are like. See if the land is good."

Los espías regresaron y dijeron:
«La tierra es hermosa.
¡Hay abundancia de comida!
Pero la gente que vive allí
¡es grande y poderosa!».

The spies returned and said,
"The land is beautiful.
It is filled with plenty of food!
But the people there are big
and strong!"

Josué y Caleb dijeron: «No se preocupen.
Dios nos ha prometido esta tierra. Nos la dará».

Joshua and Caleb said, "Do not worry.
God has promised us this land. He will give it to us."

El resto de los israelitas no estaban de acuerdo con Josué y Caleb. Entonces, Dios dijo: «Esta gente no tiene fe en mí. No les dejaré entrar en esa tierra».
Y así fue que durante los siguientes cuarenta años, el pueblo de Dios vagó por el desierto.

The rest of the Israelites did not agree with Joshua and Caleb.
Then God said to Moses, "The people do not have faith in me. They cannot enter the land."
So for the next 40 years, God's people wandered in the desert.

Josué y los espías

Josué 2

Joshua and the Spies

Joshua 2

Después de morir Moisés, Josué se convirtió en el jefe de los israelitas.

Dios los guio a la tierra prometida.

Los condujo a una ciudad llamada Jericó. La ciudad estaba protegida por altas murallas.

After Moses died, Joshua became the leader of the Israelites.

God led them into the promised land.

He led them to a city called Jericho. The city was protected by high walls.

Con todo, dos espías encontraron la manera de entrar en la ciudad.
Fueron a la casa de Rajab.
El rey de Jericó ordenó a sus soldados que capturaran a los hombres.

Still, two spies found a way into the city.
They went to Rahab's house.
The king of Jericho ordered his soldiers to capture the men.

Rajab escondió a los hombres en el techo de su casa. Cuando los soldados llegaron, ella dijo: «Los espías ya se han ido. Si se dan prisa, tal vez los alcancen».
Los soldados fueron tras los hombres.

Rahab hid the men on her roof. When the soldiers arrived, she said, "The spies have already gone. If you hurry, you may catch them."
So the soldiers ran off to find them.

«Gracias por ayudarnos», le dijeron los espías. «Cuando regresemos, prometemos salvarte a ti y a tu familia». Entonces, Rajab ayudó a los espías a escapar.

"Thank you for helping us," the spies told her. "When we come back, we promise to save you and your family."
Then Rahab helped the spies escape.

La batalla de Jericó

Josué 6

The Battle of Jericho

Joshua 6

Una vez que los espías regresaron y estaban a salvo, Dios le dijo a Josué:
«Marchen con el ejército alrededor de Jericó y que los *sacerdotes* toquen sus trompetas. Hagan eso una vez al día durante seis días».

After the spies were safely home, God told Joshua, "March your army around Jericho with the *priests* blowing their horns. Do this once a day for six days."

«Al séptimo día, el ejército deberá dar siete vueltas alrededor de la ciudad». Josué hizo exactamente como Dios le había dicho.

"On the seventh day, have your army march around the city seven times."
Joshua did exactly as God said.

Los sacerdotes tocaron sus trompetas.

Los soldados gritaron a voz en cuello.

¡Y las enormes murallas de Jericó se derrumbaron!

The priests blew their trumpets.

The soldiers shouted as loud as they could.

Then the great walls of Jericho came tumbling down!

El ejército israelita avanzó y
tomó la ciudad. Los espías
fueron fieles a la promesa que
le habían hecho a Rajab.
¡Toda su familia se salvó!

The Israelite army rushed in
and took over the city.
The spies kept their promise to
Rahab.
Her whole family was saved!

Débora marca
el camino

Jueces 4

Deborah Leads
the Way

Judges 4

Los israelitas vivieron durante muchos años en la tierra prometida. Pero se olvidaron de Dios.

Un rey malvado de otra tierra los dominaba.

Los israelitas pidieron ayuda a Dios.

The Israelites lived in the promised land for many years.
But they forgot about God.
A bad king from another land ruled over them.
The Israelites asked God for help.

Dios envió una jueza llamada Débora. Ella amaba mucho a Dios. Dios le mostró el plan para derrotar al rey malo. Ella mandó a buscar a un hombre llamado Barac y le dijo: «Dios quiere que tomes diez mil soldados y que esperes en el monte».

God sent them a judge named Deborah. She loved God very much.
God gave her a plan to defeat the bad king. She sent for a man named Barak and told him, "God wants you to take 10,000 soldiers and wait on the hill."

Los israelitas no tenían tanto
poderío como sus enemigos.
Barac rogó a Débora que lo
acompañara.
Ella era una líder muy valiente
y accedió.

The Israelites were not as
strong as their enemies.
Barak begged Deborah to go
with them.
She was a strong leader. She
agreed.

Cuando los israelitas tenían
al ejército del rey enfrente,
Débora exclamó: «¡Adelante!
¡Al ataque! ¡Dios está con
nosotros!». Los israelitas obe-
decieron y ganaron la batalla.

When the Israelites met face
to face with the king's army,
Deborah exclaimed, "Go!
Attack them now! God is with
us!" The Israelites obeyed and
won the battle.

La batalla de Gedeón

Jueces 6—7

Como el pueblo de Dios des-
obedecía las reglas de Dios
todo el tiempo, Dios dejó que
sus enemigos le robaran toda
la comida. Los israelitas volvieron a pedir ayuda a Dios.
Nuevamente, Dios respondió
sus oraciones.

Gideon's Battle

Judges 6—7

God's people kept disobeying
his rules.
So God allowed their enemies
to take all their food away.
Again, the Israelites turned to
God for help.
Again, God answered their
prayers.

Dios eligió a un hombre llamado Gedeón para ayudar a su
pueblo. Dios envió un ángel
a Gedeón. «Tú eres un guerrero valiente», dijo el ángel.
«Salvarás al pueblo de Dios».
Gedeón dijo: «Pero vengo de
una familia que no es ni rica ni
importante».

God chose a man named
Gideon to help his people.
God sent an angel to Gideon.
"You are a mighty warrior,"
said the angel. "You will save
God's people."
Gideon said, "But I'm from
a family that isn't rich or
important."

Entonces, Gedeón oró a Dios: «Necesito que me des una señal. Voy a dejar un poco de lana sobre el suelo. Si mañana la lana está mojada y el suelo alrededor está seco, te creeré». A la mañana siguiente, la lana estaba mojada y el suelo alrededor estaba seco.

Then Gideon prayed to God. "I need a sign from you. I will put some wool on the floor. Tomorrow, if the wool is wet and the ground is dry, I will believe you."
The next morning, the wool was wet and the ground was dry.

Pero Gedeón quería otra señal. Le dijo a Dios: «A ver, si la lana está seca y el suelo está mojado, estaré seguro de que tú me has elegido». A la mañana siguiente, Dios había hecho que la lana quedara seca y el suelo mojado. Ahora Gedeón estaba convencido. Dijo: «Dios, haré todo lo que me pidas».

But Gideon wanted another sign. He said to God, "Now if the wool is dry and the ground is wet, I will be sure you have chosen me." The next morning, God made the wool dry and the ground wet.
Now Gideon was sure. He said, "God, I will do whatever you say."

Más de treinta mil hombres querían unirse al ejército de Gedeón. «Son demasiados», dijo Dios. Le mostró a Gedeón cómo vencer ¡con solo trescientos hombres!

El plan parecía raro, pero Gedeón confiaba en Dios.

Over 30,000 men wanted to join Gideon's army. "That is too many," God said.
He showed Gideon how to win with only 300 men!
The plan sounded strange, but Gideon trusted God.

Durante la noche, Gedeón y sus hombres rodearon el campamento del enemigo. Tocaron las trompetas y estrellaron contra el suelo sus cántaros. Agitaron antorchas que llevaban dentro. Los enemigos se asustaron. *¡Debe de ser un ejército enorme!* pensaron. Así que huyeron. ¡El pueblo de Dios había ganado!

During the night, Gideon and his men surrounded the enemy camp. They blew trumpets and smashed clay jars. They waved burning torches in the air. Their enemies were frightened. *This must be a huge army!* they thought. So they ran away. God's people won!

Sansón

Jueces 13; 16

Los israelitas nuevamente tenían problemas. Entonces, vino un hombre muy fuerte llamado Sansón. Dios lo había elegido para salvar a los israelitas de sus enemigos, los filisteos.

Samson

Judges 13; 16

The Israelites were in trouble again. Along came a very strong man named Samson. God had chosen him to save the Israelites from their enemies, the Philistines.

Sansón sabía que mientras
no se cortara el cabello,
siempre sería fuerte.

Samson knew that as long
as he did not cut his hair, he
would always be very strong.

Sansón estaba enamorado de Dalila.

Los filisteos le dijeron a Dalila que le pagarían si averiguara el origen de la fuerza de Sansón.

Al principio, Sansón le mintió.

Samson was in love with Delilah.

The Philistines told Delilah they would pay her if she found out what made Samson so strong.

At first, Samson lied to her.

«Si me atan con cuerdas», dijo Sansón, «perderé mi fuerza».

Esa noche, mientras Sansón dormía, Dalila lo ató y se puso a gritar:

«¡Vienen los filisteos!».

Sansón se incorporó saltando y rompió las cuerdas. Dalila lo besó y le preguntó:

«¿Por qué no me dices cuál es tu secreto?».

"If you tie me up with ropes," Samson said, "I will lose my strength."

That night while Samson slept, Delilah tied him up. Then she shouted,

"The Philistines are coming!"

Samson jumped up and broke the ropes.

Delilah kissed him and asked, "Won't you tell me your secret?"

Al final Sansón se rindió y le dijo: «Mi fuerza está en mi cabello largo». Cuando Sansón se durmió, Dalila hizo que le afeitaran toda la cabeza.

¡La fuerza de Sansón lo había abandonado! Los filisteos lo capturaron y lo metieron en la cárcel.

Samson gave in and told her, "My strength is in my long hair."

When Samson was asleep, Delilah had all his hair cut off. Samson's strength was gone! The Philistines grabbed him and put him in jail.

Poco tiempo después, los filisteos estaban festejando. Trajeron a Sansón para divertirse a costa de él. Sansón oró a Dios y le pidió que le prestara fuerza solo una vez más. Dios lo hizo. Sansón empujó con todas sus fuerzas contra unas columnas. El templo se vino abajo, y Sansón derrotó a los filisteos.

A while later, the Philistines were having a big party. They brought Samson in and made fun of him.
Samson prayed to God to make him strong one last time. God did.
Samson pushed the pillars with all his might. The temple came crashing down, and Samson defeated the Philistines.

Rut y Noemí

Rut 1—4

Noemí se había criado en la tierra prometida, que también se llamaba Israel. Pero ahora vivía en otro país.

Tenía un marido y dos hijos. Rut estaba casada con uno de los hijos de Noemí.

Luego, pasó algo muy triste. El esposo de Noemí y sus hijos se murieron.

Al poco tiempo, Noemí decidió regresar a su tierra.

Ruth and Naomi

Ruth 1–4

Naomi grew up in the promised land, which was also called Israel.

But now she lived far away. She had a husband and two sons.

Ruth was married to one of the sons. Then something sad happened.

Naomi's husband and sons died.

Not long after that, Naomi decided to go back to her homeland.

Noemí le dijo a Rut que regresara con sus padres, pero Rut no quería dejarla. Ella amaba mucho a Noemí.
«Yo iré adonde tú vayas», dijo Rut. «Tu casa será mi casa. Tu Dios será mi Dios».
Entonces, Rut se fue con Noemí a Israel.

Naomi told Ruth to return to her parents, but Ruth did not want to leave her.
She loved Naomi so much.
"I will go wherever you go," Ruth said. "Your home will be my home. Your God will be my God."
So Ruth went with Naomi to Israel.

Como necesitaban alimento para comer, Rut salía todos los días a recoger los granos que quedaban tirados en los campos. Un hombre bueno llamado Booz era el dueño de estos terrenos. Un día, él vio a Rut en el campo. Quería ayudarla. Así que dejaba caer más espigas para que Rut las recogiera.

They needed food to eat. So each day, Ruth gathered left-over grain from the fields. A good man named Boaz owned the land. One day, he saw Ruth in the field. He wanted to help her. So he left extra grain for Ruth to gather.

Booz se enamoró de Rut. Se
casaron y tuvieron un bebé
varón que llamaron Obed.
Dios había bendecido a Rut
y a la abuela Noemí con una
hermosa familia nueva.

Boaz fell in love with Ruth.
They got married and had a
baby boy named Obed.
God had blessed Ruth and
Grandma Naomi with a brand-
new family.

La oración de Ana

1 Samuel 1.1–20

Ana amaba a Dios.
Quería tener un bebé,
pero no podía tener hijos.

Hannah's Prayer

1 Samuel 1:1–20

Hannah loved God. She wanted
to have a baby, but she wasn't
able to have any children.

Ana y su esposo fueron al
tabernáculo. Ella oró a Dios:
«Si me das un hijo varón,
yo lo criaré para que
te sirva toda su vida».

Hannah and her husband went
to the tabernacle. She prayed
to God, "If you will give me
a baby boy, I will see that he
serves you all his life."

Elí era un sacerdote. Vio a Ana mientras oraba. Ella explicó: «Estoy clamando al Señor porque quiero que responda mi oración».

Elí la consoló: «Vete en paz, y que Dios te conceda lo que le has pedido».

Eli was a priest. He saw Hannah praying. She explained, "I am crying out to the Lord because I want him to answer my prayer."

Eli gently told her, "Go in peace—and may God give you what you ask for."

Y así fue. Ana y su esposo tuvieron un hijo varón. Agradecieron a Dios por el niño.
Lo llamaron Samuel.

Sure enough, Hannah and her husband had a baby boy. They thanked God for their new son.
They named him Samuel.

Una voz en la noche

1 Samuel 3

Cuando Samuel era un niño pequeño, Ana lo llevó al tabernáculo a vivir.
Ella había prometido a Dios que Samuel lo serviría toda su vida. El sacerdote Elí ahora se encargaría de cuidar a Samuel.
Le enseñaría a Samuel acerca de Dios.

A Voice in the Night

1 Samuel 3

When Samuel was a little boy, Hannah brought him to live at the tabernacle.
She had promised God that Samuel would serve him all his life. The priest Eli would now take care of Samuel.
He would teach Samuel about God.

Una noche mientras Samuel
dormía, escuchó una voz:
«¡Samuel!». Corrió adonde
estaba Elí y dijo: «Aquí
estoy». Pero Elí dijo: «No te
llamé yo».
Entonces, Samuel se volvió a
acostar.

One night while Samuel was
sleeping, he heard a voice say,
"Samuel!" He ran to Eli and
said, "Here I am."
But Eli said, "I did not call
you."
Then Samuel went back to bed.

Dos veces más Samuel escuchó la voz que lo llamaba por nombre. Cada vez, corrió adonde estaba Elí. Por fin Elí le dijo a Samuel: «Creo que Dios te está hablando. La próxima vez di: "Sí, Señor, te escucho"». Así que Samuel se volvió a acostar.

Samuel heard a voice call his name two more times. Each time, Samuel ran to Eli. Finally, Eli told Samuel, "I think God is speaking to you. Next time, say, 'Yes, Lord, I am listening.'" Then Samuel went back to bed.

«¡Samuel! ¡Samuel!», dijo nuevamente la voz. Esta vez Samuel respondió: «Sí, Señor, te escucho». A partir de ese momento, Samuel entregó mensajes al pueblo de Dios. Fue un profeta de Dios especial.

"Samuel! Samuel!" the voice said again. This time, Samuel answered, "Yes, Lord, I am listening." From that moment on, Samuel gave messages to God's people. He was a special prophet of God.

El primer rey de Israel

1 Samuel 8—10

Cuando Samuel ya era viejo,
el pueblo de Dios dijo:
«Queremos tener un rey que
nos gobierne». Samuel pidió
ayuda a Dios. Dios le dijo a
Samuel que advirtiera al pueblo
acerca de todos los problemas
que tendrían con un rey.

Israel's First King

1 Samuel 8–10

When Samuel was an old man,
God's people said, "We want a
king to rule over us."
Samuel asked God for help.
God told Samuel to warn the
people about all the trouble a
king could bring.

Un rey obligaría a los jóvenes a unirse a su ejército, y la gente tendría que dar al rey las mejores cosas que tuvieran para mantenerlo. Samuel advirtió al pueblo, pero no quisieron hacerle caso. Entonces, Dios le dijo a Samuel que les diera un rey.

A king would make the young men join his army, and the people would have to give the best things they owned to support the king.
Samuel warned the people, but they still would not listen.
Then God told Samuel to give them a king.

Dios condujo a Samuel a un hombre llamado Saúl. Samuel derramó aceite sobre la cabeza de Saúl. Era una señal de que Saúl había sido elegido por Dios para ser el nuevo rey. Saúl se escondió porque era tímido.

God led Samuel to a man named Saul. Samuel poured oil on Saul's head.
This was a sign that Saul was God's choice for their new king.
Saul hid because he was shy.

Pero lo encontraron y Samuel le dijo al pueblo: «Aquí tienen a su rey». Todos vitorearon y gritaron: «¡Viva el rey!».

The people found him. Then Samuel said, "Here is your king." Everyone cheered and shouted, "Long live the king!"

Un buen corazón

1 Samuel 15.1—16.13

A Good Heart

1 Samuel 15:1–16:13

Saúl fue un buen rey por casi veinte años. Entonces, comenzó a desobedecer a Dios. Dios se arrepintió de haber hecho rey a Saúl. Samuel también lamentaba la situación.

Saul was a good king for about 20 years. Then he began to disobey God.
God was sorry he made Saul the king. Samuel was sad about it too.

Dios envió a Samuel a un hombre llamado Isaí para buscar un nuevo rey.
Cuando Samuel se encontró con Isaí, le dijo: «Me gustaría conocer a tus hijos».

God sent Samuel to a man named Jesse to find a new king.
When Samuel met Jesse, he said, "I would like to meet your sons."

Cuando Samuel los vio, pensó:
Qué hombres tan fuertes.
Dios dijo: «Yo no me fijo
en la apariencia de una
persona, me fijo en cómo
es por dentro. Yo miro su
corazón».

When Samuel saw them, he
thought, *These are strong-look-
ing men.*
God said, "I do not look at the
outside of a person. I look at
the inside of a person. I look at
the heart."

Samuel preguntó: «Isaí, ¿tienes otro hijo?».
Isaí dijo: «Sí, se llama David. Está en el campo con las ovejas».
Samuel pidió que lo buscaran.

Samuel asked Jesse, "Do you have another son?"
Jesse said, "Yes. His name is David. He is out in the field with the sheep."
Samuel asked to see him.

Tan pronto como llegó David, Dios le dijo a Samuel: «Este es. Quiero que él sea el próximo rey».
Samuel *ungió* a David. Derramó aceite sobre la cabeza de David, y David fue lleno del poder de Dios.

As soon as David arrived, God told Samuel, "He is the one I want to be the next king." Samuel *anointed* David. He poured oil on David's head, and David was filled with God's power.

David y Goliat

1 Samuel 17.1–51

Los filisteos eran enemigos de
Dios. Su ejército se reunió para
luchar en contra del ejército del
rey Saúl. Un soldado gigante
llamado Goliat los desafiaba:
«¡Llamen a su mejor soldado
para pelear conmigo!».

David and Goliath

1 Samuel 17:1–51

The Philistines were enemies
of God.
Their army came to fight King
Saul's army.
A giant soldier named Goliath
yelled, "Bring out your best
soldier to fight me!"

«Si su soldado más fuerte
me derrota, seremos sus
esclavos», gritaba. «Si yo lo
venzo, ¡ustedes serán nuestros
esclavos!». Los soldados del
rey Saúl le tenían miedo.
No querían pelear contra el
gigante.

"If your strongest soldier
defeats me, we will be your
slaves!" he boomed.
"If I defeat him, you will be
our slaves!" King Saul's
soldiers were afraid.
They did not want to fight the
giant.

Mientras, el joven David traía comida a sus hermanos, que eran soldados en el ejército del rey Saúl.
Cuando David llegó al campamento, vio a Goliat. David escuchó el desafío del gigante.

Meanwhile, young David was taking food to his brothers. They were soldiers in King Saul's army.
When David reached the camp, he saw Goliath. David heard the giant's challenge.

«Yo no tengo miedo de luchar contra ese gigante», dijo David. El rey Saúl mandó llamar a David y le dijo: «Tú no puedes pelear contra el gigante. Eres demasiado joven». David le respondió: «Dios me acompañará».

"I am not afraid to fight the giant," said David. King Saul called for David and told him, "You cannot fight the giant. You are too young." David replied, "God will be with me."

El rey Saúl le entregó su
armadura a David, pero le
quedaba muy grande y era
muy pesada. David no estaba
acostumbrado a usar armadura.

King Saul gave his *armor*
to David, but it was big and
heavy. David wasn't used to
wearing armor.

David fue al río y escogió
cinco piedras.
Luego, se plantó delante de
Goliat. El gigante se rio de él,
pero a David no le importó
y le dijo: «Yo vengo a ti en
el nombre del SEÑOR, quien
gobierna sobre todo».

David went to a nearby stream
and picked up five stones.
He stood before Goliath.
The giant laughed at him, but
David didn't care. He said, "I
come before you in the name of
the LORD who rules over all."

David puso una piedra en la honda, corrió hacia el gigante y lanzó la piedra.

David put a stone in his sling and ran toward the giant. Then he let the stone fly.

La piedra le dio a Goliat en la frente, y ¡el gigante se desplomó sobre el suelo! Los filisteos vieron que su héroe estaba muerto. Salieron corriendo.

It hit Goliath's forehead, and he fell to the ground! The Philistines saw that their hero was dead. They ran away.

Los mejores amigos

1 Samuel 16.14–23; 18—20

Best Friends

1 Samuel 16:14–23; 18–20

El rey Saúl estaba de mal humor. Sus siervos le pidieron a David que tocara el arpa para el rey. Como la música lo hacía sentir mejor, el rey invitó a David a vivir en el palacio.

King Saul became grumpy. His servants asked David to play his harp for the king. The music cheered him up, so the king invited David to live in the palace.

David se hizo amigo del príncipe Jonatán, el hijo del rey Saúl, y de la hermana de Jonatán, Mical.

David became friends with King Saul's son, Prince Jonathan, and Jonathan's sister, Michal.

David ganó muchas batallas para el rey.
La gente decía que David era mejor guerrero que el rey.
El rey Saúl estaba enojado y celoso. *Todo el mundo quiere más a David que a mí,* pensó.

David won many battles for the king.
The people said David was a better fighter than the king.
This made King Saul very angry and jealous. *Everyone likes David more than me*, he thought.

El rey Saúl estaba tan enojado que arrojó una lanza a David, pero David se escapó.

King Saul became so angry that he threw a spear at David, but David escaped.

Un día, el príncipe Jonatán le advirtió a David: «Debes huir muy lejos». Se prometieron que siempre serían muy buenos amigos.

Then one day, Prince Jonathan warned David, "You must run far away."
They promised to always be best friends.

El rey David

2 Samuel 1.1—2.4; 1 Reyes 2.1–3

Saúl persiguió a David, pero nunca lo pudo agarrar. Dios protegía a David.
Un día, David recibió una triste noticia.
El rey Saúl y el príncipe Jonatán habían muerto en batalla.

King David

2 Samuel 1:1–2:4; 1 Kings 2:1–3

Saul chased David, but he never caught him. God watched over David.
Then one day, David heard some sad news.
King Saul and Prince Jonathan had died in battle.

El pueblo recordó lo que Dios les había dicho y fueron a buscar a David.
«David, ¡tú eres ahora nuestro rey!», gritaban.

The people remembered what God had told them, and they went to find David.
"David, you are now our king!" they exclaimed.

El rey David gobernó sobre
Israel durante cuarenta años.
Escribió muchas canciones
acerca Dios. Esas canciones
son los *salmos*. Incluso hizo
planes para construir un
templo para Dios. David
fue un hombre conforme al
corazón de Dios.

King David ruled over Israel
for 40 years. He wrote many
songs about God, called
psalms. He even had plans to
build a temple for God.
David was a man who was
dear to God's heart.

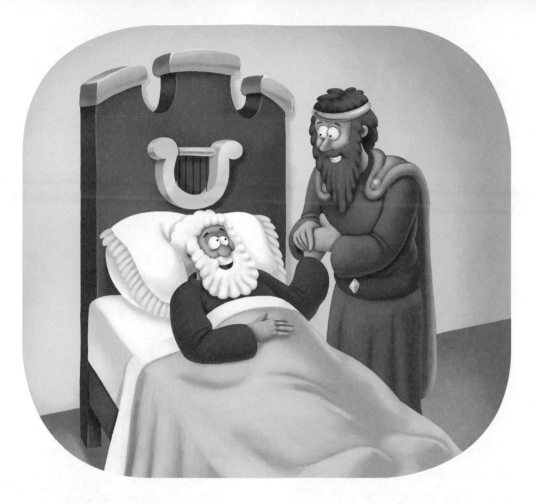

Cuando el rey David era mayor, le dijo a su hijo Salomón: «Tú serás el próximo rey de Israel. Sé fuerte y obedece a Dios de todo corazón. Y así Dios te bendecirá».

When King David was old, he told his son Solomon, "You will be the next king of Israel. Be strong and obey God with all your heart. Then he will bless you."

El Señor es mi pastor

Salmos 23

Esta es una de las canciones que escribió el rey David acerca de Dios:
El Señor es mi pastor.
Me da todo lo que necesito.
En verdes pastos me hace descansar. Junto a tranquilas aguas me conduce; me da nuevas fuerzas.

The Lord Is My Shepherd

Psalm 23

This is one of King David's songs about God:
The Lord is my shepherd.
He gives me everything I need.
He lets me lie down in fields of green grass. He leads me beside quiet waters.
He gives me new strength.

Me guía por sendas de justicia
por amor a su nombre.
Aun si voy por valles oscuros,
no tengo miedo.
Tú, Dios, estás a mi lado.
Tu vara de pastor me
reconforta.

He guides me in the right paths
for the honor of his name.
Even though I walk through
the darkest valley, I will not be
afraid.
You, God, are with me. Your
shepherd's rod and staff com-
fort me.

Me preparas un banquete
en presencia de mis enemigos.
Derramas aceite sobre mi
cabeza.
Mi copa se desborda.

You prepare a feast for me
right in front of my enemies.
You pour oil on my head.
My cup runs over.

Sé que tu bondad
y amor me seguirán
todos los días de mi vida,
y en la casa del Señor
viviré para siempre.

I am sure that your goodness
and love will follow me all the
days of my life.
And I will live in the house of
the Lord forever.

Un rey sabio

1 Reyes 3.5—10.13

El rey Salomón amaba mucho
a Dios.
Dios le habló en un sueño.
«Pídeme lo que quieras», le
dijo Dios.

The Wise King

1 Kings 3:5–10:13

King Solomon loved God very
much.
God spoke to him in a dream.
"Ask for anything you want,"
God said.

El rey Salomón respondió:
«Dame sabiduría para
reconocer la diferencia entre el
bien y el mal».
A Dios le agradó que Salomón
le pidiera eso. «Te daré
sabiduría», dijo Dios. «Pero,
además, te daré riquezas y
esplendor».

King Solomon answered,
"Give me wisdom so that
I will know the difference
between right and wrong."
God was pleased with
Solomon's answer.
"I will give wisdom to you,"
God said. "I will also give you
riches and honor."

El rey Salomón fue la persona más sabia del mundo. Compuso tres mil *proverbios*, o dichos de sabiduría, y escribió más de mil canciones. Sabía muchas cosas acerca de las plantas y los animales.

King Solomon was wiser than any other person. He spoke 3,000 *proverbs*, or wise sayings, and wrote over 1,000 songs. He knew many things about plants and animals.

El rey Salomón fue muy famoso. Venían personas de todo el mundo a visitarlo. La reina de Sabá vino desde muy lejos para hacerle preguntas.

King Solomon was famous. People from all over the world came to see him.
The queen of Sheba came from far away to ask him questions.

El rey Salomón le respondió todas sus preguntas. Entonces, la reina dijo: «Tú sí que eres un rey sabio. ¡Alabado sea el Señor tu Dios!».

King Solomon answered all of her questions. Then the queen said, "You truly are a wise king. May the Lord your God be praised!"

El rey Salomón mandó que miles de trabajadores construyeran un templo para Dios.
Cuando lo terminaron, ¡era bellísimo!
El rey Salomón planeó una celebración.

King Solomon ordered thousands of workers to build a temple for God.
When the temple was finished, it was beautiful!
King Solomon planned a celebration.

Todas las personas de Israel venían a ver el templo. Estaban felices de tener un nuevo lugar en el cual adorar.

Decían: «Dios es bueno. ¡Su amor es para siempre!».

All the people of Israel came to see the temple. They were happy to have a new place to worship.

They all said, "God is good. His love lasts forever!"

Dios cuida a Elías

1 Reyes 16.29—17.7

God Watches Over Elijah

1 Kings 16:29–17:7

Después de morir Salomón, Israel tuvo más reyes. Uno de esos reyes se llamaba Acab. No amaba a Dios. El rey Acab adoraba a los ídolos.

After Solomon, many other kings ruled over Israel. One king was named Ahab. He did not love God. King Ahab worshiped idols.

Dios tenía un profeta llamado Elías.

Dios le daba mensajes especiales a Elías para que se los transmitiera al pueblo.

God had a prophet named Elijah.

God gave Elijah special messages to tell the people.

Elías le dijo al rey Acab: «Dios está enojado contigo porque no lo sirves».

Elijah told King Ahab, "God is angry with you because you do not serve him."

Y continuó diciéndole: «No lloverá durante mucho tiempo. Los cultivos se secarán y el pueblo pasará hambre». El rey Acab estaba muy enojado con Elías.

Then Elijah told the king, "It will not rain for a very long time. The crops will dry up, and your people will go hungry." King Ahab was very angry with Elijah.

Dios le dijo a Elías que huyera al desierto. Guio a Elías hasta un arroyo. Elías bebía agua del arroyo todos los días. Cada día Dios le enviaba pájaros con comida. Elías se quedó allí hasta que el arroyo se secó.

God told Elijah to escape to the desert. He led Elijah to a brook. Each day, Elijah drank from it, and each day, God sent birds with food. Elijah stayed there until the brook dried up.

Elías ayuda a una viuda

1 Reyes 17.8–16

Elijah Helps a Widow

1 Kings 17:8–16

Dios mandó a Elías que fuera a un pueblo cercano. Allí encontraría a una mujer que cuidaría de él.
Cuando Elías llegó, vio una viuda que recogía leña. Le pidió agua y pan.

God told Elijah to go to a nearby town. There he would find a woman who would take care of him. When Elijah arrived, he saw a widow gathering sticks. He asked her for some water and bread.

La mujer dijo: «Mi hijo y yo apenas tenemos harina y aceite para una última comida».
Elías respondió: «No temas. Dios no dejará que pases hambre».

The woman said, "My son and I only have enough flour and oil for one last meal."
Elijah replied, "Don't be afraid. God will not let you go hungry."

La mujer le sirvió agua
y le hizo un panecillo.
Como ella cuidó de Elías,
Dios cuidó de ella. ¡La harina
y el aceite de la mujer nunca
se acabaron!

The woman poured him some
water and made him some
bread.
Because she took care of Elijah, God took care of her. The
woman's flour and oil never
ran out!

Fuego del cielo

1 Reyes 18

Fire From Heaven

1 Kings 18

Acab todavía era rey de Israel. Oraba a un ídolo llamado Baal. Le suplicaba a Baal que trajera lluvia, pero no llovía.
Se perdían las cosechas.
La gente clamaba: «¡Tenemos hambre!».

Ahab was still king of Israel. He prayed to an idol called Baal. He asked Baal to bring rain, but rain did not fall.
The crops did not grow.
The people cried, "We are hungry!"

El profeta Elías le llevó al rey Acab un mensaje de Dios. Elías dijo: «No hay lluvia porque tú adoras una estatua en vez de adorar al verdadero Dios».
El rey Acab se enojó mucho cuando Elías le dijo eso.

The prophet Elijah brought King Ahab a message from God. Elijah said, "There is no rain because you worship a statue instead of the true God!"
This made King Ahab very angry.

Elías quería mostrar al pueblo que su Dios era el único Dios verdadero.
Elías les hizo un reto.
Él y el rey Acab y todos los israelitas subieron al monte Carmelo.

Elijah wanted to show the people that his God was the one true God.
So Elijah gave them a challenge.
He and King Ahab and all the Israelites marched up Mount Carmel.

Elías les dijo a los adoradores de Baal: «Construyan un *altar* para su dios. Yo construiré un altar para mi Dios».
Luego, colocaron una ofrenda en cada altar.

Elijah told the worshipers of Baal, "Build an *altar* for your god. I will build an altar for my God."
Then they placed an offering on each altar.

Los adoradores de Baal gritaban a su dios para que enviara
fuego. Bailaban alrededor del
altar, pero no pasaba nada.
Elías comenzó a burlarse de
ellos: «Tal vez Baal se fue de
vacaciones».

The worshipers of Baal cried
out for their god to send fire.
They danced around the altar,
but nothing happened.
Elijah teased Baal's priests,
"Maybe Baal is on vacation!"

Elías cavó una zanja alrededor de su altar y mojó todo con agua. Había agua incluso dentro de la zanja. Elías oró. De pronto descendió fuego del cielo.

El *sacrificio* se quemó.

El altar de piedras se quemó. ¡Hasta el agua de la zanja se evaporó!

Elijah dug a trench all around his altar.

He poured water over everything. Water even filled the trench. Elijah prayed. Suddenly fire came down from heaven.

The *sacrifice* burned up.

The stone altar burned up. Even the water in the trench was gone!

Cuando el pueblo vio lo que había pasado, se inclinaron y adoraron al único y verdadero Dios. Poco después, Dios hizo que volviera a llover.

When the people saw what had happened, they bowed down and worshiped the one true God. Before long, God allowed it to rain again.

Un carro de fuego

1 Reyes 19.19–21; 2 Reyes 2.1–13

Un hombre llamado Eliseo
estaba arando en el campo.
Dios eligió a Eliseo para que
ayudara a Elías.

Chariot of Fire

1 Kings 19:19–21; 2 Kings 2:1–13

A man named Elisha was
plowing the field. God chose
Elisha to be Elijah's helper.

Durante muchos años, viajaron juntos, contándoles a muchas personas acerca del amor de Dios.

Over the years, they traveled together. They told many people about God's love.

Un día, llegaron a un río y se detuvieron.

One day, they stopped beside a river.

Elías se quitó el manto y golpeó el agua. El río se partió en dos y ambos lo cruzaron en seco.

Elijah took off his coat and struck the water with it. The river opened up! They walked across on a dry path.

Elías ya era viejo y pronto
Dios lo llevaría al cielo.
Elías le preguntó a Eliseo si
quería pedirle algo.
Eliseo respondió: «Quiero el
doble del espíritu que Dios te
ha dado».

Elijah was getting older. God
was preparing to take him to
heaven.
Elijah asked Elisha if there
was anything he wanted. Elisha answered, "I want a double
portion of the spirit God has
given you."

De repente, un carro de fuego con caballos de fuego descendió del cielo y los separó. Elías subió al cielo en un torbellino, para estar con Dios. El manto de Elías cayó al suelo y Eliseo lo recogió. Golpeó el agua con el manto y el río se partió.

Entonces, Eliseo supo que Dios había concedido su petición.

Suddenly a fiery chariot pulled by fiery horses came down from the sky. It separated the two of them, and Elijah went up to heaven in a whirlwind to be with God. Elijah's coat fell to the ground. Elisha picked it up. He struck the water with it, and the water parted. Then Elisha knew God had granted his request.

Vasijas de aceite

2 Reyes 4.1–7

Eliseo ayudó a muchas personas. Un día, se encontró con una mujer que estaba muy triste.

«Ayúdame, por favor. Debo dinero a un hombre», dijo la mujer.

Jars of Oil

2 Kings 4:1–7

Elisha helped many people. One day, he met a woman. She was very upset. She said, "Please help me. I owe a man some money."

«Si no le pago, se llevará a mis hijos como esclavos», explicó la mujer. Eliseo le preguntó: «¿Qué tienes en casa?».
Ella dijo: «Solo tengo un poco de aceite».

"If I do not pay him," the woman said, "he will make my sons become his slaves!" Elisha asked her, "Do you own anything?"
She said, "I have a little oil."

Eliseo dijo: «Consigue vasijas vacías de tus amigos. Luego, entra en la casa y echa aceite en todas las vasijas».

La mujer obedeció, y con el poquito aceite que tenía Dios llenó todas las vasijas.

Elisha said, "Gather some empty jars from your friends. Then go inside and pour your oil into them."

The woman obeyed, and God made her tiny bit of oil fill all the jars!

Entonces, la mujer vendió el aceite y pudo pagar al hombre. Con el dinero que le sobró, pudo mantener a su familia.

She sold all the oil and paid the man back. She took care of her family with the leftover money.

El cuarto para Eliseo

2 Reyes 4.8–17

Eliseo iba a menudo a la ciudad de Sunén. Se hizo amigo de un matrimonio que vivía allí.

Elisha's Room

2 Kings 4:8–17

Elisha often traveled to the town of Shunem. He became friends with a nice couple who lived there.

Una tarde, mientras Eliseo visitaba, sus amigos tenían una sorpresa: «Hemos construido un cuarto en nuestra casa para ti».

One evening, while Elisha was visiting, the couple surprised him. They said, "We built a room in our house just for you."

Eliseo estaba muy agradecido por sus amigos. Oró para que fueran felices. Eliseo le dijo a la mujer: «Dentro de un año tendrás un hijo».

Elisha was so thankful for his friends. He prayed for them to be happy.
Elisha said to the woman, "A year from now you will have a child."

Efectivamente, al año siguiente Dios les había dado un hermoso niño varón.

Sure enough, a year later God gave them a beautiful baby boy.

Naamán se sana

2 Reyes 5.1–15

Naaman Is Healed

2 Kings 5:1–15

Naamán era un importante jefe del ejército. Era un soldado valiente, pero tenía un problema. Sufría de una espantosa enfermedad de la piel que se llama *lepra*.

Naaman was a great army commander. He was a brave soldier, but he had a problem. He had a terrible skin disease called *leprosy*.

Un día, la esposa de Naamán dijo: «Mi sierva me ha dicho que deberías ver al profeta Eliseo. Él podrá sanarte».

One day, Naaman's wife said, "My servant told me you should go see the prophet Elisha. He can heal you."

Naamán fue a la casa de Eliseo. Eliseo envió un mensajero para que le dijera: «Zambúllete siete veces en el río Jordán. Así tu piel sanará».

Naaman reached Elisha's home. Elisha sent out a man with this message: "Dunk yourself in the Jordan River seven times. Then you will be healed."

Al principio, Naamán pensó que era una idea tonta, pero sus criados le dijeron: «Por favor, hágalo. No es una cosa difícil». Así que Naamán se zambulló siete veces en el río Jordán. Cuando salió, ¡se había sanado!

At first, Naaman thought it was a silly idea. But his servants said, "Please go. This is not a hard thing to do." So Naaman dunked himself in the Jordan River seven times. When he was done, Naaman's skin disease was gone!

Naamán estaba tan emocionado que corrió adonde estaba Eliseo para agradecerle.
Naamán dijo: «El Dios de Israel es el único y verdadero Dios».

Naaman was so excited that he ran to thank Elisha for curing him.
Naaman said, "Israel's God is the only true God!"

Josías, el niño que fue rey

2 Reyes 22.1—23.3

Un niño llamado Josías se convirtió en rey de Judá cuando tenía solo ocho años. Josías amaba a Dios. Muchos reyes malos habían gobernado antes que él.

Boy King Josiah

2 Kings 22:1–23:3

A boy named Josiah became the king of Judah when he was only eight years old. Josiah loved God. Many bad kings had ruled before him.

El templo de Jerusalén estaba casi en ruinas porque hacía años que la gente no adoraba allí. El rey Josías decidió restaurarlo. Quería que su pueblo volviera a adorar a Dios en el templo.

The temple in Jerusalem had started to crumble. People had not worshiped there for many years. King Josiah decided to fix it up. He wanted his people to worship God in the temple again.

Así fue que el rey Josías contrató trabajadores para que lo repararan. Un día, mientras los hombres estaban trabajando, un sacerdote encontró un pergamino escondido en la pared. El sacerdote lo mostró al rey.

So King Josiah hired workers to repair it.
One day, as the men were working, a priest found a scroll hidden in the wall.
The priest showed the scroll to the king.

Era el *libro de la ley*. El rey Josías convocó a todo el pueblo. Luego, les leyó las leyes de Dios.

It was the *Book of the Law*. King Josiah called everyone together. Then he read them God's laws.

Todo el pueblo hizo un pacto entre sí y prometió a Dios: «Prometemos obedecer siempre las leyes de Dios».

The people all made a promise to each other and to God: "We will always obey God's laws."

239

Una reina valiente

Ester 1—10

The Brave Queen

Esther 1–10

Ester era *judía*. Esto significaba que era israelita. Vivía en la tierra de Persia, junto con su primo mayor, Mardoqueo.

Esther was *Jewish*. That means she was an Israelite. She lived in the land of Persia with her older cousin Mordecai.

El rey de Persia necesitaba una nueva reina. Anunció: «Tráiganme las mujeres más hermosas de mi reino». Ester fue una de las mujeres enviadas al palacio. Cuando el rey conoció a Ester, la eligió para ser su reina.

The king of Persia needed a new queen. He announced, "Bring me the most beautiful women from all over my kingdom." Esther was one of the women sent to the palace. When the king met Esther, he chose her to be his queen.

Amán, el principal asistente del rey, odiaba a los judíos. Los judíos eran el pueblo de Dios.

Amán quería que todos se arrodillaran ante él. Mardoqueo se negó a arrodillarse ante Amán porque Mardoqueo solo se arrodillaba ante Dios.

Haman was the king's chief helper. He hated the Jewish people. They were God's people.

Haman wanted everyone to bow down to him. Mordecai refused to bow down to Haman. Mordecai would only bow down to God.

Amán fue a ver al rey. Le dijo: «Los judíos son gente mala. Deberías firmar una ley para ayudarme a deshacernos de ellos». Así fue que el rey firmó la nueva ley. ¡El pueblo de Dios corría peligro muy grave!

Haman went to the king. He said, "The Jews are bad people. You should sign a law that will help me get rid of them." So the king signed the new law. God's people were in great danger!

Mardoqueo se enteró de la nueva ley. Corrió a decírselo a Ester: «Debes hacer algo para salvarte a ti y a todo el pueblo de Dios. Tal vez Dios te ha puesto como reina por esta razón».

A Ester, entonces, se le ocurrió una idea. Era un plan arriesgado para ella.

Mordecai heard about the new law. He ran to tell Esther, "You must save yourself and the rest of God's people. Perhaps God has made you the queen for this reason."

So Esther came up with a plan. It would be very risky for her.

Ester invitó al rey y a Aman a una cena especial. Entonces, ella le preguntó al rey: «¿Por qué quiere Amán deshacerse de mí?». El rey estaba sorprendido. Ella dijo: «Yo soy judía. Amán te engañó para que firmaras una nueva ley autorizándolo a exterminar a todos los judíos».

Esther invited the king and Haman to a special dinner. Then she asked the king, "Why does Haman want to get rid of me?"
The king was surprised. She said, "I am Jewish. Haman tricked you into signing a new law that would get rid of all the Jews."

El rey les dijo a sus guardias: «¡Arresten a Amán!».
Luego, nombró a Mardoqueo como su nuevo asistente principal. A la reina Ester le dijo: «Redactaré una nueva ley que garantice la seguridad tuya y de tu pueblo». ¡Dios usó a Ester para salvar a su pueblo!

The king told his guards, "Arrest Haman!"
Then he made Mordecai his new chief helper. He told Queen Esther, "I will make a new law that will keep you and your people safe."
God used Esther to save his people!

El horno en llamas

Daniel 3

El ejército del rey Nabucodonosor había derrotado a los israelitas. Ahora él gobernaba sobre
ellos. El rey Nabucodonosor
construyó una estatua de oro
y, luego, hizo una ley mala. La
ley decía: «Cuando escuchen
la música, todos deben arrodillarse y adorar la estatua. Los
que desobedezcan serán arrojados a un horno en llamas».

Fiery Furnace

Daniel 3

King Nebuchadnezzar's army
had defeated the Israelites.
Now he was their ruler.
King Nebuchadnezzar built a
golden statue. Then he made
a bad law. It said, "When the
music plays, everyone must
bow down and worship the
statue. Those who disobey
will be thrown into the fiery
furnace."

La música comenzó a tocar. La gente se arrodilló y adoró la estatua. Pero Sadrac, Mesac y Abednego se negaron: «Solo podemos adorar al verdadero Dios», dijeron. ¡El rey se enfureció!

The music began to play. The people fell down and worshiped the statue. But Shadrach, Meshach, and Abednego refused. "We only worship the true God," they said. The king was mad!

El rey dijo: «¡Calienten el horno al máximo!». Mandó arrojar al horno a los tres hombres. Pero, cuando el rey miró dentro del horno, ¡había cuatro hombres caminando! Uno de ellos se parecía a un ángel de Dios.

The king said, "Make the furnace extra hot!" He had the three men thrown inside. Yet, when the king looked into the furnace, there were four men walking around! One of them looked like an angel from God.

El rey les gritó:
«¡Salgan de allí! ¡Su Dios los
salvó!».
El fuego no les había hecho
nada. ¡Ni siquiera olían a
humo! El rey los nombró
funcionarios en su reino.

The king shouted to the men,
"Come out! Your God has
saved you!"
The fire had not hurt them.
They did not even smell like
smoke! So the king made them
rulers in his kingdom.

Daniel y los leones

Daniel 6

Darío se convirtió en el nuevo
rey de Babilonia.
Daniel era su principal
asistente. Los demás asistentes
del rey no querían a Daniel.

Daniel and the Lions

Daniel 6

Darius became the new king of
Babylon.
Daniel was his chief helper.
The king's other helpers did
not like Daniel.

Le dijeron al rey: «Eres un rey sensacional. Deberías hacer una nueva ley que diga que, durante los próximos treinta días, todos deben orar solo a ti. Si desobedecen, serán arrojados al foso de los leones».

They said to the king, "You are such a wonderful king. You should make a new law that for the next 30 days, everyone must pray only to you. If they disobey, they will be thrown into the lions' den."

El rey Darío hizo la nueva ley, pero Daniel siguió orando a Dios porque Daniel amaba a Dios. Los ayudantes del rey lo pillaron mientras oraba.

King Darius made the new law, but Daniel kept praying to God because Daniel loved God. The king's helpers caught him praying.

Le contaron al rey Darío:
«Ahora debes arrojar a Daniel
al foso de los leones».
El rey se dio cuenta de que lo
habían engañado, pero tenía
que obedecer su nueva ley.

They told King Darius, "Now
you must throw Daniel into the
lions' den."
The king knew he had been
tricked, but he had to obey his
new law.

Arrojaron a Daniel al foso de los leones.

Él no tenía miedo. Sabía que Dios lo cuidaría. El rey Darío le dijo: «Espero que tu Dios te salve».

Esa noche, el rey no pudo dormir. Estaba muy preocupado por Daniel.

Daniel was thrown into the lions' den.

He was not afraid. He knew God would take care of him. King Darius told Daniel, "I hope your God will save you."

That night, the king could not sleep. He was too worried about Daniel.

Al amanecer, el rey fue corriendo al foso de los leones. «¿Pudo salvarte tu Dios de los leones?», gritó. «¡Sí!», respondió Daniel. «Mi Dios envió a su ángel para que me protegiera». Daniel, entonces, regresó al palacio y el rey Darío mandó que todo el mundo honrara y respetara a Dios.

At sunrise, the king hurried to the lions' den. "Has your God saved you from the lions?" he called. "Yes!" answered Daniel. "My God sent his angel to protect me."
So Daniel returned to the palace. Then King Darius ordered everyone to honor and respect God.

Jonás y el enorme pez

Jonás 1.1—3.10

Jonah and the Big Fish

Jonah 1:1—3:10

Jonás era un profeta de Dios. Un día, Dios le ordenó: «Ve a la gran ciudad de Nínive. Diles que dejen de hacer cosas malas».

Jonah was a prophet of God. One day, God told Jonah, "Go to the big city of Nineveh. Tell them to stop doing bad things."

Pero Jonás se fue para otro lado. No quería ir a Nínive. En cambio, se subió a un barco para cruzar el mar. Dios envió una gran tormenta para detener a Jonás. Los marineros estaban aterrados. ¡Creían que el barco se iba a hundir!

But Jonah ran away. He did not want to go to Nineveh. Instead he got on a boat to sail across the sea.
God sent a big storm to stop Jonah. The sailors on the boat were afraid. They thought the boat was going to sink!

Jonás les dijo a los marineros: «Mi Dios mandó esta tormenta. Si me arrojan al mar, volverá la calma».

Jonah told the sailors, "My God has sent this storm. If you throw me into the water, the sea will become calm again."

Así que los marineros lanzaron a Jonás al mar embravecido. Al instante, el mar se calmó.

So the sailors threw Jona into the raging sea. Instantly, the sea became calm.

Justo entonces, Jonás vio venir un enorme pez. ¡Glug! El pez se lo tragó.

Just then, Jonah saw a big fish coming! Gulp! The fish swallowed Jonah.

Durante tres días y tres noches, Jonás estuvo dentro del pez. Oró a Dios:
«Por favor, perdóname».

For three days and nights, Jonah was inside the fish. He prayed to God,
"Please forgive me."

Entonces, Dios mandó al pez que escupiera a Jonás en tierra firme. Dios le volvió a decir a Jonás: «Ve a Nínive y dile a la gente que dejen de hacer cosas malas».

Then God told the fish to spit Jonah onto dry land. God told Jonah a second time, "Go and tell the people of Nineveh to stop doing bad things."

Esta vez, Jonás le hizo caso a Dios. El pueblo de Nínive se arrepintió de las cosas malas que habían hecho y Dios los perdonó.

This time, Jonah obeyed God. The people in Nineveh were sorry for doing bad things, so God forgave them.

El Nuevo Testamento
The New Testament

Historias bíblicas para niños
Timeless Bible Stories

Un ángel visita
a María

Lucas 1.26–38

Dios envió al ángel Gabriel a visitar a una joven que se llamaba María.
Ella se asustó. Era la primera vez que veía un ángel.

An Angel
Visits Mary

Luke 1:26–38

God sent the angel Gabriel to visit a young woman. Her name was Mary.
She was scared. She had never seen an angel before.

Gabriel dijo: «No tengas miedo. Tú eres muy especial para Dios. Pronto quedarás embarazada y tendrás un hijo. Le pondrás por nombre Jesús. Él será llamado el Hijo del Dios Altísimo».

Gabriel said, "Don't be afraid. You are very special to God. You will become pregnant and give birth to a son. You must name him Jesus.
He will be called the Son of the Most High God."

María preguntó:
«Pero, ¿cómo puede ser?
No estoy casada».

Mary asked,
"How can it be so?
I am not married."

Gabriel respondió: «Para Dios no hay nada imposible».

Gabriel answered, "With God, all things are possible."

María dijo: «Yo amo a Dios. Haré lo que él quiera que haga».

Mary said, "I love God. I will do what he has chosen me to do."

El nacimiento del niño Jesús

Lucas 2.1–7

María amaba a José. María
y José pronto se casarían.
José vivía en Nazaret,
pero su familia era de Belén.

Baby Jesus Is Born

Luke 2:1–7

Mary loved Joseph. Mary and
Joseph were going to be
married soon.
Joseph lived in Nazareth, but
his family lived in Bethlehem.

Un nuevo emperador llamado César ordenó que todas las personas volvieran a su tierra de origen. Quería saber cuánta gente había en su reino. Así fue que María y José fueron a Belén.

A new leader named Caesar ordered all people to go back to their homeland. He wanted to count all the people in his kingdom. So Mary and Joseph went to Bethlehem.

María estaba por tener al bebé. Cuando llegaron a Belén, buscaron un lugar seguro donde dormir, pero todas las posadas estaban completas.

Mary was going to have her baby soon. When they arrived in Bethlehem, they looked for a safe place to sleep, but all the inns were full.

Por fin, un hombre los pudo
ayudar.
Dijo: «No me quedan cuartos,
pero, si lo desean, pueden
dormir en el establo».

Finally, a man was able to help
them.
He said, "I do not have any
rooms left,but you are wel-
come to sleep in the stable."

José preparó un lugar cómodo para que María descansara. Mientras estaban allí, nació el pequeño Jesús.

Joseph made a warm place for Mary to rest. While they were there, little baby Jesus was born.

María envolvió a Jesús en
pañales y lo acostó con cariño
en un pesebre.

Mary wrapped Jesus in strips
of cloth and gently laid him in
a manger.

La visita de los pastores

Lucas 2.8–20

La noche en que Jesús nació, había unos pastores que cuidaban sus ovejas.

De pronto, un ángel se les apareció y la luz de Dios brilló alrededor.

Shepherds Visit

Luke 2:8–20

On the night Jesus was born, shepherds were watching their sheep.

Suddenly, an angel stood before them, and God's light shined all around.

277

El ángel dijo: «No tengan miedo. Les traigo una noticia alegre para todas las personas. Hoy, en la ciudad de Belén, ¡ha nacido un *Salvador*! Está acostado en un pesebre».

The angel said, "Do not be afraid. I bring joyful news to all people. Today, in the town of Bethlehem, a *Savior* has been born! He is lying in a manger."

Luego, apareció un coro de ángeles.
Cantaban: «¡Gloria a Dios en las alturas! ¡Paz y buena voluntad a todos en la tierra!».

Then a choir of angels appeared.
They sang, "Glory to God in the highest! Peace and good-will to everyone on earth!"

Los pastores se apuraron para
llegar a Belén. Allí encontraron
al niño Jesús.
Les contaron a María y José
lo que el ángel había dicho.

The shepherds rushed to Bethlehem.
There they found baby Jesus.
They told Mary and Joseph
what the angel said.

Mientras regresaban con sus ovejas, los pastores iban contando lo que habían visto y oído. Regresaron alabando a Dios.

As they returned to their sheep, the shepherds told everyone what they had seen and heard. All along the way, the shepherds shouted praises to God.

Simeón y Ana conocen al niño Jesús

Lucas 2.25–38

Simeon and Anna Meet Baby Jesus

Luke 2:25–38

María y José llevaron al niño Jesús al *templo*. Allí se encontraron con un hombre piadoso llamado Simeón.

Mary and Joseph took baby Jesus to the *temple*. There they met a godly man named Simeon.

Simeón tomó a Jesús en brazos y alabó a Dios. Sabía que Jesús era el Salvador de todo el mundo. Luego, Simeón bendijo a Jesús, a María y a José.

Simeon took Jesus in his arms and praised God. He knew Jesus was the Savior of all people. Then Simeon blessed Jesus, Mary, and Joseph.

Había una profetisa llamada Ana que vivía en el templo. Ella oraba a Dios todos los días.

A prophet named Anna lived at the temple. She prayed to God every day.

Cuando Ana vio al niño Jesús, agradeció a Dios. Les dijo a todos en el templo: «Este es el Hijo de Dios, ¡el Salvador del mundo!».

When Anna saw baby Jesus, she thanked God. She told everyone in the temple, "This is God's Son, the Savior of the world!"

La estrella brillante y tres visitas

Mateo 2.1–12

Cuando nació Jesús, Dios puso una estrella especial en el cielo. Unos sabios que vivían muy lejos vieron esta estrella. Sabían que era una señal de Dios indicando que había nacido un nuevo rey.

The Bright Star and Three Visitors

Matthew 2:1–12

When Jesus was born, God put a special star in the sky. Some Wise Men who lived far away saw this star.
They knew it was a sign from God that a new king had been born.

Los sabios siguieron la estrella. En su camino, se detuvieron en la ciudad de Jerusalén para ver al rey Herodes. Los sabios querían preguntarle acerca del niño rey.

The Wise Men followed the star. On their way, they stopped in the city of Jerusalem to see King Herod. The Wise Men wanted to ask him about the baby king.

Pero Herodes era un rey malvado. Intentó engañar a los
sabios. «Deben encontrarlo y
decirme dónde está para que
también pueda adorarlo», les
dijo.

Now, Herod was a mean king.
He tried to trick the Wise Men.
"You must find him for me so
I can worship him too," he
said.

La estrella guio a los sabios hasta Belén. Allí encontraron al pequeño Jesús.
Lo adoraron y le dieron regalos dignos de un rey: oro y especias fragantes.

The star led the Wise Men to Bethlehem. There they found little Jesus.
They worshiped him and gave him gifts fit for a king: gold and sweet-smelling spices.

Un ángel les apareció en sue-
ños a los sabios. Les advirtió:
«No vuelvan a ver al rey
Herodes».
Por ende los sabios regresaron
a su hogar por otro camino.

An angel appeared to the Wise
Men in a dream. He warned
them, "Do not go back to King
Herod."
So the Wise Men went home
on a different road.

Un rey enojado

Mateo 2.13–23

An Angry King

Matthew 2:13–23

Cuando los sabios no volvían, el rey Herodes se enojó mucho.

When the Wise Men did not return, King Herod became very angry.

Les gritó a sus soldados:
«¡Encuéntrenme a ese niño!
¡Yo soy el único rey de los
judíos!».

He yelled at his soldiers,
"Go and find the boy!
I will be the only king of the
Jews!"

Pero el ángel de Dios advirtió a José en un sueño: «Toma a tu familia y huye a Egipto. No regreses hasta que yo te diga que pasó el peligro».

But God's angel warned Joseph in a dream, "Take your family and escape to Egypt. Do not return until I tell you it is safe."

Esa noche, José y María
emprendieron el viaje a Egipto,
con el niño Jesús.

That night, Joseph and Mary
left for Egypt with baby Jesus.

Unos años más adelante, el ángel de Dios le dijo a José en un sueño: «El rey Herodes ha muerto. Ahora sí pueden volver de Egipto». Entonces, José, María y Jesús se marcharon de Egipto y volvieron a su hogar en Nazaret.

Years later, God's angel said to Joseph in a dream, "King Herod is dead. Now, it is safe to leave Egypt."
So Joseph, Mary, and Jesus left Egypt and went back home to Nazareth.

¡Se perdió Jesús!

Lucas 2.41–52

Jesús creció en Nazaret. Todos los años, iba con su familia a Jerusalén a celebrar la fiesta de la *Pascua*.

Jesus Is Lost!

Luke 2:41–52

Jesus grew up in Nazareth. Every year, Jesus and his family would go to Jerusalem to celebrate the *Passover* Feast.

Jesús tenía doce años, y
fueron a la fiesta como era
su costumbre. Había mucha
gente en las calles.

When Jesus was twelve, they
went to the Feast as usual.
The streets were crowded
with people.

En el camino de regreso a Nazaret, María y José no podían encontrar a Jesús. Preguntaron a sus parientes y amigos: «¿Han visto a Jesús?». Pero nadie sabía dónde estaba.

On the way back home to Nazareth, Mary and Joseph couldn't find Jesus. They asked their relatives and friends, "Have you seen Jesus?" But no one knew where he was.

María y José regresaron a
Jerusalén.
Buscaron a Jesús por todas
partes.

Mary and Joseph went back to
Jerusalem.
They looked and looked for
Jesus.

299

Finalmente, después de tres días, ¡lo encontraron! Jesús estaba en el templo, hablando con los maestros. Los maestros estaban asombrados. Jesús era muy sabio para ser un muchacho tan joven.

Finally, after three days, they found him! Jesus was talking with the teachers in the temple. The teachers were amazed. Jesus was very wise for such a young boy.

María y José corrieron a Jesús. «¡Estábamos muy preocupados!», dijo María.

Mary and Joseph rushed to Jesus. "We were so worried about you!" said Mary.

Jesús sabía que Dios era su Padre. Dijo: «Tenía que estar en la casa de mi Padre». Jesús amaba y obedecía también a sus padres. Regresó con ellos y crecía en fuerzas y en sabiduría.

Jesus knew God was his Father. He said, "I had to come to my Father's house."
He loved and obeyed his parents too. So he returned home with them and grew stronger and wiser.

Juan bautiza a Jesús

**Mateo 3.1–17; Marcos 1.1–11;
Lucas 3.1–22; Juan 1.1–34**

John Baptizes Jesus

**Matthew 3:1–17; Mark 1:1–11;
Luke 3:1–22; John 1:1–34**

Juan había nacido poco tiempo antes de Jesús. Eran primos.

Cuando Juan creció, se fue a vivir al desierto y comía insectos y miel.

John was born just before Jesus was. They were cousins.

When John grew up, he lived in the desert and ate bugs and honey.

Juan le hablaba a la gente acerca de Dios. La gente le hacía muchas preguntas acerca de las cosas que estaban bien y las que estaban mal. Juan les decía que debían ser buenos, bondadosos y sinceros.

John told the people about God. They asked him many questions about what is right and what is wrong.
John told them to be good and kind and honest.

Juan predicaba el perdón de Dios. Muchas personas decidieron seguir a Dios.
Juan las *bautizaba* en el río.

John preached about God's forgiveness. Many people decided to follow God.
John *baptized* the people in a river.

Juan dijo a la gente que se preparara para una persona especial que los salvaría de sus pecados. Un día Jesús vino al río. Juan sabía que Jesús era esa persona especial. Jesús le dijo: «Necesito que me bautices». Juan se sorprendió, pero Jesús le dijo: «Es justo que lo hagas».

John told the people to get ready for a special person who would save them from their sins. One day, Jesus came to the river. John knew Jesus was that special person.
Jesus told him, "I need to be baptized by you." John was surprised, but Jesus said, "It is right for you to do this."

Juan, entonces, llevó a Jesús al río Jordán y lo bautizó. El *Espíritu Santo* descendió del cielo en forma de una paloma. Se posó sobre Jesús. Jesús sonrió. Luego, Dios dijo: «Este es mi Hijo, y lo amo. Estoy muy complacido con él».

So John took Jesus into the Jordan River and baptized him. The *Holy Spirit* came down from heaven in the form of a dove. It landed on Jesus. Jesus smiled. Then God said, "This is my Son, and I love him. I am very pleased with him."

Jesús elige a sus discípulos

Mateo 4.18–22; 9.9; 10.1–4; Marcos 1—3; Lucas 5—6

Jesús comenzó a hablar a la gente acerca de Dios. Sabía que tenía mucho trabajo que hacer, así que fue en busca de ayudantes.

Jesus Chooses His Disciples

Matthew 4:18–22; 9:9; 10:1–4; Mark 1–3; Luke 5–6

Jesus began to tell people about God.
He knew he had a lot of work to do, and he went to find some helpers.

308

Mientras Jesús caminaba por la orilla del mar, vio unos pescadores. Jesús los llamó: «Vengan. Síganme. Yo haré de ustedes pescadores de personas».

As Jesus was walking along the seashore, he saw some fishermen.
Jesus called to them, "Come. Follow me. I will make you fishers of people."

En seguida dejaron sus barcas y siguieron a Jesús. Sus nombres eran Pedro, Andrés, Jacobo y Juan.

Right away, they left their boats and followed Jesus. Their names were Peter, Andrew, James, and John.

Luego, Jesús se encontró con un cobrador de impuestos llamado Mateo. Su trabajo era cobrar los impuestos de la gente y entregárselos al rey. Mateo también dejó su trabajo para seguir a Jesús.

Later, Jesus met a tax collector named Matthew. His job was to get the tax money from the people and give it to the king. Matthew quit his job to follow Jesus too.

JUDAS
JUDAS

SIMÓN
SIMON

TADEO
THADDAEUS

JACOBO HIJO DE ALFEO
JAMES SON OF ALPHAEUS

TOMÁS
THOMAS

JESÚS
JESUS

BARTOLOMÉ
BARTHOLOMEW

FELIPE
PHILIP

Jesús eligió a algunas personas más. Sus nombres eran Felipe, Bartolomé, Tomás, y otro hombre llamado Jacobo.

Jesus chose some more people. Their names were Philip, Bartholomew, Thomas, and another man named James.

JUAN
JOHN

JACOBO HIJO DE ZEBEDEO
JAMES SON OF ZEBEDEE

PEDRO
PETER

MATEO
MATTHEW

ANDRÉS
ANDREW

Luego, se les unieron Tadeo, Simón y Judas. Ahora Jesús tenía doce nuevos seguidores. Los llamó sus *discípulos*. Jesús les enseñó acerca del amor de Dios.

Thaddaeus, Simon, and Judas joined them too. Jesus now had twelve new followers. He called them his *disciples*. Jesus taught them about God's love.

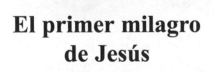

El primer milagro
de Jesús

Juan 2.1–11

Jesús fue a una boda junto con su madre María y sus discípulos.

Jesus'
First Miracle

John 2:1–11

Jesus went to a wedding with his mother Mary and his disciples.

María oyó que algunos sirvientes decían: «Se acabó el vino. ¿Qué vamos a hacer?».
María les dijo: «Hagan lo que Jesús les diga».

Mary heard the servants say, "There is no more wine. What can we do?"
Mary told the servants, "Do what Jesus tells you to do."

Jesús dijo: «Llenen seis tinajas de agua. Saquen un poco y llévenselo al encargado».

Jesus said, "Fill up six jars of water. Dip out a cup and give it to your master."

Cuando lo hicieron, vieron que en vez de agua había vino. Los sirvientes estaban asombrados. Cuando el encargado del banquete probó el vino, le dijo al novio: «¡Has guardado el mejor vino para el final!». Los discípulos también se maravillaron. Era el primer *milagro* de Jesús.

When they did, they saw wine instead of water! The servants were amazed. When their master tasted the wine, he told the groom, "You have saved the very best wine for last!" The disciples were also amazed.
This was Jesus' first *miracle*.

Jesús enseña en una montaña

Mateo 5.1–12; 6.25–34;
Lucas 6.17–23; 12.22–31

Toda clase de gente fue a ver
a Jesús: niños y niñas, madres
y padres, abuelas y abuelos.
Todos querían escuchar lo que
enseñaba.

Jesus Teaches on a Mountain

Matthew 5:1–12; 6:25–34;
Luke 6:17–23; 12:22–31

All sorts of people went to
see Jesus. Children, mothers,
fathers, grandmas, and
grandpas.
They all wanted to hear what
he was teaching.

«Miren los pájaros», dijo Jesús. «¿Acaso guardan su alimento en graneros? No. Dios los alimenta».

"Look at the birds," said Jesus. "Do they store up food in a barn? No. God feeds them."

«Miren las flores», dijo Jesús. «No trabajan ni se hacen ropa. Dios las viste con verdes hojas y preciosos pétalos».

"Look at the flowers," said Jesus. "They don't work or make clothes. God dresses them in lush leaves and pretty petals."

Luego, Jesús dijo: «Ustedes son mucho más importantes que los pájaros. Son mucho más importantes que las flores. Así que no se preocupen. Si Dios cuida de las aves y de las flores, ¡cómo no va a cuidar de ustedes!».

Then Jesus said, "You are much more important than birds. You are much more important than flowers. So do not worry. If God takes care of them, God will take care of you."

El Padrenuestro

Mateo 6.9–13; Lucas 11.1–4 (NVI)

Cuando Jesús estuvo en la
montaña, enseñó a la gente
cómo debían orar. Dijo:
«Padre nuestro que estás en el
cielo, santificado sea tu nombre,
venga tu reino,
hágase tu voluntad
en la tierra como en el cielo.
Danos hoy nuestro pan
cotidiano.
Perdónanos nuestras deudas,
como también nosotros hemos
perdonado a nuestros deudores.
Y no nos dejes caer en
tentación, sino líbranos del
maligno».

Amén.

The Lord's Prayer

Matthew 6:9–13; Luke 11:1–4 (NIV)

When Jesus was on the mountain, he taught the people how
to pray.
Jesus said,
"Our Father in heaven,
hallowed be your name,
your kingdom come,
your will be done
on earth as it is in heaven.
Give us today our daily bread.
Forgive us our debts,
as we also have forgiven our
debtors.
And lead us not into temptation, but deliver us from the
evil one."

Amen.

La fe de un capitán

Mateo 8.5–13

Jesús bajó de la montaña y
fue a una ciudad cercana. Lo
seguían grandes multitudes que
querían verlo.

A Captain's Faith

Matthew 8:5–13

Jesus came down the mountain
to a nearby city.
Crowds of people gathered to
see him.

Un capitán del ejército dijo:
«Señor Jesús, mi siervo está
muy enfermo. Por favor,
¿podrías ayudarlo?». Jesús dijo:
«Iré a tu casa para sanarlo».

An army captain said, "Lord
Jesus, my servant is very sick.
Please, will you help him?"
Jesus said, "I will go to your
house and heal him."

El capitán respondió: «No es necesario que vengas a mi casa. Basta que lo ordenes y mi siervo se sanará».

The captain replied, "You do not need to go to my house. Just say the word and my servant will be healed."

Jesús estaba asombrado. «No conozco nadie que tenga una *fe* tan grande», dijo. Luego, Jesús le dijo al capitán: «¡Ve! Tu siervo ya se sanó». El capitán corrió a su casa. ¡Qué contento estaba cuando vio que su siervo se había sanado!

Jesus was amazed. "I have not found anyone whose *faith* is so strong," he said. Then Jesus said to the captain, "Go! Your servant is healed." The captain ran home. He was happy to see his servant well again!

Un agujero en el techo

**Mateo 9.1–8; Marcos 2.1–12;
Lucas 5.17–26**

Jesús se encontraba predicando en una casa. Se había reunido mucha gente porque todos habían oído que él sanaba a los enfermos.

A Hole in the Roof

**Matthew 9:1–8; Mark 2:1–12;
Luke 5:17–26**

Jesus was at a house preaching. Many people gathered there because they heard he was healing the sick.

La casa estaba llena de gente. Muchos tuvieron que pararse afuera. No había lugar, ni siquiera en la puerta.

The house was overflowing with people. Many had to stand outside. There was no room left, not even outside the door.

Cerca vivía un hombre que no podía caminar. Estaba paralizado. Sus amigos creían que Jesús podría sanarlo.

Down the road lived a man who could not walk. He was paralyzed. His friends believed Jesus could heal him.

Lo llevaron a la casa.
Todavía había mucha gente.
Así que lo llevaron al techo.

They carried him to the house.
It was still too crowded. So
they carried him up to the roof.

Los amigos del hombre abrieron un agujero en el techo y
bajaron al hombre hasta donde
estaba Jesús. Jesús vio que
los hombres tenían fe. Sabía
cuánto amaban a su amigo.

The man's friends made a
hole and lowered him down to
Jesus.
Jesus saw that the men had
faith. He knew how much they
loved their friend.

Jesús le dijo al hombre: «Tus pecados quedan perdonados». El hombre su puso en pie y ¡caminó! La gente alabó a Dios.

Jesus said to the man, "Your sins are forgiven." The man stood up and walked! The crowd praised God.

Jesús calma la tormenta
Mateo 8.23–27

Jesus Calms the Storm
Matthew 8:23–27

Jesús y sus discípulos se subieron a una barca. Querían cruzar el lago.

Jesus and his disciples got into a boat. They wanted to cross the sea.

Jesús se quedó dormido.
Las olas mecían suave-
mente la barca.

Jesus took a nap.
The waves gently rocked
the boat back and forth.

De pronto se levantó una tormenta. Las olas sacudían la barca y el viento los azotaba de todos lados.

Suddenly a great storm came up. Waves splashed over the boat. Winds whipped around the disciples.

Despertaron a Jesús y gritaron: «¡La barca se hunde! ¿No te importa?».

They woke Jesus up and shouted, "The boat is sinking! Don't you care?"

Jesús les preguntó: «¿Por qué tienen tanto miedo? ¿No tienen nada de fe?». Entonces, Jesús ordenó a la tormenta que parara. En seguida todo quedó tranquilo.

Jesus asked, "Why are you so afraid? Don't you have any faith at all?"
Then Jesus told the storm to stop. Right away it was calm.

Los discípulos no salían de su asombro. Se decían unos a otros: «¿Quién es este hombre Jesús? ¡Hasta el viento y las olas le obedecen!».

The disciples were amazed. They said to each other, "Who is this man Jesus? Even the wind and the waves obey him!"

Dos milagros

**Mateo 9.18–26; Marcos 5.21–43;
Lucas 8.40–56**

Two Miracles

**Matthew 9:18–26; Mark 5:21–43;
Luke 8:40–56**

Un día, un hombre llamado
Jairo vino a ver a Jesús.
«¡Jesús! Ven y sana a mi hija
que se está muriendo», le
pidió.

One day, a man named Jairus
came to see Jesus. He cried,
"Jesus! Please come heal my
daughter. She is dying."

«Si tan solo tocas a mi hija, se sanará», dijo Jairo. Entonces, Jesús y sus discípulos fueron con Jairo.

"If you would just touch my daughter," Jairus said, "she would be healed." So Jesus and his disciples went with Jairus.

Mucha gente acompañaba a Jesús mientras iba a la casa de Jairo.

A large crowd followed Jesus as he walked to Jairus's house.

Justo entonces, una mujer se metió entre la gente y se acercó a Jesús. Hacía doce años que estaba enferma. Los médicos no la podían sanar.

Just then, a woman pushed through the crowd toward Jesus. She had been sick for twelve years. The doctors could not heal her.

La mujer creía que Jesús podría sanarla. Pensó: *Sé que si pudiera tocar su manto, me sanaría.*

The woman believed that Jesus could heal her. She thought, *I know if I just touch his clothes, I will be healed.*

Entonces, la mujer se acercó a Jesús, extendió su brazo y lo tocó.
¡En ese mismo instante se sanó! Jesús se detuvo y se volvió.

As the woman got closer to Jesus, she reached out and touched him.
She was healed at that moment! Jesus stopped and turned around.

«¿Quién me tocó?», preguntó
Jesús. «Sentí que de mí salió
poder».
La mujer se arrodilló ante
Jesús y dijo: «Yo te toqué».
Jesús dijo: «Tu fe te ha sanado.
Vete en paz».

"Who touched me?" Jesus
asked.
"I felt power go out of me."
The woman knelt before Jesus
and said, "I am the one who
touched you."
Jesus said, "Your faith has
made you well. Go in peace."

Finalmente, Jesús llegó a la casa de Jairo. La gente decía que era demasiado tarde. La niña ya había muerto.

Finally Jesus arrived at Jairus's house.
The people said it was too late.
His daughter had already died.

Jesús dijo: «Jairo, confía en mí. Tu hija no está muerta; está durmiendo».

Jesus said, "Jairus, trust me. Your daughter is not dead. She is sleeping."

Jesús sacó a todo el mundo de la casa. Entonces, Jairo y la madre acompañaron a Jesús al cuarto de la niña. Jesús se arrodilló junto a ella y dijo: «Despierta, mi niña».

Jesus told everyone to leave the house. Then Jairus and his wife went with Jesus into the girl's bedroom. Jesus knelt down beside her and said, "Wake up, my child."

La niña abrió los ojos en
seguida y se levantó.
Jairo y su esposa rebosaban de
gozo.

Right away she opened her
eyes and climbed out of bed!
Jairus and his wife were over-
come with joy.

La red de los pescadores

Mateo 13.47–49

A Fishermen's Net

Matthew 13:47–49

Jesús contó una historia: «Un día, unos pescadores se subieron a su barca y salieron a pescar».

Jesus told a story. "One day," he said, "some fishermen took their boat out."

«Echaron su red al agua. Había todo tipo de peces nadando en el lago».

"They threw their net into the water. All kinds of fish swam in the lake."

«Cuando regresaron a la orilla, sacaron su red del agua para revisar qué habían recogido», dijo Jesús.

"When the fishermen returned to shore, they dragged their net out of the water and looked through their catch," said Jesus.

«Se quedaron con todos los peces buenos y desecharon los malos», continuó Jesús. «El reino de Dios es como esa red de los pescadores».

"They kept all the good fish and tossed out all the bad fish." Jesus said, "The fishermen's net is like God's kingdom."

«Todos quieren ser parte de su reino. Pero los ángeles vendrán y separarán a las personas justas de las personas malvadas».

"Everyone wants to be part of his kingdom. But the angels will come and separate the godly people from the ungodly people."

«Las personas justas vivirán conmigo en el cielo para siempre».

"The godly people will live in heaven with me forever."

Jesús alimenta a miles

Mateo 14.13–22; Marcos 6.30–44;
Lucas 9.10–17; Juan 6.1–15

Jesus Feeds Thousands

Matthew 14:13–22; Mark 6:30–44;
Luke 9:10–17; John 6:1–15

Jesús y sus discípulos estaban cansados. Necesitaban descansar en un lugar tranquilo. Así que se subieron a una barca y se alejaron un poco de la orilla. Pero la gente los seguía.

Jesus and his disciples were tired. They needed a quiet place to rest. So they got into a boat and pushed off from shore. A crowd followed the boat.

357

Más de cinco mil personas
habían venido para ver a Jesús.
Aunque estaba cansado, Jesús
quería ayudarlos. Salió de la
barca y comenzó a bendecir y
a sanar a muchas personas.

Over 5,000 people had come
to see Jesus. Even though he
was tired, Jesus wanted to help
them. He climbed out of the
boat, and he began to bless and
heal many people.

Más tarde, los discípulos le dijeron a Jesús. «Se está haciendo tarde. Esta gente debería volver a sus hogares para cenar».

Later that day, the disciples said to Jesus, "It is getting late. These people should go home and eat dinner."

Jesús respondió: «Nosotros podemos alimentarlos. Fíjense si alguien tiene un poco de comida para compartir».

Jesus replied, "We can feed them. See if anyone has any food to share."

Los discípulos encontraron a un niño. Tenía cinco panes y dos pescaditos.
Jesús dijo: «Tráiganme al muchacho».

The disciples found one boy. He had five loaves of bread and two small fish.
Jesus said, "Bring the boy to me."

Los discípulos preguntaron: «Pero ¿cómo vamos a alimentar a tanta gente con tan poco alimento?». Jesús dijo: «Ya verán. Hagan que se sienten todos». Entonces, Jesús tomó el pan y dio gracias a Dios.

The disciples asked, "How will so little food feed this many people?" Jesus said, "You will see. Have the people sit down." Then Jesus took the bread and gave thanks to God.

Los discípulos repartieron el pan y los pescados a todos. Para su asombro, ¡sobraron doce canastas!

His disciples gave bread and fish to everyone. To their surprise, twelve baskets were left over!

Jesús camina sobre el agua

Mateo 14.22–33; Marcos 6.45–51; Juan 6.15–20

Jesús les dijo a sus discípulos que él los alcanzaría luego.

Jesus Walks on Water

Matthew 14:22–33; Mark 6:45–51; John 6:15–20

Jesus told his disciples to go on ahead of him.

Entonces, Jesús subió a una montaña para orar. El cielo se nubló y se levantó una tormenta. Jesús vio que los discípulos en la barca estaban en apuros.

Then Jesus walked up a mountainside to pray. Storm clouds filled the sky.
Jesus could see the disciples in the boat. They were having trouble.

El viento rugía y soplaba. El mar estaba picado y las olas sacudían la barca.

The wind swooshed. The waves sloshed. The boat was tossed about.

De pronto, los discípulos vieron que alguien se acercaba a la barca, caminando sobre el agua. ¡Pensaron que era un fantasma!

Suddenly, the disciples saw someone walking on the water toward them.
They thought it was a ghost!

Jesús los llamó: «Soy yo.
¡No tengan miedo!». Los discípulos no estaban tan seguros.
Pedro dijo: «Si de veras eres
Jesús, déjame caminar hasta
donde tú estás». Jesús respondió: «¡Ven!».

Jesus called out to them,
"It is I. Do not be afraid!"
The disciples still weren't sure.
Peter said, "If you really are
Jesus, let me walk out to you."
Jesus replied, "Come!"

Pedro bajó de la barca. Comenzó a caminar sobre el agua hacia Jesús. Pero cuando se fijó en el viento y las olas, se asustó. De pronto, comenzó a hundirse. «Señor, ¡sálvame!», gritó Pedro. Jesús le tendió la mano y lo levantó.

Peter stepped out of the boat. He began walking on the water toward Jesus. Then Peter looked at the wind and the waves. He became afraid. Suddenly he started to sink. "Lord, save me!" Peter cried out. Jesus reached out and pulled Peter up.

«¿Por qué no confiaste en mí?», preguntó Jesús a Pedro. Se subieron a la barca y la tormenta se calmó. Los discípulos adoraron a Jesús. Dijeron: «Es cierto: ¡tú eres el hijo de Dios!».

"Why didn't you trust me?" Jesus asked Peter. They climbed into the boat and the storm stopped. The disciples worshiped Jesus. They said, "Truly you are the son of God!"

Jesús sana a un mendigo ciego

Juan 9.1–12

Jesús y sus discípulos vieron a un mendigo ciego. Había nacido ciego. Los discípulos preguntaron a Jesús: «Maestro, ¿este hombre pecó, o pecaron sus padres? ¿Es por eso que está ciego?».

Jesus Heals a Blind Beggar

John 9:1–12

Jesus and his disciples saw a blind beggar.
He had been blind since he was born. The disciples asked Jesus, "Teacher, did this man sin? Or did his parents?
Is that why he is blind?"

«Nadie pecó», explicó Jesús. «Esto pasó para que la obra de Dios fuera evidente en su vida». Entonces, Jesús escupió en el suelo e hizo un poco de barro con sus manos. Con delicadeza cubrió los ojos del ciego con el barro.

"No one sinned," said Jesus. "This happened so that God's work could be shown in his life." Then Jesus spit on the ground and made mud out of it with his hands. He gently spread the mud on the blind man's eyes.

Jesús le dijo al hombre:
«Ve al estanque de *Siloé*
y lávate el barro de la cara».

Then Jesus told the man,
"Go to the Pool of Siloam
and wash off the mud."

Tan pronto como se lavó el
barro de los ojos, ¡el hombre
pudo ver! Todos estaban asombrados. Querían saber más
acerca de Jesús.

As soon as the mud was
washed off, the man could see!
Everyone was amazed.
They wanted to find out more
about Jesus.

Dinero en un pescado

Mateo 17.24–27

Había llegado el momento de pagar el impuesto del templo. Este dinero se usaba para reparar el templo.

Money in a Fish

Matthew 17:24–27

It was time to pay the temple tax. This money was used to fix up the temple.

375

Un día, unos recaudadores de impuestos le dijeron a Pedro: «¿Así que Jesús no paga el impuesto del templo?». Pedro respondió: «Por supuesto que lo paga».

One day, some tax collectors said to Peter, "Jesus does not pay the temple tax, does he?" Peter replied, "Of course he does."

Antes de que Pedro pudiera preguntarle qué hacer, Jesús le dijo: «Aunque soy el Hijo de Dios, pagaré el impuesto. Ve a pescar. Saca el primer pez que pique. Ábrele la boca y encontrarás una moneda. Tómala y dásela a los cobradores de impuestos. Con eso pagaré mi impuesto y el tuyo».

Before Peter could ask Jesus what to do, Jesus told him, "Even though I am the Son of God, I will pay the tax. Go fishing. Take the first fish you catch. Look in its mouth and you will find a coin. Take it and give it to the tax collectors. It will pay my tax and yours."

Pedro le abrió la boca al primer pez que pescó y ¡dentro había una moneda! Era exactamente lo que necesitaban para pagar a los cobradores de impuestos.

Peter caught a fish. He opened its mouth and found a coin inside!
It was exactly enough to pay the tax collectors.

El buen samaritano

Lucas 10.25–37

Un día, un experto en la ley puso a prueba a Jesús. Dijo: «Yo sé que la ley dice que debo amar a Dios con todo mi corazón y amar a mi prójimo como a mí mismo. Pero ¿quién es mi prójimo?».

The Good Samaritan

Luke 10:25–37

One day, a lawyer put Jesus to the test. He said, "I know the law says to love God with all my heart and to love my neighbor as myself. But who is my neighbor?"

Jesús le contó esta parábola: «Un hombre iba camino a la ciudad de Jericó. Unos ladrones lo agarraron y lo golpearon. Le robaron todo lo que tenía».

Jesus told him this parable: "A man was on his way to the city of Jericho. Some robbers beat him. They stole everything he had."

380

«El hombre estaba herido. Necesitaba ayuda. En eso pasó un sacerdote. El sacerdote vio al hombre, pero no se detuvo. Después, pasó un hombre que ayudaba en el templo. Vio al hombre, pero tampoco se detuvo. También vino un samaritano. Cuando vio al hombre herido, se detuvo. El samaritano limpió las heridas del hombre».

"The man was hurt. He needed help. Along came a priest. The priest saw the man, but he did not stop. Along came a helper in the temple. He saw the man but did not stop. Along came a Samaritan man. When he saw the hurt man, he stopped. The Samaritan man cleaned up the man's wounds."

«Levantó al hombre y lo puso sobre su propio burro, y lo llevó a una posada donde se quedaron. El samaritano cuidó al hombre herido toda la noche», dijo Jesús.

"He lifted the man onto his own donkey and took him down the road to an inn. They stayed at the inn. The Samaritan man took care of the hurt man all night long," said Jesus.

«En la mañana, el samaritano le dio dos monedas de plata al mesonero y le dijo: "Cuídemelo hasta que yo vuelva"».

"In the morning, the Samaritan man gave the innkeeper two silver coins and said, 'Take good care of him until I return.'"

Cuando Jesús terminó de contar la historia, preguntó: «¿Cuál de estas tres personas te parece que fue el prójimo?». El experto respondió: «El que cuidó del hombre herido». Jesús dijo: «Anda entonces y haz lo mismo».

After Jesus finished the story, he asked, "Which one of the three men was the neighbor?" The lawyer answered, "The one who took care of the hurt man." Jesus said, "Go and do as he did."

María y Marta

Lucas 10.38–42

María, Marta y su hermano Lázaro eran amigos de Jesús.

Mary and Martha

Luke 10:38–42

Mary, Martha, and their brother Lazarus were friends with Jesus.

Un día Jesús fue a visitarlos. María se sentó a los pies de Jesús para escucharlo largo rato.

One day, Jesus came over to visit. Mary sat at his feet and listened to him for a long time.

Mientras, Marta estaba
ocupada cocinando y limpiando.
¡Tenía muchísimo que hacer!

Meanwhile, Martha was busy
cooking and cleaning.
There was so much to do!

Cuanto más escuchaba María a Jesús, más enojada estaba Marta. Dijo: «Yo estoy trabajando y trabajando en la cocina ¡y María no hace nada!».

The longer Mary listened to Jesus, the madder Martha got. She said, "I am busy in the kitchen while Mary is doing nothing!"

«Jesús, ¿por qué no le dices a mi hermana que me ayude?», se quejó Marta.

"Jesus, please tell my sister to help me," Martha whined.

«Marta, Marta», dijo Jesús.
«No te alteres. María ha
elegido lo mejor. Ella está
escuchándome».

"Martha, Martha," said Jesus,
"You should not be upset.
Mary has chosen what is
better. She is listening to me."

La oveja perdida

Mateo 18.10–14; Lucas 15.3–7

Algunas personas se preguntaban quién era el más importante para Dios. Entonces, Jesús les contó una parábola.

The Lost Sheep

Matthew 18:10–14; Luke 15:3–7

Some people wondered who was most important to God. So Jesus told them a parable.

391

«Piensen en un pastor.
¿Qué hace el pastor?
Cuida a sus ovejas.
Les da la comida y
el agua que necesitan».

"Think about a shepherd.
What does he do? He watches
over his sheep. He gives them
plenty of food, and he gives
them plenty of water."

«Las cuenta para asegurarse de que estén todas. Cuando se pierde una, sale a buscarla. La busca en el establo. La busca en el arroyo. La busca en las colinas. La busca por todas partes».

"He counts them up to make sure they are all there. If one is lost, he looks for it. He looks in the barn. He looks near the stream. He looks in the hills. He looks everywhere."

393

«El pastor no se da por vencido. ¡Por fin encuentra la oveja perdida!».

"The shepherd does not give up. At last, he finds the little lost sheep!"

«La lleva con el rebaño.
Luego llama a sus amigos:
"Vamos a hacer fiesta.
¡Encontré la oveja que
se me había perdido!"».

"He carries the sheep back.
He calls his friends together
and says, 'Let's celebrate!
My lost sheep has been
found!'"

Luego Jesús dijo: «Dios ama a cada uno de sus hijos como el pastor ama a sus ovejas. Cuando uno de sus hijos peca, es como una oveja que se ha perdido, y Dios se pone muy triste. Pero cuando esa persona deja de pecar y vuelve a Dios, él se pone muy, muy contento. Celebra como un pastor que encuentra su oveja perdida».

Then Jesus said, "God loves every one of his children like a shepherd loves his sheep. When one of them sins, it is like a sheep that has gone astray, and God is very sad. But when the person turns away from sin and comes back to God, he is very, very happy. He celebrates like a shepherd who has found his lost sheep."

El hijo perdido

Lucas 15.11–32

Jesús les contó otra parábola acerca del amor de Dios: «Había un hombre que tenía dos hijos. Vivían en una gran casa de campo».

The Lost Son

Luke 15:11–32

Jesus told another parable about God's love. "There was a man who had two sons," said Jesus. "He owned a big farm."

397

«El hijo menor no quería trabajar más. Quería viajar y divertirse. Así que le pidió a su padre la parte que le correspondía del dinero de la familia».

"His youngest son did not want to work anymore. He wanted to travel and have fun. So he asked his father for his share of the family money."

398

«Cuando recibió su dinero, empacó sus cosas y se marchó. ¡Estaba ansioso por conocer el mundo! Su familia se puso muy triste cuando se fue».

"The son got the money. He packed his things and left. He couldn't wait to see the world! His family was sad to see him go."

«Al principio se divirtió mucho, gastando mucho dinero. Se compró ropa muy cara y comía todo tipo de cosas ricas. Pero pronto el dinero se le acabó».

"At first he had fun spending the money. He bought expensive clothes, and he ate fancy food. But soon all the money was gone."

Tuvo que buscar trabajo y el único trabajo que encontró fue cuidar los cerdos de un granjero. Tenía tanta hambre que hasta le apeteció la comida que les daban a los cerdos. El hijo quería volver a su casa. Se dijo: "Le voy a pedir perdón a mi padre. No merezco ni que me llame su hijo. Tal vez me deje trabajar para él"».

"He had to go to work and he got a job with a pig farmer. He was so hungry that even the pigs' food looked good.
The son wanted to go back home. He said, 'I will tell my father I am sorry for what I have done.
I do not deserve to be called his son. Maybe he will let me work for him.'"

«El padre lo vio venir cuando todavía estaba muy lejos. Sus ojos se le llenaron de lágrimas y corrió a recibirlo».

"The father saw his son coming down the road. His eyes filled with tears as he ran to greet him."

El hijo dijo: «Perdóname, papá». Esa noche hicieron una gran fiesta. El padre dijo: «Mi hijo se había perdido, pero ya lo hemos encontrado».

"The son said, 'Please forgive me, Dad.' That night, they had a big party. The father exclaimed, 'My son was lost, but now he's found.'"

Jesús explicó esta historia. «Dios es como este padre. Está lleno de amor y gozo cuando alguien que estaba perdido vuelve a estar con él».

Jesus explained his story. "God is like this father. He is full of love and joy when people who are lost come back to him."

Diez leprosos

Lucas 17.11–19

Ten Lepers

Luke 17:11–19

En uno de sus viajes, Jesús se encontró con diez leprosos. Tenían el cuerpo cubierto de llagas. Los leprosos gritaban: «Jesús, ¡sánanos!».

As Jesus was traveling, he met ten lepers. Their bodies were covered with sores.
The lepers shouted, "Jesus, please heal us!"

Jesús dijo: «Vayan y presén-
tense ante los sacerdotes».
Los diez leprosos se fueron.
Mientras iban, sucedió algo
asombroso.

Jesus said, "Go. Show your-
selves to the priests." The ten
lepers left. While they were
walking away, something
amazing happened.

¡Los diez fueron sanados!
Uno de los hombres regresó
para darle las gracias a Jesús.

All ten of them were healed!
Only one man went back to
thank Jesus.

Se arrojó a los pies de Jesús
y le dijo: «¡Gracias!».
Jesús quedó preguntándose
dónde estarían los otros.
No habían vuelto para agradecerle lo que había hecho.

He threw himself at Jesus' feet
and said, "Thank you!"
Jesus wondered where the
other men were. They did not
come back to thank him.

Jesús y los niños

**Mateo 19.13–15; Marcos 10.13–16;
Lucas 18.15–17**

Jesus and the Children

**Matthew 19:13–15; Mark 10:13–16;
Luke 18:15–17**

A los niños les encantaba pasar
tiempo con Jesús.

The children loved to spend
time with Jesus.

Pero los discípulos no lo
podían entender. Decían:
«Váyanse. No molesten a
Jesús. Está demasiado
ocupado».

But the disciples didn't
understand.
They said, "Stop. Do not
bother Jesus. He is just too
busy."

Jesús les dijo a los discípulos: «Dejen que los niños se me acerquen. No los echen. Ustedes tienen que ser como estos pequeños si quieren entrar en el reino de Dios».

Jesus told the disciples, "Let the children come to me. Do not keep them away. You must become like these little children if you want to enter God's kingdom."

Luego Jesús bendijo
a los niños.

Then Jesus blessed
the children.

Un hombre muy bajito

Lucas 19.1–10

La gente salía a la calle para ver a Jesús. Zaqueo también quería verlo, pero era demasiado bajito. Entonces, se trepó a un árbol.

A Short Man

Luke 19:1–10

People crowded the streets to see Jesus. Zacchaeus wanted to see too, but he was too short. So he climbed up a tree.

Cuando Jesús pasó debajo del árbol, levantó la vista y dijo: «Zaqueo, baja. Quiero ir a tu casa». Zaqueo se apresuró a bajar del árbol.

As Jesus was passing by, he looked up and said, "Zacchaeus, come down. I want to go to your house." Zacchaeus scrambled down the tree.

Zaqueo era un recaudador de impuestos. Su trabajo consistía en cobrar el impuesto de la gente y entregárselo al rey. Nadie lo quería. Aunque no lo podía creer, estaba muy feliz porque Jesús quería ir a su casa.

Zacchaeus was a tax collector. His job was to get the tax money from the people and give it to the king. Nobody liked him. He was surprised but happy that Jesus wanted to come to his house!

Había mucha gente fuera de la casa de Zaqueó. La gente preguntaba, indignada: «¿Por qué está Jesús en esa casa?».

A crowd of people stood outside the house. They grumbled, "Why is Jesus in there?"

Zaqueo le dijo a Jesús: «Daré mi dinero a los pobres. Y devolveré el dinero a quienes he estafado. De hecho, les voy a devolver más dinero que el que les robé». Jesús estaba feliz porque Zaqueo quería reparar el daño que había hecho.

Zacchaeus told Jesus, "I will give money to the poor. And I will pay back anyone I have cheated. In fact, I will give them back more money than I took."
Jesus was happy that Zacchaeus was going to make things right.

Lázaro recupera la vida

Juan 11.1–44

Un día, Jesús recibió un mensaje de María y Marta. «Jesús, ven pronto. Lázaro está muy enfermo». Pero Jesús se quedó dos días más en el lugar donde estaba.

Lazarus Lives Again

John 11:1–44

One day, Jesus received a message from Mary and Martha. "Jesus, please come quickly. Lazarus is very sick." But Jesus stayed where he was for two more days.

Entonces Jesús fue a la ciudad donde vivían María y Marta. Marta salió a recibirlo. Estaba llorando.

Then Jesus traveled to the place where Mary and Martha lived.
Martha went to meet him. She was crying.

Marta le dijo a Jesús: «Mi querido hermano ha muerto. Si hubieras estado aquí, habrías podido sanarlo».
Jesús estaba triste. Él lloró también.

Martha said to Jesus, "My dear brother has died. If you had been here, you could have healed him."
Jesus was sad. He cried too.

Luego Jesús fue hasta la tumba de Lázaro. Pidió a unos hombres que quitaran la piedra. Jesús oró en voz alta: «Padre, sé que tú siempre me escuchas. Ahora muestra a todos que tú me enviaste».

Then Jesus walked over to Lazarus's tomb. He told some men to roll away the stone. Jesus prayed out loud, "Father, I know you always hear me. Now, show everyone that you have sent me."

Entonces, Jesús gritó:
«¡Lázaro, sal fuera!». Lázaro
salió de la tumba. ¡Estaba
vivo! Todo el mundo estaba
asombrado. Ese día mucha
gente creyó en Jesús.

Then Jesus shouted, "Lazarus,
come out!" Lazarus walked
out of the tomb. He was alive
again! Everyone was amazed.
Many people believed in Jesus
that day.

Un regalo para Jesús

Juan 12.1–8

A Gift for Jesus

John 12:1–8

Una tarde, Jesús y sus discípulos se encontraban de visita en casa de María, Marta y Lázaro.

One evening, Jesus and his disciples were visiting Mary, Martha, and Lazarus.

María derramó sobre los pies
de Jesús un perfume muy caro.
Luego le secó los pies con su
cabello.

Mary poured some expensive
perfume on Jesus' feet. Then
she dried his feet with her hair.

Judas era uno de los discípulos. Dijo: «Ese perfume debió costar mucho dinero. María debería haberlo vendido y entregado el dinero a los pobres».

Judas was one of the disciples. He said, "That perfume cost a lot of money. Mary should have sold it and given the money to the poor."

Pero Jesús sabía que en realidad Judas quería el dinero para sí mismo. Jesús respondió: «María hizo bien. Ella me honró. A los pobres siempre los tendrán con ustedes, pero a mí no siempre me tendrán».

Jesus knew the truth—that Judas wanted the money for himself. Jesus replied, "Mary did what is right. She honored me. You will always have the poor among you. But you won't always have me here."

El verdadero rey

**Mateo 21.1–11; Marcos 11.1–11;
Lucas 19.29–42; Juan 12.12–19**

Jesús y sus discípulos fueron
a Jerusalén para la fiesta de
la Pascua. Jesús pidió a dos
discípulos que le trajeran un
burrito. Les indicó dónde lo
encontrarían.

The True King

**Matthew 21:1–11; Mark 11:1–11;
Luke 19:29–42; John 12:12–19**

Jesus and his disciples went
to Jerusalem for the Passover
Feast. Jesus told two disciples
to bring him a donkey.
He told them where to find it.

Jesús entró en Jerusalén
montado en un burrito.

Jesus rode the donkey to
Jerusalem.

Lo recibió una gran multitud. | A big crowd welcomed him.

La gente agitaba ramas de palmera y las ponía en el camino por donde pasaba Jesús.

People waved palm branches and put them on the road in front of Jesus.

Gritaban: «¡Hosana! ¡Hosana! ¡Bendito el rey de Israel!».

They shouted, "Hosanna! Hosanna! Blessed is the king of Israel!"

A los líderes de Jerusalén
no les agradaba Jesús.
Observaban cuánta gente lo
seguía y estaban enojados.
Tenían celos.

The leaders in Jerusalem did
not like Jesus. They saw how
many people were follow-
ing him, and they were angry
about it. They were jealous.

La ofrenda de una viuda pobre

Marcos 12.41–44; Lucas 21.1–4

Jesús y los discípulos fueron al templo, donde podían observar a la gente echar su dinero en las alcancías de las *ofrendas*.

A Poor Widow's Gift

Mark 12:41–44; Luke 21:1–4

Jesus and the disciples went to the temple area. They watched people drop money into the *offering* box.

La gente rica echaba grandes cantidades de dinero.

The rich people put a lot of money into the box.

Luego Jesús vio a una pobre
viuda.
Ella echó dos moneditas en la
alcancía. «La ofrenda de esa
mujer es más grande que la de
los demás», susurró Jesús a
sus discípulos.

Then Jesus saw a poor *widow*.
She put two small coins into
the box. "This woman's gift
is greater than all the others,"
Jesus whispered to his disciples.

«Aunque esa mujer es pobre, ella dio todo el dinero que tenía. La gente rica daba mucho dinero, pero todavía les sobra mucho más».

"Even though the woman is poor, she gave all the money she had. The rich people gave a lot of money, but they still have plenty left over."

Jesús les lava los pies a los discípulos

Juan 13.3–30

Jesús y sus discípulos se reunieron para una cena especial durante la Pascua. Jesús sabía que pronto los dejaría.

Washing the Disciples' Feet

John 13:3–30

Jesus and his disciples gathered together for a special Passover meal. Jesus knew he would be leaving them soon.

Después de cenar, Jesús se quitó el manto. Se ató una toalla a lacintura. Luego echó agua en un recipiente. Lavó y secó los pies de los discípulos, uno por uno.

After supper, Jesus removed his outer clothing. He wrapped a towel around his waist. Then he filled a bowl with water. Jesus washed and dried the disciples' feet, one by one.

Llegó el turno de Pedro. Él le dijo a Jesús: «Señor, no eres tú quien debería lavar mis pies». Jesús respondió: «Tengo que lavarte los pies para que seas parte de mi reino». Luego les dijo a todos: «Así como yo les lavé los pies a todos ustedes, ustedes deben lavarse los pies unos a otros». Jesús quería mostrar con este gesto cómo sus amigos deberían amarse y servirse unos a otros.

Then it was Peter's turn. He said to Jesus, "Lord, you should never wash my feet." Jesus answered, "I must wash your feet for you to be part of my kingdom." Then he said to them all, "As I have washed your feet, you must wash each other's feet." By doing this, Jesus showed his friends how to love and serve each other.

Jesús les dijo: «Uno de ustedes me traicionará esta noche». Sus discípulos estaban conmocionados y dijeron: «¡Nunca haríamos eso!».

Jesus told them, "One of you will turn against me tonight." His disciples were shocked and said, "We would never do that!"

«¿Quién te va a traicionar?», preguntó Juan. «Aquel a quien yo le dé este pedazo de pan», dijo Jesús. Se lo entregó a Judas y dijo: «Haz lo que debes hacer». Judas se marchó rápidamente.

"Who will turn against you?" John asked. "The one I give this piece of bread to," said Jesus. He handed it to Judas and said, "Do what you must." Judas quickly left.

La última cena

Mateo 26.17–29; Marcos 14.12–25;
Lucas 22.7–19; Juan 13—14

Luego Jesús hizo otra cosa.
Tomó un pan y lo bendijo.
Luego lo partió en pedacitos
y lo repartió entre los discípulos para que comieran. Jesús
dijo: «Este pan es mi cuerpo.
Cada vez que lo coman,
piensen en mí».

The Last Supper

Matthew 26:17–29; Mark 14:12–25;
Luke 22:7–19; John 13–14

Then Jesus did something else.
He picked up a loaf of bread
and blessed it. Then he broke it
into pieces.
He gave the bread to his disciples to eat. Jesus said, "This
bread is my body. Every time
you do this, think of me."

De la misma manera, tomó una copa de vino y la bendijo. Luego la repartió entre los discípulos para que bebieran. «Esta es mi sangre, que se derrama para perdonar los pecados de muchos».

In the same way, he took a cup of wine and blessed it. He gave it to the disciples to drink. "This is my blood. It is poured out to forgive the sins of many."

«Ha llegado la hora en que debo irme. A donde yo voy, ustedes todavía no pueden ir. Yo voy al *cielo*, a prepararles un nuevo hogar hermoso. Pero volveré pronto».

"The time has come for me to go away. Where I am going, you cannot go yet. I am going to *heaven* to prepare a wonderful new home for you. But I will return to you soon."

«Al principio, ustedes estarán muy tristes. Pero no tengan miedo. Pronto comprenderán y serán llenos de gozo».

"At first, you will be very sad. But do not be frightened. Soon you will understand and you will be filled with joy."

El arresto y la crucifixión de Jesús

Mateo 26—27; Marcos 14—15;
Lucas 22—23; Juan 18—19

Judas fue a hablar con los líderes. Les preguntó: «¿Cuánto me pagarán si les ayudo a capturar a Jesús?». Le dijeron: «Treinta piezas de plata». Así que Judas tomó el dinero y urdió un plan.

Jesus Is Arrested and Crucified

Matthew 26–27; Mark 14–15;
Luke 22–23; John 18–19

Judas went to the leaders. He asked, "How much will you pay me if I help you capture Jesus?" They said, "Thirty pieces of silver." So Judas took the money and made a plan.

Jesús había ido a orar en su jardín favorito. Los discípulos lo acompañaron. Jesús oró: «Padre, si es tu voluntad, estoy dispuesto a entregar mi vida para que todas las personas que confían en mí sean salvas de sus pecados».

Jesus had gone to his favorite garden to pray. The disciples went along.
Jesus prayed, "Father, if it is your will, I am ready to give my life so that all the people who trust in me will be saved from their sins."

De pronto apareció Judas con unos soldados. Pedro quería proteger a Jesús, pero Jesús le dijo: «No. Debo dejar que esto suceda». Todos los discípulos huyeron y los soldados arrestaron a Jesús.

Soon, Judas arrived with some soldiers. Peter wanted to protect Jesus.
But Jesus said, "No. I must allow this to happen." All the disciples ran away, and the soldiers arrested Jesus.

Llevaron a Jesús a los líderes.
Los líderes dijeron: «Tú dices
que eres el Hijo de Dios.
No te creemos».

They took Jesus to the leaders.
The leaders said, "You say that
you are the Son of God.
We do not believe you."

Los soldados se hicieron cargo de Jesús. Le hicieron cargar una pesada cruz de madera.
Lo llevaron a un lugar que se llamaba la Calavera (*Gólgota*). Allí clavaron a Jesús a la cruz.

The soldiers took charge of Jesus. They made him carry a big wooden cross.
They took him to a place called The Skull (*Golgotha*). There they nailed Jesus to the cross.

Jesús murió en la cruz. | Jesus died on the cross.

Todas las personas que amaban
a Jesús estaban muy tristes.
Pero se habían olvidado algo
importante. ¡Jesús había dicho
que lo volverían a ver pronto!

Everyone who loved Jesus
was very sad. But they forgot
something important. Jesus
had said he would see them
again soon!

¡Jesús resucitó!

Mateo 28.1–10; Marcos 16.1–10; Lucas 24.1–11; Juan 20.1–18

Después de morir Jesús, unos amigos suyos pusieron su cuerpo en una tumba. Sellaron la entrada con una gran piedra redonda. Soldados vigilaban la tumba.

Jesus Is Risen!

Matthew 28:1–10; Mark 16:1–10; Luke 24:1–11; John 20:1–18

After Jesus died, some of his friends laid his body in a big tomb.
They sealed it shut with a large round stone. Soldiers guarded the tomb.

A los tres días, la tierra tembló. Un ángel del Señor descendió del cielo y retiró la piedra de la tumba. Luego el ángel se sentó en la piedra.

Three days later, the earth shook. An angel of the Lord came down from heaven and pushed the stone away from the tomb. Then the angel sat on the stone.

Cuando los soldados vieron al
ángel, se cayeron al suelo.

When the soldiers saw the
angel, they fell to the ground.

María iba caminando a la tumba con algunas de sus amigas. Vieron al ángel que les dijo: «No tengan miedo. Jesús no está aquí. ¡Ha resucitado!».

Mary was walking to the tomb with some of her friends. They saw the angel, who said, "Do not be afraid. Jesus is not here. He has risen!"

«¡Vayan y cuéntenle a Pedro y a los demás discípulos que Jesús vive!».

"Go and tell Peter and the other disciples that Jesus is alive!"

Mientras regresaban, las mujeres vieron a Jesús. Se arrodillaron y lo adoraron. Jesús sonrió y les dijo: «Vayan y díganles a todos que los veré en Galilea». María corrió a dar la noticia a los discípulos.

On their way, the women saw Jesus.
They fell to their knees and worshiped him. Jesus smiled and said, "Go tell the others that I will see them in Galilee."
So Mary ran to tell the disciples.

Jesús regresa

Juan 20.19–20

Los discípulos se habían ence-
rrado en un pequeño cuarto
porque temían que los líderes
enviaran soldados para arres-
tarlos.

Jesus Returns

John 20:19–20

The disciples had locked themselves in a small room because
they were afraid the leaders
would send soldiers to arrest
them.

De pronto ¡se les apareció
Jesús! Jesús dijo: «La paz sea
con ustedes». Pensaron que era
un fantasma, pero Jesús dijo:
«Toquen mis manos y mis
pies, para comprobar que soy
yo de verdad».

Suddenly, Jesus appeared to
them!
He said, "Peace be with you."
They thought he was a ghost.
But Jesus said, "Touch my
hands and my feet so that you
will know it is really me."

¡Los discípulos vitoreaban!
Estaban muy, pero muy contentos de ver a Jesús de nuevo.

The disciples cheered! They
were very, very happy to see
Jesus again.

La red se llena de pescados

Juan 21.1–14

A Net Full of Fish

John 21:1–14

Pedro se fue a pescar con algunos discípulos. Estuvieron toda la noche en la barca, intentando pescar, pero no pescaron ni siquiera un pescadito.

Peter went fishing with some of the disciples. They fished from their boat all night, but they did not even catch one fish.

Temprano en la mañana, alguien los llamó desde la orilla: «¿No han sacado ningún pescado para comer?».
«No», contestaron. «Tiren la red a la derecha de la barca», dijo el hombre.

Early the next morning, someone from the shore shouted, "You have not caught any fish, have you?"
"No," they replied. "Cast your net to the right side of the boat," the man said.

Así lo hicieron y ¡la red se llenó de peces! Entonces, Pedro supo que el hombre era Jesús. Se tiró al agua y nadó a la orilla.

As soon as they did, their net was full of fish! Then Peter knew the man was Jesus. He jumped out of the boat and swam to shore.

Jesús le preguntó: «¿Me amas?». «Tú sabes que te amo», dijo Pedro. «Si me amas, cuida bien a los que son míos», dijo Jesús.

Jesus asked him, "Do you love me?" Peter said, "You know I do."
Jesus said, "If you love me, then take good care of my people."

Jesús se va al cielo

**Mateo 28.16–20; Lucas 24.44–51;
Hechos 1.6–11**

Jesus Goes to Heaven

**Matthew 28:16–20, Luke 24:44–51;
Acts 1:6–11**

Jesús había dicho a sus discípulos: «Di mi vida para que ustedes pudieran estar conmigo en el cielo. Allá voy para prepararles un nuevo hogar hermoso. Cuando vuelva la próxima vez, los llevaré conmigo». Había llegado el momento de irse.

Jesus had told his disciples, "I gave my life so that you could be with me in heaven. I am going there to prepare a wonderful new home for you. When I come back the next time, I will take you with me." But now it was time for Jesus to leave.

Jesús dijo: «Dios me ha dado poder absoluto en el cielo y en la tierra. Vayan y cuenten a todos las buenas noticias. Hagan nuevos discípulos. Bautícenlos y enséñenles a obedecer mis *mandamientos*. No se olviden de esto: siempre estaré con ustedes».

Jesus said, "God has given me complete power over heaven and earth. Go and tell everyone the good news. Make new disciples. Baptize them and teach them to obey my *commandments*. Don't ever forget, I will always be with you."

«Vayan a Jerusalén y esperen allí», dijo Jesús. «Allí recibirán el Espíritu Santo. Él les dará poder para hablar a todos acerca de mí. Ahora debo irme al cielo. No tengan miedo».

"Go to Jerusalem and wait there," said Jesus. "The Holy Spirit will come to you. He will give you power to tell people about me. Now the time has come for me to go to heaven. Do not be afraid."

Entonces, Jesús fue llevado al cielo en una nube. Los discípulos se quedaron mirando al cielo por largo rato.

Then Jesus went up toward heaven in a cloud. His disciples stared at the sky for a long time.

De repente, se aparecieron
dos ángeles. Les preguntaron: «¿Qué hacen allí parados
mirando al cielo? Jesús vendrá
otra vez de la misma manera
que lo han visto irse».

All of a sudden, two angels
appeared.
They asked, "Why are you
standing here looking at the
sky? Jesus will return the same
way you saw him go."

Entonces, los discípulos se acordaron de lo que Jesús les había dicho. Regresaron a Jerusalén y esperaron la venida del Espíritu Santo.

Then the disciples remembered what Jesus had said. They returned to Jerusalem and waited for the Holy Spirit to come.

La venida del Espíritu Santo

Hechos 2

Había miles de personas en Jerusalén que habían ido a celebrar la fiesta judía de *Pentecostés*. Venían de muchos países y hablaban diferentes idiomas. Los discípulos de Jesús también se encontraban allí. Estaban orando juntos.

The Holy Spirit Comes

Acts 2

Thousands of people went to Jerusalem to celebrate a Jewish holiday called *Pentecost*. They came from many countries and spoke many different languages. Jesus' disciples were staying there. They were praying together.

De pronto, el cuarto se llenó de un tremendo ruido. Fue como si soplara un fuerte viento.
El *Espíritu Santo* se les apareció como lenguas de fuego sobre cada uno de ellos.

Suddenly, a noise filled the room. It sounded like a strong wind blowing.
The *Holy Spirit* appeared as tongues of fire on each of them.

Comenzaron a hablar en idiomas que no conocían.
La gente de Jerusalén escuchó el ruido y vino a ver qué estaba pasando.

They started talking in languages they did not know.
The people in Jerusalem heard the noise and came to see what was happening.

La muchedumbre estaba perpleja y preguntaban: «¿Cómo pueden hablar nuestros idiomas?». Pedro dijo: «Los profetas anunciaron que esto sucedería».

The crowd was amazed and asked, "How are you able to speak our languages?" Peter said, "The prophets told us this would happen."

Entonces, Pedro les explicó el plan de Dios. «Dios envió a Jesús para salvar a todo el mundo de todo lo malo que hemos hecho».

Then Peter told them about God's plan. "God sent Jesus to save everyone from the bad things we have done."

La gente preguntó: «¿Qué deberíamos hacer?». Pedro respondió: «Pídanle a Jesús que les perdone los pecados y bautícense en el nombre de Cristo Jesús».

The people asked, "What should we do?" Peter replied, "Ask Jesus to forgive you for your sins and be baptized in the name of Jesus Christ."

Aquel día, tres mil personas creyeron en Jesús. Los discípulos las bautizaron a todas.

On that day, 3,000 people believed in Jesus. The disciples baptized all of them.

La primera iglesia

Hechos 2.42–47

Los nuevos creyentes estudiaban con los discípulos. Aprendieron muchas cosas acerca de Dios y de los planes de Dios.

The First Church

Acts 2:42–47

The new believers studied with the disciples. They learned many things about God and God's plans.

Oraban juntos. | They prayed together.

Cantaban cantos y
alababan a Dios.

They sang songs
and praised God.

Comían juntos y juntos cele-
braban la Cena del Señor.
Compartían todo lo que
tenían. Dios agregaba más
y más creyentes a la iglesia
todos los días.

They ate meals and celebrated
the Lord's Supper together.
They shared everything they
had with each other. God
added more and more believers to the church every day.

El hombre paralítico

Hechos 3.1–10

Un día, Pedro y Juan iban al templo. Vieron un hombre que no podía caminar. Desde su nacimiento, nunca había caminado. El hombre pedía limosna.

The Lame Man

Acts 3:1–10

One day, Peter and John were going to the temple. They saw a man who could not walk. He had not been able to walk his whole life. The man was begging for money.

Pedro le dijo: «No tenemos plata ni oro. Pero lo que tenemos te damos. En el nombre de Jesús, ¡levántate y anda!».

Peter told him, "We have no silver or gold. But we will give you what we do have. In Jesus' name, stand up and walk!"

485

Inmediatamente el hombre se paró saltando. ¡Tenía fuerza en las piernas! Comenzó a caminar y a saltar, alabando a Dios.

Immediately, the man jumped up. His legs were strong! He began walking and leaping and praising God.

La gente que lo conocía estaba asombrada. Pedro les dijo: «No fuimos nosotros quienes hicimos caminar a este hombre. Fue Jesús». Muchas más personas creyeron en Jesús ese día.

All the people who saw him were amazed. Peter told the people, "We did not make this man walk. Jesus did." Many more people believed in Jesus that day.

Un hombre convertido

Hechos 9.1–19

A Saulo no le agradaban los seguidores de Jesús. Iba de camino para meter a algunos de ellos en la cárcel.

A Changed Man

Acts 9:1–19

Saul did not like Jesus' followers. He was on his way to put some of them in jail.

De pronto, una luz cegadora lo rodeó. Saulo cayó al suelo. Una voz potente preguntó: «Saulo, ¿por qué me persigues?». Saulo se asustó. Llamó: «¿Quién eres?». La voz respondió: «Yo soy Jesús, el que tú persigues».

Suddenly, a bright light flashed around him. Saul fell to the ground. A loud voice asked, "Saul, why are you against me?" Saul was afraid. He cried out, "Who are you?" The voice replied, "I am Jesus, the one you are against."

«Ve a Damasco y allí te dirán lo que debes hacer». Cuando Saulo se levantó, no podía ver.

"Go to Damascus and you will be told what to do." When Saul got up, he could not see.

Los hombres que acompaña-
ban a Saulo lo condujeron a
la ciudad. Jesús también había
aparecido a un hombre llamado
Ananías. Jesús lo envió a ver a
Saulo.

Some men who were traveling
with Saul led him to the city.
Jesus had also appeared to a
man named Ananias. Jesus led
Ananias to Saul.

Ananías impuso las manos sobre Saulo y dijo: «Jesús me envió. Ya puedes ver. ¡Seas lleno del Espíritu Santo!». ¡Inmediatamente Saulo pudo ver! Luego Ananías lo bautizó.

Ananias laid his hands on Saul and said, "Jesus sent me to you. You may see again. Be filled with the Holy Spirit." Immediately Saul could see! Then Ananias baptized him.

Después de esto, Dios le cambió el nombre a Saulo y lo llamó Pablo. ¡Era un hombre nuevo! En vez de odiar a los seguidores de Jesús, los amaba. Y él también se convirtió en un seguidor.

After this, God changed Saul's name to Paul. He was a new man! Instead of hating Jesus' followers, he loved them. And he became a follower too.

Los viajes de Pablo

Hechos 9.20–43

Paul's Journeys

Acts 9:20–43

Pablo viajó por muchos lados. Enseñó a todas las personas con quienes se topaba acerca de Jesús. Los nuevos creyentes se llamaban *cristianos* porque eran seguidores de Cristo Jesús.

Paul traveled far and wide. He taught everyone he met about Jesus. The new believers were called *Christians* because they were followers of Jesus Christ.

Pablo viajó con diferentes ayudantes. Compartió las buenas
noticias con todas. Bautizó a
muchas personas.

Paul traveled with different
helpers. He shared the good
news with everyone he met.
He baptized many people.

En sus viajes, Pablo comenzó
muchas iglesias.

During Paul's travels,
he started many churches.

A veces caminaba kilómetros y kilómetros.

Sometimes he would walk for miles and miles.

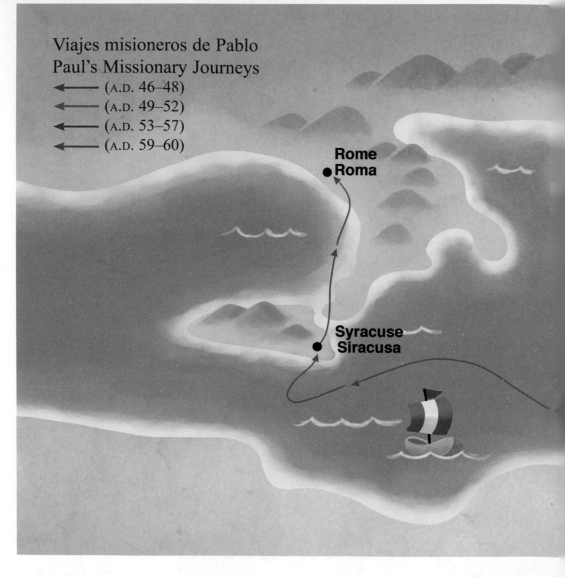

Viajes misioneros de Pablo
Paul's Missionary Journeys
- (A.D. 46–48)
- (A.D. 49–52)
- (A.D. 53–57)
- (A.D. 59–60)

Rome
Roma

Syracuse
Siracusa

Otras veces, se subía a un
barco y cruzaba los mares.

Other times, he would take
a boat across the seas.

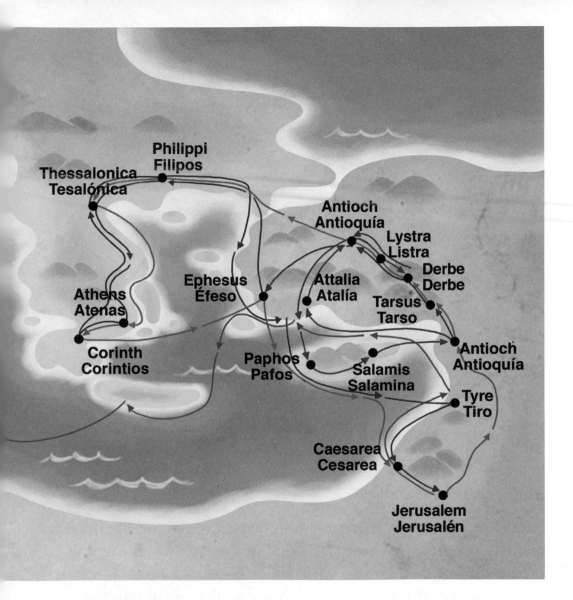

Contaba a todos acerca del amor de Jesús por todo el mundo.

He told everyone about Jesus' love for them.

Un terremoto
en la cárcel

Hechos 16.24–34

Earthquake
in Prison

Acts 16:24–34

Algunas personas no querían que Pablo y su amigo Silas predicaran acerca de Jesús. Un día los metieron en la cárcel. Pero ellos no estaban preocupados. Sabían que Dios los cuidaría.

Some people did not like Paul and his friend Silas preaching about Jesus.
One day, they were thrown into prison. But they were not worried. They knew God would take care of them.

500

Esa noche, Dios mandó un terremoto. Fue una sacudida tan grande que todas las puertas de la cárcel se abrieron y se soltaron las cadenas de todos los presos. El carcelero pensó que todos se habían escapado. ¡Le entraba terror!

That night, God sent an earthquake.
It shook so hard that all the prison doors opened up and all the prisoners' chains fell off. The guard thought everyone had escaped. He was terrified!

Pablo le dijo al carcelero: «No te preocupes. Estamos todos aquí». El carcelero no lo podía creer. Invitó a los dos hombres a su casa.

Paul told the guard, "Do not worry. We are still here." The guard was amazed.
He invited the two men to his house.

El carcelero y su familia aprendieron acerca de Jesús y decidieron seguirlo.

Al día siguiente, Pablo y Silas los dejaron para contarle a más gente acerca de Jesús.

The guard and his family learned about Jesus and decided to follow him.

The next day, Paul and Silas left to tell more people about Jesus.

¡Jesús viene!

Apocalipsis 1.1–2; 21.2–4

Muchos años después, el discípulo Juan vivía en una isla. Mientras estuvo allí tuvo una visión de un ángel.

Jesus Is Coming!

Revelation 1:1–2; 21:2–4

Many years later, the disciple John lived on an island. While he was there, an angel came to him in a vision.

504

En la visión, una luz muy brillante rodeó a Jesús. Jesús le habló a Juan y le dijo: «No tengas miedo. Escribe un libro acerca de lo que ves y envíalo a las iglesias».

In the vision, a bright light surrounded Jesus. He spoke to John, "Do not be afraid. Write a book about what you see and send it to the churches."

505

En la visión, Juan vio a Dios sentado en su trono. Un arco iris deslumbrante lo rodeaba. Juan vio que todo lo malo del mundo había llegado a su fin.

In the vision, John saw God sitting on his throne. A rainbow sparkled all around him. John saw that everything bad on the earth had come to an end.

Luego Juan vio un cielo nuevo y una tierra nueva. Dios dijo: «Ya no habrá más muerte ni tristeza ni llanto ni dolor. Yo viviré con mi pueblo para siempre».

Then John saw a new heaven and a new earth. God said, "There will be no more death or sadness or crying or pain. I will live with my people forever."

Y Jesús prometió:
«Volveré pronto».

Then Jesus promised,
"I am coming back soon."

La Biblia para principiantes

DICCIONARIO / DICTIONARY

Algunas de las palabras en este libro pueden ser nuevas para ti. En las historias las verás escritas en letra itálica. Con este diccionario podrás saber lo que significan.

Altar: Plataforma o lugar elevado en el cual se ofrecían regalos o sacrificios a Dios.

Amén: En hebreo esta palabra significa «así sea» o «que se haga verdad».

Armadura: Una cobertura externa especial, parecida a una ropa, que se hace con metal y cuero. Las personas la usaban para protegerse en las batallas.

Ejército: Un grupo de personas que pelean en la guerra.

Bautizar: Salpicar o cubrir a una persona con agua, o vertérsela por encima. Es una señal de que esa persona pertenece a Dios.

Cielo: 1. El lugar donde vive Dios. 2. El lugar donde se encuentran el sol, la luna y las estrellas. 3. El lugar adonde van los cristianos después de morir.

Codornices: Pequeñas aves que los israelitas comieron cuando estuvieron en el desierto.

Cristianos: Las personas que creen que Jesús ha perdonado sus pecados y que algún día vivirán con él para siempre en el cielo.

Día de reposo: El séptimo día de la semana en el que los judíos descansaban y adoraban a Dios.

Discípulo: Una persona que sigue a su maestro y hace lo que él le indica.

Some of the words in this book may be new to you. Throughout the stories you will see these words in italics. You can find out what they mean by using this dictionary.

Altar: A platform or raised place on which a gift, or sacrifice, was offered to God.

Amen: A Hebrew word that means "so be it" or "let it become true."

Anoint: 1. To pour olive oil on people or things. This sets them apart for God. 2. To pour oil on people as part of praying for their healing. 3. A sign of God's blessing or favor.

Armor: A special outer covering like clothes made of metal and leather. People wore it to help keep them safe in battle.

Army: A group of people who fight in wars.

Baptize: To sprinkle, pour on, or cover a person with water. It is a sign that the person belongs to Jesus.

Book of the Law: The first five books of the Bible; Genesis, Exodus, Leviticus, Numbers, and Deuteronomy.

Christians: People who believe Jesus has forgiven their sins and will someday live with him forever in heaven.

Commandment: A law or order that God gives.

Disciple: A person who follows a teacher. This person does what their teacher says to do.

Espíritu Santo: El Espíritu de Dios que crea la vida. Ayuda a la gente a hacer el trabajo de Dios. Ayuda a la gente a creer en Jesús, a amarlo y a vivir como él.

Fe: Confiar y creer en Dios. Saber que Dios es real, a pesar de que no se puede ver.

Israelitas: Gente de la nación de Israel. El pueblo escogido de Dios.

Judío: Otro nombre para las personas de Israel.

Libro de la ley: Los primeros cinco libros de la Biblia: Génesis, Éxodo, Levítico, Números y Deuteronomio.

Lepra: Una palabra usada en la Biblia para describir distintos tipos de enfermedades e infecciones de la piel. Durante los tiempos de la Biblia, los leprosos tenían que vivir en comunidades separadas para no contagiar a otros.

Maná: Comida especial enviada del cielo. Tenía sabor de galleta endulzada con miel. Cuando los israelitas salieron de Egipto, Dios les dio el maná en el desierto.

Mandamiento: Ley u orden que Dios da.

Milagro: Algo extraordinario que sucede y que solo puede hacer Dios, como calmar una tormenta o devolverle la vida a alguien.

Ofrenda: Algo que las personas le dan a Dios. Era y sigue siendo parte de la adoración al Señor.

Pascua: Una fiesta celebrada cada año para recordar el tiempo en que Dios liberó a los israelitas de Egipto. Se refiere también a cuando Dios «saltó por encima» de las casas que estaban marcadas con sangre.

Pentecostés: 1. Una celebración judía que se celebra cincuenta días después de la Pascua. 2. El día en que el Espíritu Santo descendió sobre los cristianos de una forma especial.

Faith: Trust and belief in God. Knowing God is real, even though we can't see him.

Heaven: 1. The place where God lives. 2. The sky. 3. Where Christians go after they die.

Holy Spirit: God's Spirit who creates life. He helps people do God's work. He helps people to believe in Jesus, to love him and to live like him.

Israelites: People from the nation of Israel. God's chosen people.

Jewish: Another name for a person from Israel.

Leprosy: A word used in the Bible for many different skin diseases and infections. People with leprosy during Bible times had to live in separate communities so they wouldn't infect others.

Manna: Special food sent from heaven. It tasted like wafers, or crackers, sweetened with honey. God gave it to the Israelites in the desert, after they left Egypt.

Miracle: An amazing thing that happens that only God can do. This includes such things as calming a storm or bringing someone back to life.

Offering: Something people give to God. It was and is a part of their worship.

Passover: A feast that was celebrated every year to remember the time when God set the people of Israel free from Egypt. God "passed over" their homes if they were marked with blood in the doorways.

Pentecost: 1. A Jewish celebration held 50 days after Passover. 2. The day the Holy Spirit came in a special way to live in Christians.

Priest: A man who offered gifts and prayers to God on behalf of himself or other people. He often worked in the holy tent or the temple.

Proverbios: 1. Dichos sabios. 2. (en mayúsculas) El libro en la Biblia que contiene muchos dichos sabios.

Sacerdote: Un hombre que ofrecía regalos y oraciones a Dios en su nombre y en el de otras personas. Frecuentemente trabajaba en un lugar sagrado, el tabernáculo o el templo.

Sacrificio: 1. Sacrificar: Ofrecer algo a Dios como regalo. 2. Algo que se ofrece a Dios, que se otorga como un regalo de adoración. Ver también *ofrenda.*

Salmos: Poemas de alabanza, oración o de instrucción. El libro de Salmos está lleno de estos poemas.

Siloé: Un estanque de agua en Jerusalén, donde algunas veces ocurrían milagros.

Salvador: El que nos rescata de nuestros pecados. Es uno de los nombres que se le da a Jesucristo.

Tabernáculo: Un santuario móvil de adoración. Cuando los israelitas estuvieron en el desierto, su tabernáculo era una carpa.

Templo: El edificio donde los judíos adoraban a Dios y le ofrecían sus sacrificios. Dios se hizo presente allí de manera especial.

Ungir: 1. Verter aceite de oliva sobre personas o cosas. Era una forma de separarlas para Dios. 2. Verter aceite sobre una persona como parte de orar por su sanación. 3. Una señal de favor o bendición de Dios.

Viuda: Una mujer a la que se le murió su esposo.

Proverbs: 1. Wise sayings. 2. (cap) A book of the Bible that contains many wise sayings.

Psalms: A poem of praise, prayer, or teaching. The book of Psalms is full of these poems.

Quail: Small birds the Israelites ate when they were in the desert.

Sabbath: The seventh day of the week when the Jews rested and worshiped God.

Sacrifice: 1. To give something to God as a gift. 2. Something that is given to God as a gift of worship. See also *offering.*

Siloam: A pool in Jerusalem where miracles sometimes happened.

Savior: The One who saves us from our sins. A name belonging to Jesus Christ.

Tabernacle: A traveling house of worship. When the Israelites were in the desert, their tabernacle was a tent.

Temple: The building where the Jewish people worshiped God and brought their sacrifices. God was present there in a special way.

Widow: A woman whose husband has died.

Nos agradaría recibir noticias suyas.

Por favor, envíe sus comentarios sobre este libro

a la dirección que aparece a continuación.

Muchas gracias.

Vida@zondervan.com

www.editorialvida.com

Oil City Library

Oil City, Pa.

Memorial Book
in memory of

Maude H. (Peg) Gault

presented by
The children of:
Truman and Isabelle Reed

ART OF THE
CAROUSEL

published by

CAROUSEL ART, INC.
GREEN VILLAGE, NEW JERSEY 07935

Library of Congress Catalog Card Number 82-90507

Color separations by Scantrans Pte. Ltd.

Printed in Singapore

Printed by Kok Wah Press Pte Ltd

ART OF THE

CAROUSEL

BY
CHARLOTTE DINGER

DESIGNED BY WILLIAM MANNS

EDITED BY BETTY-MAY SMITH

AUTHOR'S COLLECTION PHOTOGRAPHED BY RICHARD C. CARTER

Acknowledgements

I am indebted to the management and staff of museums and amusement parks throughout the country, the artists' families, and my many carousel friends whose invaluable assistance made this book possible.

In particular, I would like to thank: Jon Abbott, Nancy Alley, Charles Bennett, May Bowman, Al Burlew, Bill, Patty and Cindy Carlone, Erica Carmel, Joyce Carmel, John Caruthers, Marguerite Cerny, Joan and Jack Cole, Kit Denton, Elizabeth Dewar, Douglas Duncan, Ann Engelhardt, Sondra Evans, Sue and Edwin Ferren III, Camille Flankey, Nina and Maurice Fraley, Gay and Jack Friel, Neil Fulghum, Steve Gilman, Pat and Peter Greenstein, Bob Guenthner, Alma Heiss, Ann Heiss, Allan Herschell, Linda and Sam High III, Al Hofer, Carol Holden, Barney Illions, Holger Jensen, Gloria and George King, Carol Koch, Bruce Kneevals, Joe Leonard, Bill Manns, Edo McCullough, Victor Michaels, Esther Mindes, Arlene and Joe Mucerino, Ed Openshaw, Leonard Pavia, Beverly Pollen, Don Rand, Allan Recht, Dorothy Reed, Relic Design, Albert Ricci, Peggy Seehafer, George Siessel, Arthur Simmons, Betty-May Smith, Joy Smith, Rose Crane Sokolow, Carla and Dale Sorensen, William Steen, Sidney Stein, Joanne Steinberg, Marianne Stevens, Richard Strinsky, Jo and Rol Summit, Helene Sutter, Marge Swenson, Swen Swenson, Wilda Taucher, Jean and Noel Thompson, Anita Toenniges, Judy and Gray Tuttle, Tina and Bob Veder, Carol Volger, Mary Lawrence and Walter Youree, Carole Zensius, Bill Zensius, Pat and Bob Zensius.

A special thanks to Geoff Weedon and Richard Ward, authors of Fairground Art, published by White Mouse Editions, Ltd., London, 1981, for their photographs and assistance; and to their publishers Narisa Chakrabongse and Allen Levy for permitting the use of their material.

Contents

Dedication

To the young at heart
who find the carousel a
never-ending joy.

Introduction

"Carousel animals are a lovely part of our heritage, showing as much vision as many of our most respected sculptures."

David L. Shirey, Art Critic
THE NEW YORK TIMES
© 1976 by The New York Times Company
reprinted by permission

The fanciful carousel has charmed people of all ages...of all lands, but it reached its most outstanding success and beauty through the talent and creativity of American craftsmen.

In late nineteenth century America, an enthusiastic "City Beautiful" movement was underway giving birth to imposing parks, streets, squares, malls, monuments and public buildings. American artists, architects and sculptors captured the spirit of this cultural Renaissance by breaking from European tradition to seek their own direction and freedom of expression. The country's rich and diverse history was portrayed on murals, paintings, sculptures and statuary throughout the land. Cowboys and Indians represented the West; Revolutionary and Civil War heroes were exalted and glorified; and America's aspirations were symbolized by the "virtuous woman" in the forms of Columbia and Liberty.

It was during this energetic period of self-discovery that the American carousel developed into a unique artistic achievement. Roaring lions, menacing sea serpents and plump cherubs glided among flashing mirrors and glittering lights. Tiny frogs, dressed in short pants and bow ties, showed wit and whimsy as they cavorted with ponderous bison and gangling giraffes. Saddle decorations ranged from satirical to sublime as Abraham Lincoln and Teddy Roosevelt vied with leering monkeys and languid mermaids for attention. Overlooked for nearly a century, the quality and originality of carousel art had been lost in the kaleidoscope of the whirling ride.

Created by gifted hands, loving hearts, and forgotten names of a bygone era, the carousel is now a recognized and respected American art form.

Come, take a whirl with me...but, this time, observe, appreciate, and treasure the unique magic and artistic splendor of this wondrous ride.

Climb aboard, and see the carousel as you have never seen it before!

A stunning William Dentzel carousel, circa 1922. The Dentzel carousel with "jester head shields," a crown-like outer facade, splendid horses and chariots, and delicately painted ceiling panels, is an architectural masterpiece. *Photo-Philadelphia Toboggan Company, Sam High III*

Chapter 1
Development of the Carousel

In the 17th and 18th centuries, young French noblemen trained for jousting tournaments as servants pushed them round and round a centerpole. This device appears to be the forerunner of the carousel and its game of "catching the brass ring." *Drawing by Nancy Alley*

Although the concept of the carousel has been recorded since early Byzantine times, the word has been traced to twelfth century Arabian games of horsemanship called *carosellos* or "little wars." Introduced to Europe by Spanish and Italian crusaders, the contests were tests of dexterity and equestrian skill involving the tossing of fragile perfumed clay balls from one rider to another. The object of the game was to deftly catch the delicate balls to avoid the unmanly mark of the loser — a bath of sweetly scented fragrance.

The popular games spread to France; and, by the sixteenth century, they had expanded into lavish tournaments of pageantry and drama called *Carrousels*. Designers, wigmakers, seamstresses and artisans of the court spent months preparing elaborate costumes and decorations for these magnificent spectacles.

Le Grande Carrousel, the most celebrated of all Carrousels, was planned by Louis XIV in 1662, to impress his young mistress, Louise de la Valliere. Cheered by thousands and heralded by choirs and trumpet fanfares, quadrilles of cavaliers demonstrated their equestrian talents as allegorical dances and scenic displays were performed. Even today, the Arc du Carrousel commemorates the location of this grand Parisian event.

In the late seventeenth century, young French noblemen, astride legless wooden "horses," trained for spearing contests by lancing rings as they rode around a center pole. This training device appears to be the forerunner of our present day carousel and its game of "catching the brass ring." As the ride evolved into a popular form of entertainment, French peasants paid to ride crudely constructed carousels, while the aristocracy

Historical photographs, drawings, and statues of war heroes on horseback inspired American carousel carvers. The decorations on horses parading in Le Grande Carrousel of 1662 show similarities to trappings found on American carousel figures over two centuries later. *Drawing-Nancy Alley*

circled in elegant seats resembling fancy chariots, bicycles, or boats. Until the late nineteenth century, rotation power was supplied by a horse, mule, or man pushing, pulling, or cranking the mechanism.

The amusement flourished in England, and it was there that the invention of steam as a motive power revolutionized the development of the carousel. In the 1860's, Frederick Savage, an engineer-machinist, designed a portable center-mounted steam engine which could carry the weight of three or four rows of horses on platforms that reached forty-eight feet in diameter. He followed this device with a patent for overhead gears which gave an up-and-down piston-type motion to the horses we now call jumpers. Portable Savage roundabouts were an enormous success and traveled to fair grounds throughout England.

Early carousels with carved animals were in use in Germany by 1838 but were not produced in large numbers. In 1883, a German businessman, Fritz Bothman, impressed with the success of the steam-powered English roundabouts, began manufacturing machines on a grand scale; and carousels became a popular amusement throughout Europe.

Meanwhile, early nineteenth century American wheelwrights, carpenters, and blacksmiths, in their off-season, were constructing carousels carrying benches or crude loglike horses suspended by chains. These rides were usually placed in picnic groves, which were the center of sporting events and social activities in rural areas. As early as 1800, an advertisement for a wooden horse "circus ride" appeared in a Salem, Massachusetts, newspaper and mentioned similar devices already established in Philadelphia, New York, Baltimore and Boston. The ad not only extolled the innocent pleasure and great satisfaction of the circus ride, but stated that riding it was highly recommended by physicians as an aid in circulating the blood.

Similar amusement rides appeared by the 1850's in the seaside resort of Long Branch, New Jersey, and in two parks in New York City. The motive power for the carousel installed in New York's Central Park was supplied by a horse circling in an underground pit beneath the wooden platform. At the sound of a tapping stick from above, the animal dutifully stopped and started the carousel.

In 1864, eighteen year-old Gustav Dentzel arrived

An English roundabout, typical of those that traveled to
fairgrounds throughout Britain. *Photo - Geoff Weedon and
Richard Ward*

A small primitive horse typical of those carved in the first half of
the nineteenth century. Horses and wooden chair swings,
suspended by iron rods or chains, swung out as the simple device
revolved. The horse has an iron patch covering deteriorated wood
on a section of its head no doubt fashioned by a blacksmith.
From the author's collection.

Typical two abreast "flying horse" carousel operating at Lake
Pleasant in Montaque, Massachusetts. circa 1870. *Photo-Margaret
Woodbury Strong Museum, Rochester, New York*

Late nineteenth century Dentzel carousel. Rocking tubs or gondolas, similar to those found on European carousels, were replaced in America by stationary chariots before the turn of the century. *Photo-Nelson Ferris*

from Germany and opened a cabinet shop in Philadelphia. Gustav's father, Michael, a wheelwright by trade, who had success carving horses and building carousels in Germany, influenced the young woodworker to try his hand at constructing carousels in America. Three years later, in 1867, the young entrepreneur formed the G.A. Dentzel Company and pioneered the carousel industry in America.

As business prospered, Dentzel moved to larger quarters and employed some of the most talented carvers ever to wield a chisel. One was Daniel Carl Muller, whose finely detailed figures are among the most admired of all carousel carvings. Although early Dentzel carousels combined elegant horses and a variety of menagerie animals, including lions, tigers and giraffes, the hiring of master craftsman Salvatore Cernigliaro introduced whimsical rabbits, cats and bears to Dentzel carousels. It was *Cherni* who first created lavish trappings of flowers, bells, bows, and intricate halters and straps.

Six years after Dentzel erected his first carousel, a Danish woodworker employed in a furniture factory in Brooklyn was inspired to try his hand at carving wooden animals. In 1876, Charles Looff, working alone in his spare time, carved, painted, and assembled the first carousel to be installed in the most celebrated amusement center in the country, Coney Island.

Looff's carousel, with its gaudy, sweetly-appealing horses, was installed in a popular beach pavillion and was a resounding success. The young carver's next carousel was commissioned for Charles Feltman's huge beer-garden restaurant, which had blossomed from a simple boardwalk hot dog stand. Like a magnet, the glittering new carousel drew thousands of daily visitors. At the turn of the century, the famous ride was partially destroyed by fire. Amusement genius, William Mangels, and Russian carver, Marcus Charles Illions, were hired to restore the landmark Feltman carousel. Illions, who learned his craft under the direction of Frederick Savage,

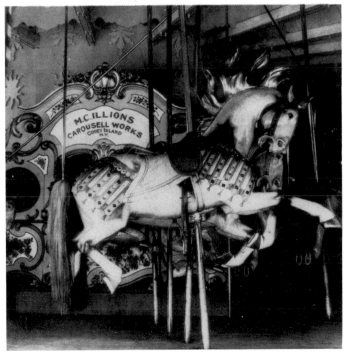

"Presidents" Carousel produced around 1890 by pioneer Coney Island carver, Charles Looff. Horses show German influence of eagle back saddles, tassels, and etched mirrored jewels. (Photographed in Lakeside Park, Syracuse, New York, in 1903) *Photo-Joseph Carrolo*

One of America's most famous carousels was housed in the huge Feltman's restaurant complex in Coney Island. The Feltman carousel was a favorite of many celebrities at the turn of the century, including Diamond Jim Brady, Lillian Russell, and Lily Langtry. *Photo-Bill Carlone*

One of the many flamboyant carousels produced by M.C. Illions that dotted Coney Island in its heyday. Horses, typical of Illions' style, are wildly animated with exciting gold leaf manes, elaborately carved ornamentation and a profusion of multi-colored, facted jewels. *Photo-Bernard Illions*

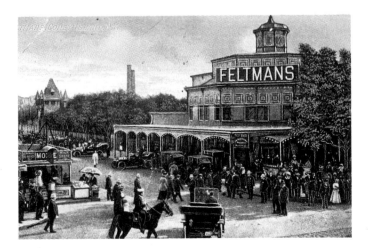

Trolley owners, wishing to stimulate week-end and evening business, built amusement parks at the "end of the line." Dressed in their Sunday finery, this crowd boards the trolley to Kennywood Park, located on the outskirts of Pittsburg in West Mifflin, Pennsylvania. *Photo-Kennywood Park*

breathed new life into the famous ride. His wildly animated, bejewelled animals caused a sensation; and Illions' carousels spread throughout Coney Island.

In 1882, Allan Herschell, part owner of a company that made machinery and boilers, visited New York City, where he saw an operating carousel. He returned to his home in North Tonowanda, New York, determined to build a *steam-riding gallery.* His company (first known as the Armitage Herschell Company, then the Herschell-Spillman Company, and, finally, the Allan Herschell Company) except for a few large park machines, constructed very popular small portable carousels. Produced in great numbers, these carousels traveled to country fairs and carnivals in rural farming communities.

The invention of the trolley increased the demand for carousels as trolley owners, wishing to stimulate weekend and evening business, built amusement parks at the "end of the line."

In 1893, as the popular new ride spread across the country, "Colonel" Charles Wallace Parker, a colorful figure from Abilene, Kansas, decided that the time was right to build carousels in the Midwest. As orders poured in for his portable *Carry-us-alls,* the Colonel expanded his business to include a full line of carnival equipment. Parker horses, reflecting the Midwestern influence, were often adorned with rifles, ears of corn and sunflowers. It has been reported that the most notable employee of the C.W. Parker Company was Dwight David Eisenhower, who, at the age of fourteen, sanded horses in the Parker factory located near his home in Abilene.

Philadelphia businessman, Henry B. Auchy, inspired by the success of Gustav Dentzel, formed the Philadelphia Toboggan Company for the purpose of building carousels and coasters in 1903. Daniel and Alfred Muller, who had left the Dentzel firm, were hired to supply the fledgling company with their first horses and menagerie animals. During its long and successful history, the Philadelphia Toboggan Company employed a number of exceptional carvers, including Frank Carretta, who joined the firm in 1912. Under the direction of Carretta, the company produced sturdily crafted carousels that were exquisite in beauty and design.

Around 1905, Charles Carmel opened a woodworking shop just a short distance from Coney Island. Carmel, an outstanding artist who had carved carousel animals for both Looff and Mangels, supplied lovely

Produced in great numbers at a cost of around $2,000, portable Herschell-Spillman "Steam Riding Galleries" traveled around the world, circa 1905. *Photo-Nelson Ferris*

Steam-driven Parker carousel built in Abilene, Kansas. An early "grasshopper" mechanism, attached to pole and platform, allowed the horses to go up and down. *Photo-Don Rand and Ed Openshaw*

15

Early Philadelphia Toboggan Company carousel, circa 1905. The carousel was photographed after some of the standing figures were converted to jumpers, explaining their awkward leg positions. With the introduction of overhead gears, which allowed horses to move up and down, many stationary carousels were returned to factories for conversion. *Photo -Philadelphia Toboggan Company, Sam High III*

Carousel at Rye's Playland, Rye, New York, is a showcase for the exciting carousel figures carved by Charles Carmel, circa 1910, Jeweled horses laden with armour, feathers, tassels and flowers are a Carmel "tour de force." *Photo-George King*

Elongated, wild-eyed, aggressive horses, typical of Stein and Goldstein, are on the carousel operating at Sportland Pier in Wildwood, New Jersey, circa 1912. *Photo-George King*

One of Dare's most outstanding carvings, a sea horse with agate eyes, circa 1890. *From the Eleanor and Mabel Van Alstyne Collection, Smithsonian Institute, Washington, D.C.*

A typical Dare horse with swirling marble eyes, innocent expression, plump face, flat nostrils, and static pose. *Photo-Marge Swenson from the Sharkey Collection*

spirited figures to a number of firms that constructed machinery and frames.

Two years later, in 1907, Solomon Stein and Harry Goldstein, who met while carving carousel figures for the William Mangels Company, joined forces in Brooklyn and formed the Artistic Carousel Manufacturers. They carved aggressive looking steeds, laden with roses and intricate ornamentation. The largest carousels, built to carry over one hundred people, were produced by Stein and Goldstein.

A number of less significant companies played a role in the development of the American carousel. The most prominent of these firms was the New York Carousal Manufacturing Company, founded in Brooklyn by Charles Dare. Dare was manufacturing a wide variety of amusement devices by 1890, but it appears that his company produced only a small number of carousels compared to major carving shops. Dare figures were varied and included lions, camels, elephants, deer and donkeys, in addition to horses with swirling glass marble eyes.

Other firms, including Norman and Evans, Bungarz Steam Wagon and Carrousele Works, and the United States Merry-Go-Round Company, produced carousels on a limited scale; but their efforts resulted in few significant carvings.

While fire, storm and neglect destroyed many carousels, accidents also took their toll. This barnstorming pilot made an unexpected landing at the Johnny Jones Carnival on top of a 1917 portable Philadelphia Toboggan Company carousel (#40). *Photo-Philadelphia Toboggan Company, Sam High III*

A fascinating group of riders "enjoying" an early Gustav Dentzel carousel. *Photo-Nelson Ferris*

Fine fiberglass reproduction of a large, outside row jumper from the Philadelphia Toboggan Company carousel at Disneyworld, Orlando, Florida. The carousel, which formerly operated at Olympic Park, Maplewood, New Jersey, now has a mixture of wooden and fiberglass horses. *Photo-Arlene and Joseph Mucerino*

The handcrafted carousel prospered through the twenties, but the lovingly guided chisel of the carousel sculptor was put aside forever when mass production techniques and the Great Depression dealt the industry a fatal blow. Small cast aluminum carousel animals have been manufactured since that time, and now fine horses and menagerie figures of all sizes are being reproduced in fiberglass.

Accidents, fires, storms and neglect have taken their toll, but approximately 300 handcrafted carousels are still operating throughout the United States. As museums, collectors, and preservationists draw attention to the beauty of carousel art, concerned citizens are raising necessary funds to preserve and maintain operating carousels in their communities. This growing spirit of public awareness and concern may be the salvation of the American handcrafted carousel.

19

Magnificent Stein and Goldstein "Lead" horse—always the most elaborately decorated figure on the carousel. Delicate roses carved in deep relief temper the angry, forceful expression of this large stander. *From the author's collection*

Chapter 2

Collecting Carousel Art

The extremely rare and beautiful Dentzel hippocampus with the head of a horse and the body of a fish. Mythical sea creatures were carved by both European and American carvers, but not in profusion, since children preferred the less intimidating horses. *Photo- The Redbug Workshop*

Beauty, rarity, size, proportion, animation, condition and intricacy of the carving are important considerations in evaluating a carousel figure. As is true with any antique or collectible, it is important to purchase the best quality you can afford, since one outstanding carving is much more satisfying and is a better investment than two or three of ordinary quality. However, no matter how rare or exceptional the figure is to others, the primary consideration is *your* emotional reaction—the animal must excite and delight you.

Due to their superior artistry, American carousel animals are the most valued by collectors. American figures can be identified by their more elaborately carved right side - the side facing the viewer, while the left side of most European animals is the more ornate. This distinguishing feature can be explained by the counter-clockwise rotation of American carousels and the clockwise movement of all English and many European machines.

Unless the figure can be documented as particularly historic or significant, its age is not as important as the overall grandeur and artistry of the carving. While folk art collectors often prefer the more primitive early figures, an elaborately carved animal is usually far more attractive to a carousel collector than a plain one, thirty or forty years older. By 1915, many carving shops were using machines to rough out the bodies of carousel figures; but the heads, fancy trappings and fine finish work continued to be done by hand. The quality and value of the animals suffered little in the transition.

American carousel animals were produced in various sizes, graduating from the largest on the outside row

A Stein and Goldstein lavishly embellished "king" horse dressed for battle, circa 1912. A fancy gorget, elaborate head shield and layers of mail decorate this magnificent armoured horse. *From the author's collection*

A rare signed horse with initials "PTC" carved on the trappings. Although the Philadelphia Toboggan Company signed more horses than any other company, few carvers signed their work. *Photo-Philadelphia Toboggan Company, Sam High III*

to the smallest on the inside. Horses with at least three feet resting on the platform are called "standing figures." Outside row standers are the most elaborately decorated and intricately carved horses and are the most prized by collectors. They are the largest horses—usually measuring around sixty inches from the nose to the tail and approximately sixty inches in height. Horses with two back feet resting on the platform and front legs posed in the air are called "prancers"; they are usually found on the inner rows. Jumping horses, distinguished by their four bent legs which never touch the platform, are the horses that move up and down.

American standers, prancers and jumpers were carved in sizes ranging from approximately forty-two inches to over sixty inches in length, depending on their position on the carousel. Stationary figures (standers or prancers) have small pole holes measuring about three-quarters of an inch in diameter, while jumpers have larger pole holes measuring approximately one and one-half inches in diameter. Although most carousels had a mixture of standing and jumping horses, the earliest carousels (known as stationary machines) had all standing and prancing horses. Some later carousels carried all jumping horses; large, ornate outside jumpers are also highly prized by collectors.

The rarest and most sought after carousel figures are *lead* or *king* horses, signed figures, and fine menagerie animals. King or lead horses are outside row figures-large in size and very elaborate in ornamentation and detail. They are often ladened with armour or draped with roses. Carvers rarely signed their work, but a few special and highly valued animals do carry the signature of their carver or company initials on their trappings.

Figures other than horses, known as menagerie animals and among the most prized of all carvings, were never as popular as horses. Carving companies concentrated their efforts mainly on horses because children preferred them to the more intimidating lions, tigers and sea monsters. With rare exception, the whimsically appealing menagerie animals produced by Dentzel and his master carver, Salvatore Cernigliaro, are the most highly regarded by collectors. Even though menagerie figures are rarer than horses, there is a wide disparity in their quality and desirability. Sizes vary from large, showy, outside row figures to small intricately carved animals found on the inner row. While many figures are life-like in proportion and design, others are cartoonlike caricatures of the animals they portray.

The condition of a carousel figure is, of course, an important consideration. A figure in fine original paint is

An elaborately decorated stander from the Philadelphia Toboggan Company. Standers have at least three feet resting on the platform and are usually found on the outside row of the carousel. *Photo - Philadelphia Toboggan Company, Sam High III*

A Muller-Dentzel prancer with rear feet on the platform and front feet raised. Prancers were usually on the inner-rows of stationary carousels. *Photo-Dale Sorensen*

A Philadelphia Toboggan Company elaborately festooned outside-row jumper. Jumpers have four feet raised off the platform, which allows the animal to move up and down. *Photo-Philadelphia Toboggan Company, Sam High III*

the most valued, followed by a carving in good period paint. An animal with thick kelly green or shocking pink paint covering its body does not, however, discourage a collector. An experienced eye can see the quality of the carving through layers of garish *park paint*. Sometimes it's difficult to convince antique buffs that stripping and restoring a carousel animal does not decrease the value of the figure. The fact is that a quality restoration can only enhance an animal found in thick, ugly paint.

Hasty repairs employing tin patches, nails, screws and metal braces are sometimes concealed by encrusted paint. A careful and thorough examination of the figure should reveal patched areas. Minor repair problems are encountered quite often and are relatively easy to solve. However, major structural repair involving separated body seams and missing parts can be expensive to restore.

An awl or sharp pocket knife pushed into the wood surface of deteriorated areas may reveal a more serious problem. If the knife sinks easily into the wood and the area feels crumbly and soft, the figure is most likely a victim of dry rot. Since dry rot penetrates wood until its action is stopped, the affected areas must be dug out and scraped. A product which halts dry rot and hardens soft areas to a wood-like consistency is available at most marine supply stores. Eliminating dry rot in a small area is not too difficult; but, if the dry rot is extensive, consider the work and expense involved before purchasing the figure.

A problem which can be as serious as dry rot is worm, beetle or termite infestation. If the carving is being purchased in a hot humid area of the country, pay special attention in examining the animal for insect damage. Inspection of the body cavity through the pole hole may reveal traces of grainy sawdust or a honeycomb effect in the wood, both indications of insect invasion. Depending upon the duration of the infestation, damage may range from a small area to the entire animal. Termites, worms and beetles sometimes destroy all but the thin outside shell. Unless you're prepared for the worst, a figure in this condition should be avoided.

Once you've made up your mind to purchase a carousel figure, it's important to gather as much information as possible so that you'll be prepared to make a wise investment. Reading materials and addresses of collectors' organizations can be located through your local library. Carousel organizations provide historical information, restoration advice, and often include advertised figures for sale. Visit museums with permanent exhibitions of carousel figures, and watch for announcements of loan exhibitions featuring carousel art. Collectors,

too, are a prime source of information; and many will allow you to visit and photograph their collections.

Most antiques and collectibles appear with some regularity in antique shows and dealer shops, allowing prospective buyers to compare quality and prices before making their first purchase. Unfortunately, this is not too often the case with carousel animals. Dealers with limited booth space often opt to display smaller more portable items at shows, rather than large heavy carousel figures. The prospective carousel collector often feels a sense of frustration in attempting to find an animal for sale.

Collectors, though, have found a number of effective ways to locate carousel animals. First, it's important to let your friends and acquaintances know of your interest in carousel figures. Be sure to specify that you are looking for a carved wooden animal to eliminate calls about fiberglass and metal figures. It's a good idea to consult the yellow pages of your telephone directory under the heading *Amusements* or *Amusement Devices* to check if the companies listed have any suggestions or leads. Use the directory for a list of antique dealers in your area; they might have an animal for sale. If they don't, ask them for leads. Dealers are always in contact with pickers and others in the trade. Even though they may not have a figure available at the moment, their contacts may result in a purchase. Offer dealers a finder's fee of ten percent if they locate a figure that you ultimately buy from their lead. Reputable dealers specializing in carousel animals are most important to a new collector. Many have a buy-back policy and issue brochures filled with photos of figures for sale. These brochures allow you to compare quality and price.

Take your camera to as many amusement parks as you're able to visit. Photograph all of the figures on the carousel—take full shots, head shots and close-ups of carving details. Your photos will be an invaluable aid in the study and comparison of the various carvers' work. As you cover amusement parks and traveling carnivals in your area, ask park owners and carousel operators if they can supply you with leads. Lists of old amusement parks that are now nonexistent can be important. In the old days when a park closed, carousel figures were often scrapped following a fire or natural disaster. Collectors have found animals stashed away in basements or attics for years just by advertising in local papers where parks operated in years past.

Check auction gallery sales and subscribe to antique publications. Some offer a first-class mailing service for an additional fee, assuring you a first look at items offered for sale. Many collectors place ads in newspapers or magazines specializing in antiques with an offer of a

Magnificent Philadelphia Toboggan Company Roman chariot built to entice the more timid riders.

finder's fee for leads that result in the purchase of a carousel figure. Other possible sources are display houses which supply items for decorating store windows. Carousel figures are sometimes used as display props and may be available to buy. These companies can be located through the yellow pages of your phone directory under *Displays* or *Window Displays*.

It's a good idea to subscribe to both local and national amusement trade publications, since they sometimes carry ads offering carousel animals for sale. Amusement park owners usually have the names and addresses of these publications.

When you do locate an animal for sale that is close by, it's wise to make immediate arrangements to take a look. By delaying a day or two, you may find that the figure has already been sold. If the animal is located an inaccessible distance from you, it's usually possible to have a photo mailed with a *hold* on the figure until you receive the picture. Be sure to explain that the photograph you want must be taken with the animal's head to the right so that the fancy or *romance* side is visible. Ask for measurements of the horse, requesting nose to tail, shoe to ear and shoe to saddle measurements. It is very difficult to determine the size of a figure from a photograph - and size, of course, enters into the final determination.

Related adornments of the carousel add interest to a collection. These collectibles include decorative shields and panels, fancy mirrors, rounding boards, and chariot sides. Many chariots are exquisitely carved and compete well with the finest animals in artistry and design.

Most collectors find that carousel art adds a fascinating new dimension to their lives through a continual expansion of knowledge, enthusiasm, and friendship with craftsmen, dealers and fellow collectors who share a similar interest.

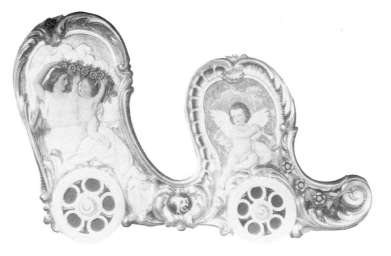

An exquisite rococo Philadelphia Toboggan Company chariot attributed to Frank Carretta, with the PTC signature carved on a medallion, circa 1915. *Photo-Philadelphia Toboggan Company, Sam High III*

25

Philadelphia Toboggan Company shop, 1920. By the twenties, a number of companies used carving machines to rough out the bodies of the animals; but the fine detailed carvings were always finished by hand. *Photo-Philadelphia Toboggan Company, Sam High III*

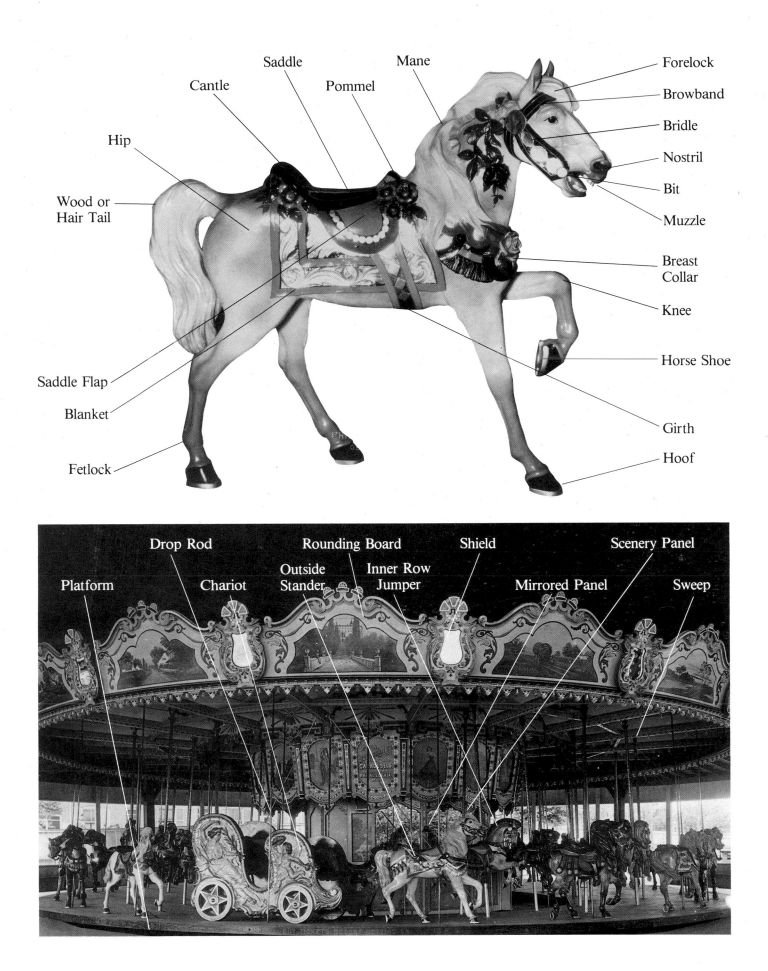

Saddle

Cantle

Pommel

Mane

Forelock

Browband

Bridle

Nostril

Bit

Muzzle

Hip

Wood or
Hair Tail

Breast
Collar

Knee

Horse Shoe

Saddle Flap

Blanket

Girth

Fetlock

Hoof

Drop Rod

Rounding Board

Shield

Scenery Panel

Outside
Stander

Inner Row
Jumper

Platform

Chariot

Mirrored Panel

Sweep

Examples of showfronts still in existence in the Netherlands. The earliest European showfronts were part of nineteenth century traveling marionette shows. By the turn of the century, Savage, Tidman, and Orton and Spooner were constructing magnificent facades that traveled to fairgrounds throughout Europe.

Large elaborate band organs, some with moving figures that "conducted" or "played" instruments in time to the music, were sometimes incorporated into enormous, portable showfronts. *Photo-Geoff Weedon and Richard Ward*

Chapter 3

European and Mexican Carousel Carvings

Small "dobby" horses, pigs, and motor cars on board a hand-cranked English kiddie ride by J.R. Anderson, circa 1905. *Photo -Malcolm Gliksten, Relic Design*

The European carousel industry appears to have originated in Germany. Records show that Michael Dentzel was in business in the 1830's; and by 1914, eleven major carousel companies were successfully established. European carousels, seldom placed on a permanent site, were built to withstand the rigors of travel from fairground to fairground. The area near Neustadt-Dresden became the hub of Germany's carousel industry. The most prominent companies were Heyn, Müller, Hübner, Buhler, and Poeppig. Horses offered by these firms were remarkably alike except for small variations in saddles and trappings.

German carousel horses were most often perky prancers or elongated jumpers with alert expressions. Decorations were attractively ornate and were often set off by mirrored *jewels*. The figures, sometimes with metal ears and carved parrots or other birds at the back of their saddles, were well proportioned; but pose variations were limited. Attractively carved German menagerie animals included goats, polar bears, giraffes, chickens, reindeer, burros, tigers, lions, swans, peacocks, lambs and ostriches. Chariots sometimes resembled gondolas or sleighs but most often were set on carved wooden wheels and ornately decorated with a variety of figures, including maidens, warriors, eagles, and cherubs.

Figures produced by carving companies located in Holland and Belgium were very similar to those crafted in Germany. German carousel company catalogs were widely distributed throughout Europe, and some of the same figures they offered for sale were found in catalogs of carving shops in other countries. While it is believed that most of these figures were German in origin, it is difficult to accurately document this as fact.

Except for the few permanently installed salon

German carousel with rocking gondolas and jumping horses by Heyn. Heyn horses have gentle pretty faces, perky expressions and decorative mirrored jewels. Horses, usually in dappled paint, are often in a prancing position supported by a rocking metal stand. *Photo-Geoff Weedon and Richard Ward*

Prancers from Josef Hubner factory on a mixed French and German carousel. Hubner horses can be distinguished from similar Heyn carvings by their tapering noses and clumps of hair on their manes. *Photo-Geoff Weedon and Richard Ward*

Double-decker German carousel with prancing horses. Two-story carousels were not too popular in America due to difficulties in quickly loading and unloading passengers. *Photo-Geoff Weedon and Richard Ward*

Heyn horse on two-story carousel built by Bothman, circa 1900. Note etched mirror ornaments and parrot saddle cantle imitated by American carvers. *Photo Geoff Weedon and Richard Ward*

German giraffe seat from child's carousel. The small carved musicians were used as decorations in the center of German kiddie carousels that carried wooden motor vehicles in place of horses. *From the author's collection*

English carousel, rotating in a clockwise direction, allowed for the proper equestrian left-sided mount which stemmed from a right-handed swordsman's need to mount without discomfort. *Photo-Geoff Weedon and Richard Ward*

Imparting a feeling of fantasy is this J.R. Anderson galloper. Note Anderson trademarks: a flower at the bridle rosette, elaborate ornamentation, scrolls, leaves, and mythical beasts flowing onto the animal's body, alert forward ears, and expressive eyes. circa 1900. *Photo-Geoff Weedon and Richard Ward*

English carousel horse and rooster by Arthur E. Anderson. Oversized buckles, a larger flower at the bridle rosette and flamboyant trappings are typical of Anderson figures. *Photo-Geoff Weedon and Richard Ward*

carousels, most European carousels rotated in a counter-clockwise direction so that the right hand was free to catch the brass ring. The ring-catching game, so popular in Europe, never took hold in England. To this day, English carousels rotate in a clockwise direction which allows for the proper left-sided equestrian mount.

English carousel figures are the easiest to identify — their more elaborately carved side is on the left, due to their clockwise rotation. Major carousel companies were the Frederick Savage Company of Kings Lynn, C.J. Spooner of Burton-on-Trent, and J.R. Anderson of Bristol. Savage was the founder of the carousel industry in England and the developer of the steam carousel. Savage horses were always jumpers or *gallopers* (as they were called in England) and often seated two passengers. Leg positions were parallel, lending a rigid, static appearance to the figure. Carvings were more fanciful than representational, but the overall effect of the lavishly decorated figures was a visual delight. Menagerie figures included roosters, dragons, pigs, ostriches, and centaurs. Centaurs, a result of a surge of patriotism during the Boer War (1899-1902), were double-seater horses with lifelike waist-up carvings of British political or military heroes in place of the usual horse's head.

Rooster by C.J. Spooner. English roosters were carved with both single and double saddles. Two-seater ostriches and roosters had hinged necks which simplified packing and storing these large figures. *From the Swen Swenson Collection*

Two-seater Savage galloper, circa 1912. The parallel leg positions, which allowed for easy packing, lent a stiff rigidity to Savage carvings. *Photo-Geoff Weedon and Richard Ward*

The most realistic, well proportioned horses produced in England were carved by Orton and Spooner. Wide round eyes, well defined muscles, pleasant, alert expressions, layered saddle carvings, and a feeling of motion mark this figure as an Orton and Spooner galloper, circa 1918. *Photo-Geoff Weedon and Richard Ward*

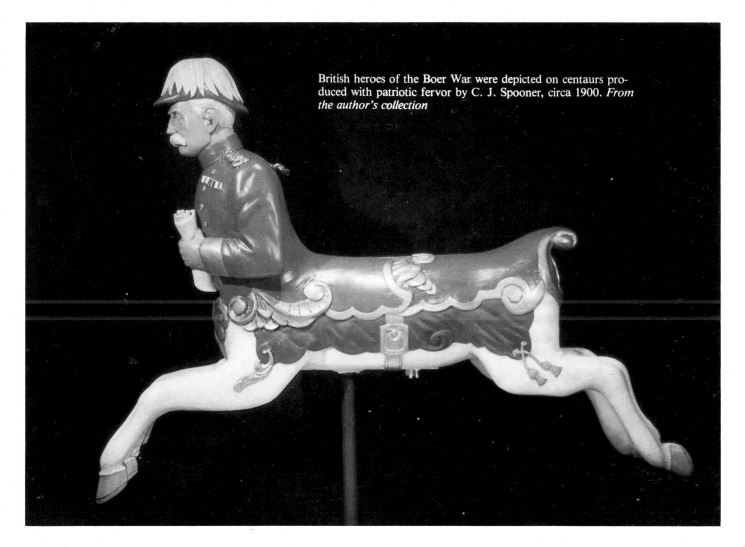

British heroes of the Boer War were depicted on centaurs produced with patriotic fervor by C. J. Spooner, circa 1900. *From the author's collection*

Savage never signed his animals, although his competitors, C.J. Spooner and J.R. Anderson, signed at least one horse on each carousel. A variety of first names were painted on ribbons flowing from the bridle of many horses; English carousel figures, similarly posed and decorated, often had metal ears. A distinctive feature of horses produced by J.R. Anderson was a large carved flower found at the bridle rosette.

The major French carousel manufacturers were Bayol, Coquereau et Maréchal, and N. Henri de Vos. Happily, for the sake of identification, company plaques were attached to the animals; and some have survived. The famous Limonaire Freres Organ Company of Paris produced a limited number of carousel figures, but the major companies were located in Angers. Early French carousel carvers concentrated their talents on horses and a variety of domesticated barnyard creatures—dogs, cats,

A brass handle protrudes from this centaur carving of a highly decorated British officer from the Boer War, circa 1900. *From the Swen Swenson Collection*

cows, rabbits, and, especially, pigs. The well-proportioned realistic French pigs with floppy ears and beribboned curly metal tails have a whimsical charm and are considered by many to be more appealing than the more ferocious looking American pigs. French cows are also especially engaging, as are some of the later French carvings of small kangaroos, elephants, wild boars and giraffes.

In the thirties, cartoon characters of Donald Duck, Goofy, Bugs Bunny, and others were carved by French craftsmen for kiddie carousels. American cartoon characters were never carved in the United States; they are either French or Mexican in origin. Animals carved in France were usually crafted from yellow woods with knots and grainy textures. Small stationary figures were sometimes bolted to the platform; instead of having poles or reins, they had U-shaped handles attached to the body.

Crestings, mirrors and decorative panels found on European carousels were stunning in their intricacy and design. Graced by lifelike carved figures, heavily decorated, huge showfront facades, some fifty feet long and twenty-five feet high, accompanied rides as they traveled from fairground to fairground. As the cinema grew in popularity, interest in fairs declined. In the twenties, it became too expensive to build, dismantle and transport the cumbersome roundabouts which, by then, were competing with mass produced thrill rides. Over the years, huge elaborately carved facades and fancy carousels were burned or left to disintegrate in showmen's yards. Unfortunately, few have survived.

A charming French dog carved by Bayol for a child's carousel. *From the Alma Heiss Collection*

Similarly designed jumpers and prancers were produced by Bayol, the largest carousel company in France. Bayol horses have simple trappings, happy faces and small brass plaques attached to saddle blankets. The cow in the background is German. French companies offered a wide variety of German menagerie figures for sale in their catalogs. *Photo-Geoff Weedon and Richard Ward*

A French kangaroo from a child's carousel carved in the twenties by Coquerau and Maréchal. The kangaroo and its companion carvings of such varied animals as foxes, cockatoos and wild boars are among the most appealing, realistic figures produced by French carvers. Trademarks of these animals are scooped saddles, blanket tassels and well-defined muscles and sinews. *From the author's collection.*

A whimsically charming French pig carved by Bayol, circa 1900. *From the Jean and Noel Thompson Collection*

French elephant in a circus pose from a stationary carousel. *From the Greenstein Collection*

Bells and tassels decorate this French Bayol donkey whose elongated saddle is large enough for two riders. A large brass handle protrudes from the neck. Bayol figures are finely carved and have a wistful charm but legs are disproportionately short. For an additional charge, this animal was available with a nodding head. *From the Swen Swenson Collection*

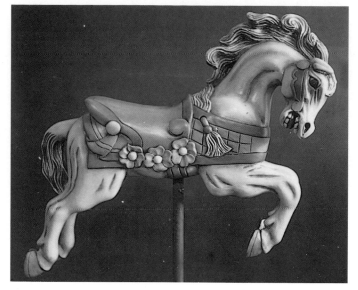

A dynamic Mexican carousel horse with a highly stylized, flying mane. The dramatic figure resembles lead horses carved by the C.W. Parker Company. *From the Youree Collection*

A small, fancy Mexican carousel horse by Flores—restored by Tobin Fraley. *From the Gerald Lamberti Collection*

Early in the twentieth century, portable carousels manufactured by the Herschell-Spillman and C.W. Parker Companies traveled to Mexico as part of gala festivals and celebrations.

As the American carousel industry was winding down in the twenties, Mucio Juarez, a carver of European furniture, pioneered the carousel industry in Mexico. Juarez's carvings, now quite difficult to find, were influenced by the traveling American carousels which he saw in his youth. When the master died, his protege, Flores, and Flores' students, Luis Ortega and Ismael Serrano, continued his carving tradition. Carousel carvings in Mexico were done under the most primitive circumstances; the craftsmen usually worked at home with the simplest of tools.

Mexican animals, carved of savino wood, are often small—usually measuring less than thirty-six inches long by twenty inches high. Ornately carved on both sides, most horses have wooden eyes and tails, prominent teeth, bulging straining muscles and oversize saddles; they somewhat resemble Parker horses. Menagerie figures are often charming replicas of a wide variety of animals, including apes, camels, polar bears, seals, rams, and coyotes. Fantasy creatures; e.g., witches, mermaids, and American cartoon characters such as Donald Duck, Mickey Mouse, Pluto, Superman and Mighty Mouse, were favorite subjects of Mexican carousel carvers in the thirties.

The art of carousel carving continued from one generation to another and is still flourishing in Mexico.

A Mexican carousel horse, stripped of paint, showing typical wooden eyes and tail, stylized mane, and poor construction details. *From the Douglas Duncan Collection*

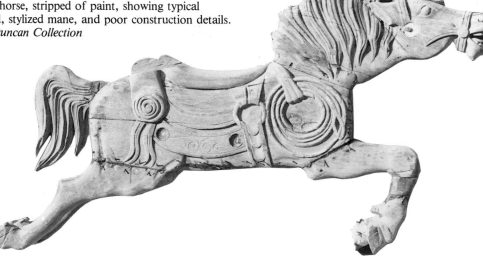

A carved re-creation of a favorite Mexican cartoon character, Mighty Mouse. American cartoon characters were never carved in the United States. *From the Douglas Duncan Collection*

Small Mexican giraffe for a child's carousel, by Ortega. *From the Youree Collection*

Tiny Mexican ape carved for a child's carousel. *From the Swenson Collection*

Country Fair Style Parker horses racked and ready to move to the next town. Portability and packability of the animals were prime considerations in the design of Country Fair Style horses. *Courtesy of Nancy Alley*

Chapter 4
American Carving Styles

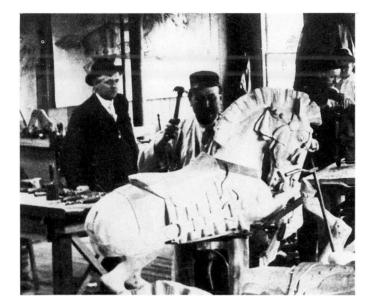

A Country Fair Style carver from the Allan Herschell Company puts the finishing touches on a large, roach-maned jumper.

There is little question that early nineteenth century American carousel carvings fall into the folk art or primitive genre. Often, with barely discernible features, early horses were crudely fashioned from logs by wheelwrights and carpenters in their spare time. Refinements such as horse hair manes and tails and upholstered saddles were added to some carousel horses by the mid-nineteenth century. Often called *flying horses,* these figures hung by chains or poles that swung out as the ride turned. Examples of these early carvings can be seen on one of America's oldest operating carousels at Watch Hill, Rhode Island.

When applied to later carousel figures produced by the major carving companies, there is a general disagreement over the term *folk art*. Perhaps James Duff, Director of the Brandywine River Museum, summed it up best when he said, "Carousel carvers were not folk artists, but highly skilled artisans who used their considerable talents to raise the craft of carving to a fine art."

Three styles evolved from the major American carving companies. The realistic, classically elegant animals carved by the G. A. Dentzel Company, the Philadelphia Toboggan Company, and the D. C. Muller and Brother Company were the trademark of the *Philadelphia Style*. Richly decorated, yet harmoniously refined, their carvings reflected the propriety of Philadelphia and its conservative Main Line. Housed in spacious park pavillions surrounded by trees and rolling carpets of manicured lawns, Philadelphia style carousels were a successful and appropriate amusement for late nineteenth century city parks.

In contrast, the heavily jewelled, gilded and lavishly

These early prancers with horsehair manes and tails were large enough for two young riders, circa 1895. *Photo-John Caruthers*

decorated animals of Charles Looff, Marcus Charles Illions, Charles Carmel, Solomon Stein and Harry Goldstein were carved in the *Coney Island Style*. The Coney Island Style reflected the glitter and flamboyance of the most celebrated amusement center in the country. Competing with a panoply of games of chance and a diversity of live entertainers, including such celebrated names as Eddie Cantor and Jimmy Durante, Coney Island carousels were created to attract and dazzle the senses.

Animals carved in the simpler *Country Fair Style* by the Herschell-Spillman Company of North Tonawanda, New York, and the C.W. Parker Company of Kansas suited the traveling and rural carousels they were designed to serve. The style was influenced by the need for packability, portability and large-scale production.

Styles became less distinctive as carvers moved from one shop to another. Successful patterns and ideas crossed over and similarities in carvings evolved.

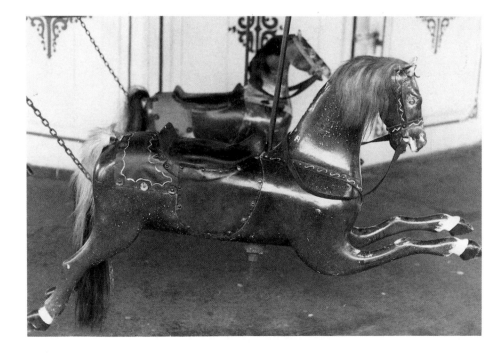

Early "flying horses" on one of America's oldest operating carousels at Watch Hill, Rhode Island. These primitive horses, in a rocking horse position, have horse hair manes and tails. As the carousel revolves, the horses, hanging from suspended rods and chains, "fly" out. *Courtesy of Albert Hofer*

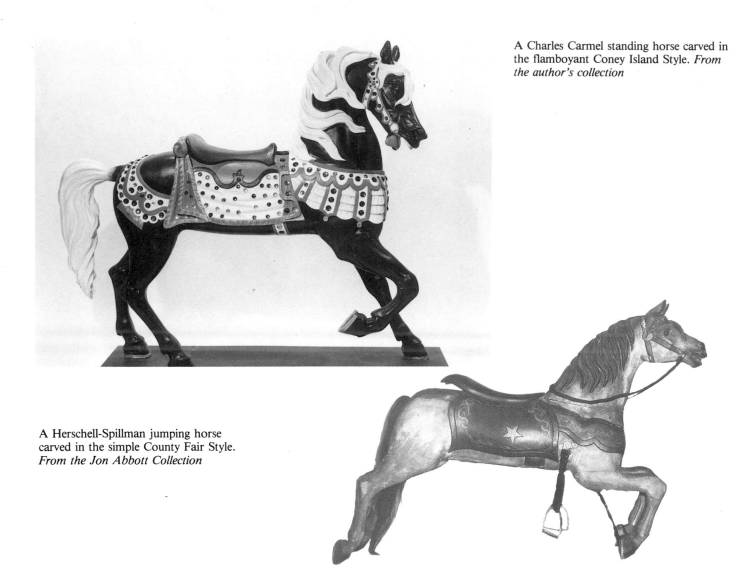

A Charles Carmel standing horse carved in the flamboyant Coney Island Style. *From the author's collection*

A Herschell-Spillman jumping horse carved in the simple County Fair Style. *From the Jon Abbott Collection*

A Dentzel standing horse carved in the elegant Philadelphia Style. *From the author's collection*

Above: The proliferation of city parks, such as Chestnut Hill Park in Philadelphia, created a growing demand for Philadelphia Style carousels. *Photo - Philadelphia Toboggan Company, Sam High III*

Below: The Country Fair Style developed as the need for traveling carousels increaed in rural towns and farm communities. *Photo -Nelson Ferris*

The Coney Island Style reflected the glitter and flamboyance of the most celebrated amusement capital in the country.

Coney Island, located nine miles south of Manhattan, has a rich and interesting history. It was on this strip of land that Henry Hudson made his first landing in 1609.

The area remained virtually undisturbed until a road leading to the first beach hotel, the Coney Island House, was constructed. By 1840, the hotel was a popular summer vacation spot for such illustrious guests as Edgar Allen Poe, Herman Melville, Jenny Lind, P.T. Barnum, Daniel Webster, Henry Clay and Washington Irving.

The sun and surf of Coney Island attracted more and more New Yorkers seeking relief from the heat and humidity of the city. Dance halls, hotels, bathhouses and beer gardens dotted the beachfront; and, by 1870, the first railroad to Coney Island was bringing over 50,000 visitors a day to the famous resort. *Photos-George Siessel*

A rare, realistic Dentzel rooster rides this splendid William Dentzel carousel, circa 1922. *Photo-George King*

Chapter 5
Gustav and William Dentzel

William Dentzel (known as "Hobby Horse" Bill). In 1909, William took over the helm of the Dentzel Company upon the death of his father and continued the standards of excellence synonymous with the Dentzel name. *Photo-Anita Toenniges*

Gustav Dentzel, the pioneer American carousel craftsman, was born in Germany on August 9, 1846. His father, Michael, a wheelwright by trade, was a successful carousel craftsman in Kreuznach, Germany, in the early nineteenth century. His carousels, consisting of a variety of carved horses and menagerie animals, were in existence in Germany by 1839. In the mid-nineteenth century, many European families, fearing the lack of opportunity and threats of war, sent their young sons to America. Michael Dentzel's three oldest sons, Jacob, Michael Jr., and Harry, left Germany for the New World by the mid-1800's, settled in the Philadelphia area, and pursued careers unrelated to the carousel.

Trained by his father in the art of woodworking and carousel building, Gustav followed his brothers to America in 1864 and opened a cabinet shop in Philadelphia. The first Dentzel carousel with wooden animals that operated in America was built in Germany by Gustav and his father, then shipped to Philadelphia and installed at Smith's Island. The carousel was a smashing success and resulted in Gustav's decision to form the G.A. Dentzel Steam and Horse Power Carousel Company in 1867.

The new ride was in such great demand that Dentzel moved his prospering business to larger quarters on Germantown Avenue in Philadelphia. Dentzel hired a number of carvers to help him in his expanding shop; his cousin, Harry Dentzel, and John Henry Muller were among the earliest Dentzel carvers. Muller and Dentzel became close friends; and when John Henry Muller died at an early age, Gustav Dentzel took his two sons, Daniel and Alfred, under his wing. The Muller brothers worked in the Dentzel shop and while both were talented carvers, Daniel had a special talent. Held in the highest esteem by

Dentzel shop employees, circa 1922. Top left: Angelo Calsamilia, paint shop foreman, top right: carver, Daniel Muller, front row center: carver, Harry Dentzel. *Photo-Anita Toenniges*

Dentzel master carver, Salvatore Cernigliaro, at the age of 30. *Photo-Marguerite Cerny*

his peers, Daniel breathed life into the wooden figures he created.

Around the turn of the century, Daniel and Alfred Muller left Gustav Dentzel, whom they felt was too stern and demanding, to work for the newly formed Philadelphia Toboggan Company. Dentzel considered their departure a lack of loyalty and never did forgive the young brothers.

SALVATORE CERNIGLIARO

In 1903, a twenty-four year-old immigrant, Salvatore Cernigliaro, arrived in America from his native Sicily. Already an experienced artist and woodcarver, *Cherni* had worked from the age of thirteen for one of Italy's leading designers and craftsmen. His experience included decorating magnificent palaces, villas and public buildings. Arriving alone, without any knowledge of the English language, the young man sought employment in

Philadelphia. When he was down to his last few dollars, he was hired by Gustav Dentzel to carve carousel figures. It was a mutually successful relationship, as Cherni created some of the most delightful carousel animals ever crafted. It was Cherni who introduced an assortment of whimsical menagerie animals, including rabbits, cats, and bears, to the American carousel.

Cherni called his toolcase and handmade carving tools his *box of gold*. He was an exceptionally fast carver who usually took one week to carve a horse. Embarrassed about showing up his slower contemporaries, Cherni sometimes took his work home. A quiet, pleasant and compassionate man, Cherni always sought perfection in his work. The artisan's final carving years were spent at the Philadelphia Toboggan Company. Following his retirement, he moved to California to be near his daughter, Marguerite. Cherni taught sculpturing in a California art school until he was 87. He died in 1974, at the age of 94, leaving behind the most appealing and beloved carousel menagerie animals ever carved.

Turn of the century carousels produced by Gustav Dentzel, the pioneer American carousel carver. *Photo-Bill Carlone*

This finely detailed miniature Dentzel carousel, carved by Harry Dentzel, was the delight of neighborhood children.

Gustav and his wife Mary had one son, William. A neighbor of the family recalls that an impressive life-sized wooden Indian stood in the Dentzel yard every spring and summer. Carved by Gustav, the Indian, which held a large bow and arrow and a real American flag, was removed and repainted during the winter months. Although the Dentzel family socialized little, Gustav enjoyed a daily "schnapps" break with a neighboring tailor at the local beer garden.

Harry Dentzel, a cousin to William, was a friendly fellow, as well as a fine carver. He was especially loved by neighborhood children for his wonderful Christmas display, which included a miniature operating Dentzel carousel, complete with 52 horses and animals and two chariots. A Christmas tree was placed in the center of the carousel; as a music box played, toy dolls in handmade finery sat astride the carved animals as they spun around the decorated tree.

Gustav Dentzel died in 1909; but the company continued to prosper under the leadership of his son, William (also known as "Hobby Horse Bill"). Bill Dentzel, a bachelor, was a charming, dapper man-about-town. Often traveling to Europe to take advantage of the German health spas, Bill seemed to enjoy life to the fullest. Although he worked in his father's shop, William did not take up the chisel once he took over the business.

A spirited jumper, typical of those found on the second row of early Dentzel carousels, circa 1900.

51

An 1885 Gustav Dentzel outside-row stander in original dappled paint. Note the long cascading mane, flipped forelock and barrel chest. *From the author's collection*

An early Dentzel stander, circa 1885, with replaced wooden tail. Horses of this period originally had hair tails. *From the Edwin Ferren III Collection*

This restored Dentzel stander was one of two horses rescued from a devastating coastal storm in 1962 in Sea Isle, New Jersey. The remainder of the carousel, including 44 figures, was bulldozed into the ground by engineers who hurriedly constructed a seawall to save the town from further flooding. *From the author's collection*

The Dentzel "Mare," with its sweet, pretty face and full, billowing mane, is one of the most popular of all inner-row horses, circa 1900. *From the Gay and Jack Friel Collection*

This "sweet face" Dentzel stander, which is considered to have one of the prettiest of all carousel heads, was carved from 1900 to 1928. An eagle with yellow glass eyes was often carved on both sides of the saddle cantle.

This Dentzel lead horse, draped with a full eagle and an American flag, survived the devastating hurricane of 1938 which destroyed over a dozen carousels along the east coast. The Muller horse, found floating in a tidal pool, once rode the Newport, Rhode Island carousel, which was demolished by the storm. Body paint is original, trappings have been redone, circa 1914. *From the author's collection*

Following the closing of the D.C. Muller & Brother Company, Daniel and Alfred Muller returned to carve for the Dentzel Company. Daniel, in charge of the shop, supervised the work of the other carvers. In the early twenties, a three-abreast Dentzel carousel cost $18,000 and a four-abreast model $24,000. In 1927, Angelo Calsamilia, the Dentzel shop painter for over twenty years, received $1,000 to paint a three-abreast carousel, including scenery panels and horses.

William Dentzel died in 1928. The stock of the Dentzel Company was bought by the Philadelphia Toboggan Company at auction. Upon his death, this tribute was printed in a Philadelphia newspaper:

"A king is dead - is the author, painter, sculptor or orator who has given pleasure to millions of adult minds any more entitled to homage than he who has brought delight to millions of children's minds?

Does it matter, after all, that the medium he employed was nothing more than a ring of painted hobby horses, to which a lot of laughing, shouting youngsters clung madly as they swung around a pole in dizzy circles? Merry-Go-Round King is no slight sobriquet to be remembered by."

The Dentzel Company, through its long history, retained the highest standards of excellence by producing overall the most elegant and revered American carousel animals.

This Dentzel lead horse, carved by Daniel Muller in 1919, is quite different from previous Dentzel standers. Eyes are wide open and set high and the soft, gentle look has been replaced by a more aggressive expression. *Photo - Bill Manns*

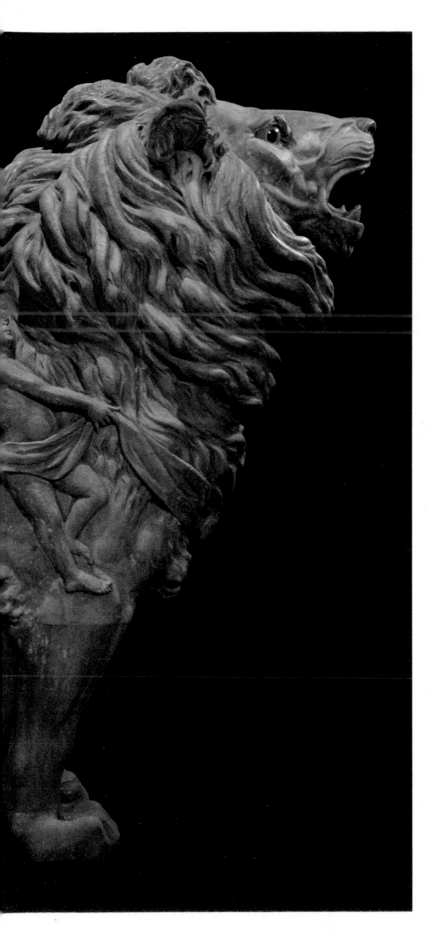

Dentzel lions, after the turn of the century, followed this classic pose and were often elaborately decorated with figures in relief. A wistful nymph on this intricately carved ''Cherni'' lion clutches a fold of fabric. Note the fine delineations of muscles and sinews. *From the author's collection*

Dentzel rabbit with thick, billowing fur and twitching ears, circa 1905. Dentzel rabbits are similarly posed, except for a few that have a front leg raised in a "flirting" position. There are two styles of heads—the style with a more rounded profile than the one shown has less deeply carved fur. *From the author's collection*

Dentzel pigs, always in this pose, sometimes sported an acorn or ear of corn on their trappings, circa 1905. *From the author's collection*

Proud pose and protruding chest are marks of the rare Dentzel zebra. Zebras are sometimes painted as, and mistaken for, horses but their tails provide the clue to their identity. *From the author's collection*

Rearing upright head, awkward stance, cascading mane and fierce roaring expression are typical features of early lions by Gustav Dentzel, circa 1885.

Under the direction of head carver, Daniel Muller, the elegant pose of Dentzel lions remained the same, but features softened and expressions became less angry. A playful cherub decorates this 1910 carving. *From the author's collection*

Dentzel bears, rare compared to cats, deer and goats, were also carved in a running position with their smiling mouths open and heads cocked to the side. *From the author's collection*

Dentzel cat in original paint, circa 1905. Note the realistic body color and muted pastel shades on the trappings. The prey of Dentzel cats included birds, fish, frogs, crabs and squid, which the felines smugly held in their mouths. *From the author's collection*

After the introduction in the late 19th century of this sleek, realistic Dentzel tiger, its classic pose never changed, circa 1910. *From the author's collection*

A rare Dentzel dog showing the fine realism of Dentzel figures, circa 1895. *From the Fraley Collection*

Very rare Dentzel kangaroo with a "hopping" mechanism built into its rear legs. *From the Albert Ricci Collection*

While sizes of Dentzel goats varied, poses remained the same. The gentle, whimsical expression of this goat, in original body paint, marks it as a Cherni carving, circa 1905. *From the author's collection*

Three giraffes produced by the Dentzel Company. The style on the left, believed to be carved by Daniel Muller, appeared on very early and very late Dentzel carousels. The giraffe above, in original paint, is circa 1895; the Cerni giraffe below was introduced after the turn of the century. *Photos above and below from the author's collection.*

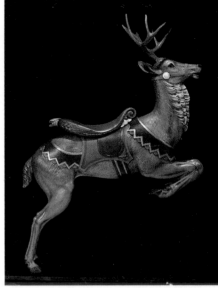

Facial expressions and features of Dentzel deer varied, but the leaping pose remained the same. Antlers were always real, circa 1895. *From the author's collection*

Dentzel deer with the soft, gentle expression of the "Cherni" period; tongue is out, nose is squared, eyes are soulful, circa 1905. *From the author's collection*

Delicately painted scenery panels, lavish mirrors, and jester head shields decorated fancy Dentzel carousels produced in the twenties.

Dentzel chariot, circa 1920. Griffins, with
the wings of an eagle and the body of a
lion, often decorated carousel carvings as a
symbol of strength and agility. Photo-Joe
Leonard

Plaster-cast cherubs surround the
centerpole housing on this 1920 Dentzel
carousel.

A large Looff jumper in a dramatic "Star Gazer" pose, circa 1905. *From the author's collection.*

Chapter 6

Charles Looff

Charles Looff, his wife Anna, and son Arthur. *Photo-Arthur Simmons*

Schleswig-Holstein, an area bordered and contested by Denmark and Germany for many years, was the birthplace of Charles Looff. Already a talented craftsman, Looff arrived in America in 1870. At the age of eighteen, he settled in Brooklyn where he obtained employment as a furniture carver. To earn extra money, the ambitious artist rented a hall at night and opened a dance studio. One of his pupils, Anna Dolle, became his bride; and their marriage resulted in six children.

Looking further to expand his horizons, Looff persuaded the owner of a successful beach pavillion in Coney Island to install a handcrafted carousel in his establishment. Toiling by day as a furniture craftsman and working alone at night in a basement room, Looff carved every figure for the carousel himself. Not only did he construct the frame and platform, but Looff painted

the animals and trim as well. Combining a mixture of horses and menagerie animals, embellished with etched mirrored ornaments, Looff originated the Coney Island style in 1876. Hordes of daily visitors to the popular seaside resort of Coney Island embraced the new ride and launched Looff into a highly successful career as a carousel craftsman.

Looff's second carousel was commissioned by Charles Feltman, an entrepreneur who made his fortune in an interesting way. In the early 1860's, Feltman, a young Coney Island pie vendor, looked for a way to increase his business with a new food that might catch the public's fancy. After a bit of experimentation, he stuffed a sausage into a roll, added some mustard and called the new gastronomical delights *red hots*. Feltman's discovery was successful beyond his wildest dreams and was the

Rare Looff outside prancer from the famous Feltman's carousel of Coney Island. Note the interior illumination shining through the large colorful faceted jewels. *From the Summit Collection*

Carver, Charles Looff, who was very fond of bears, with three of his "pets." *Photo-Wilda Taucher*

Rhode Island, the site of a magnificent carousel he had constructed in 1895. A mass of gilt and glitter, the Crescent Park carousel, embellished with cherubs and neobaroque carvings, became a showpiece for prospective customers. The carousel was housed in a domed building, designed and constructed by Looff to enhance its dazzling effect. Light danced through stained-glass windows, reflecting a rainbow of colors in mirrored panels and cut-glass jewels. The huge four-abreast carousel, painted shining white with gold leaf trim, was set off by a breathtakingly beautiful carved band organ constructed by A. Ruth and Sohn.

The talent and sculptural background of John Zalar and the business acumen of Charles Looff proved a suc-

talk and rage of Coney Island. A newspaper reporter, commenting on the new food sensation, wrote an article questioning the contents of the sausage and suggested that, for all anyone knew, it might be dog meat...voila, the America *hot dog* was born.

Enormous restaurants and grand hotels, catering to their guests' every pleasure, vied to attract the elite and celebrated personalities who vacationed at Coney Island. The largest, most elaborate restaurant, which, by 1920, could serve over a thousand patrons a day, was constructed by the wealthy and successful Charles Feltman. The enterprising Feltman installed Looff's carousel in his complex in 1880, and the ride became a celebrated landmark of Coney Island.

As the demand for his carousels increased, Looff hired a number of talented carvers. The shop's roster included some of the most revered American carousel craftsmen - among them Marcus Charles Illions, Charles Carmel and John Zalar.

In 1905, following a dispute with the city over his land, Looff moved his entire operation to Riverside,

Enormous, rare, Looff teady bear, with swiveling head. This 300 pound bear is one of the heaviest of all American carousel carvings. circa 1880. *From the Summit Collection*

Magnificent band organ produced by A. Ruth and Sohn, Waldkirch, Germany, located at Crescent Park, Riverside, Rhode Island. The organ has moving carved figures that "play" and "conduct" in time to the music. *Photo-George King*

The midway at Crescent Park, Riverside, Rhode Island, in 1907. This park is no longer in existence, but efforts are being made to preserve the splendid carousel that marks Looff's factory site. *Photo-John Caruthers*

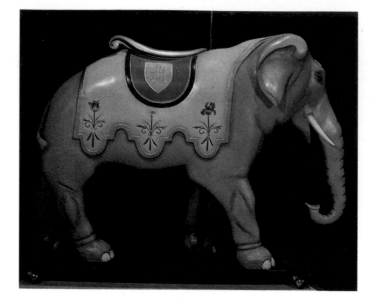

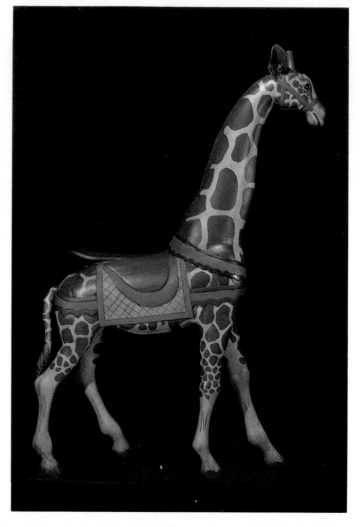

A rare Looff elephant, circa 1885. The small, realistic figure reflects Looff's interest in animals. He visited the zoo often and owned a number of exotic pets. *From the author's collection*

An 1885 giraffe with the sweet, innocent expression that typifies Looff's carvings. Looff giraffes came in all sizes and designs; some had a curving, snake-like neck; others, a long overhanging upper lip. *From the author's collection*

A Looff lion with its head turned as if to invite riders to climb aboard. The horse in the left background is typical of inner-row Looff horses before the turn of the century, circa 1895.

Looff goat in original body paint, with typical plaid or checkered blanket found on early Looff figures, circa 1880. *From the Jean and Noel Thompson Collection*

cessful combination; their carousels were in ever-increasing demand. As business prospered, Looff went into production of other amusement devices, including scenic railways, fun houses and thrill rides.

Around 1909, Looff, already a self-made millionaire, sought to expand his business even further. The energetic carver moved his family and factory to California, near the harbor in Long Beach. While the firm produced a few small portable carousels, its main concentration was on large park machines. At his Long Beach factory site, Looff and Zalar, who had joined his employer in the move, constructed a similar carousel to the one at Crescent Park; and it became the company's West Coast showpiece.

Pioneer Coney Island carver, Charles Looff, whose carousels dotted seaside resorts on both coasts, died in 1919. His imaginative menagerie animals and carousel horses, beckoning even the most timid riders to climb aboard, are the legacy he left behind.

This early Looff ''pug nose'' horse with typlical plaster rosettes and etched beveled mirror ''jewels'' was converted from a stationary prancer to a jumper.

Plaster rosettes, tassels and a plaid saddle blanket mark this horse as a Looff stander from the late nineteenth century. Looff and Dentzel, as well as German craftsmen, carved eagles and parrots at the saddle cantle.

Early Looff stander with original painted floral and scroll decorations on the trappings. Early figures often had elaborate stenciled and painted decorations on straps and blankets. *From the author's collection*

Above: Young riders line up to board a turn of the century Looff carousel. *Photo - Wilda Taucher*

Below: The appealing sensitivity of Looff's carving is evident on these late nineteenth century horses. *From the author's collection*

Dramatic outside stander on Looff's
showpiece carousel at Crescent Park,
Riverside, Rhode Island.

An exciting jeweled jumper, circa 1905, on
Looff's Crescent Park Carousel, carved by
John Zalar.

Mythical beasts and violent subjects did not escape the chisel of American carousel carvers. Gruesome dragons in a fight to the death are featured on a chariot carved by Looff's eldest son, Charles, on the carousel at Crescent Park, Riverside, Rhode Island, circa 1905.

Looff sea dragons have large, squarish heads and many exposed teeth. This vicious looking creature measures seven feet in length. *From the Albert Ricci Collection*

The rare, and greatly admired, Looff "sneaky tiger." *Photo-Richard Strinsky*

JOHN ZALAR

John Zalar was born in Austria in 1874. In his youth, he apprenticed as a sculptor of religious statues and artifacts. In 1902, at the age of twenty-eight, Zalar arrived in America and gained employment as a designer of ornamental ironwork. He married an Austrian girl, Johanna Rutar and their marriage produced six daughters.

Around 1905, John Zalar was hired to carve carousel figures for Charles Looff. His sculptural talents so impressed Looff that Zalar accompanied the pioneer Coney Island carver first on his move to Rhode Island and later to California.

Tragedy struck the Zalar family in 1915, when thirty-four year old Johanna died suddenly. John moved his six children back to New York City from California and remarried a year later. Seeking employment as a carousel carver, he moved his family to Germantown, Pennsylvania, where he lived for five years while employed by the Philadelphia Toboggan Company.

When he was forty-six, Zalar took ill with tuberculosis. In 1920, on the advice of his doctors, Zalar moved again to the warmer climate of California. As his health permitted, the craftsman continued to carve figures and chariots for the Philadelphia Toboggan Company, which he shipped all the way across country. His work was completely handcrafted as Zalar worked at home with just a simple set of tools. Philadelphia Toboggan Company records show that Zalar supplied these horses from 1921 to 1923. In 1921, he shipped four horses across country and was paid $120 per horse. The freight charge to ship the crated animals from California through the Panama Canal to Philadelphia was $4.

Zalar died in 1925, leaving behind some of the most beautiful examples of carousel art.

Looff outside stander, with a profusion of flowers at the saddle cantle, showing heavy legs, long scooped saddle and extremely stylized pose of the late Looff period. circa 1910. *From the author's collection*

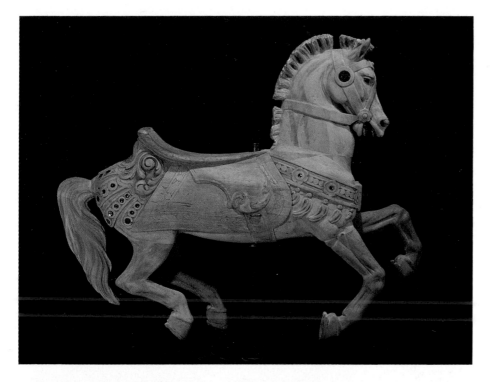

Left and opposite page: Looff outside row Trojan jumper with large deeply carved roached mane and boxy knees of the late Looff period, circa 1910. *From the author's collection*

Exaggerated pose and fancy jeweled trappings are typical of late Looff jumpers, circa 1910. This one rides the beautifully restored carousel in Spokane, Washington. *Photo-Richard Strinsky*

Looff lions were varied in size and design. Most were extremely large and muscular with intricate full manes. This lifesize lion is from the old Salem Willows carousel which formerly operated in Salem, Massachusetts, circa 1895. *Photo-George King*

This superb American buffalo is considered to be one of Looff's finest carvings. The massive, realistic animal is from the old Salem Willows carousel which formerly operated in Salem, Massachusetts. circa 1895. *Photo-George King*

A large, rare, superbly carved greyhound rides Looff's late 19th century "Presidents" carousel at Rocky Point, Rhode Island. Photo was taken in 1910. Looff used pictures of George Washington's favorite mount as a model for many of his carousel carvings. *Photo-Joseph Carrolo*

Looff's showpiece carousel at this factory site in Crescent Park, Riverside, Rhode Island. Customers chose the animals for their carousels from the varied figures displayed on this machine. *Photo-George King*

A Herschell-Spillman jumper, draped in an American flag, on the park carousel at Greenfield Village, Dearborn, Michigan.

Chapter 7
Armitage Herschell Company
Herschell-Spillman Company
Spillman Engineering Company
Allan Herschell Company

Allan Herschell. *Photo-Allan Herschell*

Allan Herschell was born in Scotland in 1851. As one of thirteen children, he left school at an early age to learn the mold-making trade. When he was nineteen, Allan arrived in America, settled in Buffalo, New York, and found employment as a foundry foreman. His fortunes took an upward turn when he and his shop associate, James Armitage, bought out their failing employer's equipment and began the production of steam engines.

Because of its strategic location on the Erie Canal, the new owners moved their business to North Tonawanda, New York, in 1873, launching the Tonawanda Engine and Machine Company. After two fires, the company was formed as the Armitage Herschell Company; and George Herschell, Allan's brother, became a partner in the firm.

In 1882, Allan Herschell visited a New York City specialist to help cure a persistent case of ague, and discovered a popular new ride, the carousel. Realizing the potential of this new amusement device, Herschell convinced his reluctant partners to plunge into the construction of steam-operated merry-go-rounds. While still fighting the opposition of his partners, Allan Herschell completed his first carousel in 1864. The young man's persistence launched the firm as a major force in the American carousel industry.

Armitage Herschell horses were charming with a sweet simplicity; legs were in a parallel position and rear legs were joined to the body by a mortise-type notch, which became a construction trademark of the company. Unlike his competitors, Herschell concentrated on portable traveling carousels which were well suited to the rigors of continual dismantling and rebuilding.

An Armitage Herschell carousel, circa 1890. There is no question that Allan Herschell patterned his first carved horses after those produced by Charles Dare. The similarity is striking. *Photo-Nelson Ferris*

This 1894 Armitage Herschell portable carousel traveled half-way around the world. *Photo-Nelson Ferris*

A typical Armitage Herschell horse, circa 1895.

A Herschell-Spillman jumper with an unusual tiger skin blanket, circa 1905.

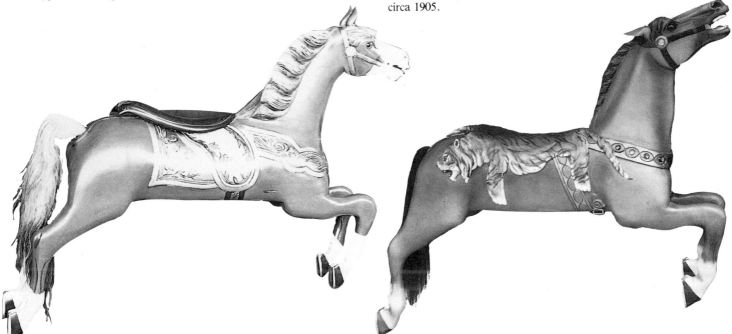

Spurred on by enormous financial success, the partners invested heavily in land which later proved to be their downfall. The collapse of the economy in 1899 and the company's heavily mortgaged assets resulted in the failure of the Armitage Herschell Company.

Allan, with his brother-in-law and new partner, Edward Spillman, gained control of the company's assets from the bank in 1903. They formed the Herschell-Spillman Company, which was to become the world's largest producer of carousels. Herschell-Spillman's $2,000 portable steam-powered carousels traveled to the four corners of the globe.

A particularly enterprising customer, J.D. Gwin of Prairie, Indiana, bought two steam driven carousels and introduced them to the island of Tahiti. Due to the unavailability of wood and coal, Gwin fueled his merry-go-rounds with coconut hulls. Successful beyond his wildest dreams, he left the island a wealthy man. Within

Herschell-Spillman portable carousel, circa 1905. Menagerie animals included a pair of pigs, roosters, zebras and dogs on many portable machines of this period. *From the Jon Abbott Collection*

A Herschell-Spillman dog from a portable carousel, circa 1902. Although more simply carved than those produced by Looff, Dentzel and PTC, Herschell-Spillman dogs have a captivating charm. A more elaborate standing dog was carved for the company's larger park carousels. *From the author's collection*

A fancy Herschell-Spillman pig on the park carousel at Greenfield Village in Dearborn, Michigan, circa 1911.

A well-proportioned Herschell-Spillman chicken from a 1902 portable carousel. *From the author's collection*

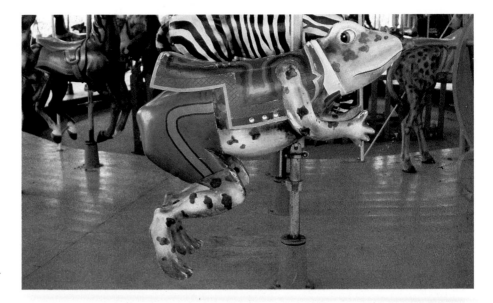

This delightful little frog, in short pants and bow tie, rides the carousel at Greenfield Village, Dearborn, Michigan.

Herschell-Spillman sea dragons, although smaller in size, show a similarity to Coney Island Style sea creatures, circa 1911.

A Herschell-Spillman goat on a permanently-installed park carousel. The hair carvings are shallow compared to goats produced by other American carousel companies.

In addition to patriotic carvings, Herschell-Spillman chariots had varied themes, including Mother Goose characters and bathing beauties.

a few years, the Tahitian investor who bought Gwin's carousels constructed a four-story hotel with the profits from the amazingly lucrative rides.

The carved figures of the Herschell-Spillman Company were very similar to the Armitage Herschell animals except for a less static, more flowing mane. The firm produced a few menagerie figures; mainly, chickens, dogs, zebras and pigs, until around 1914, when the company ventured into carving permanently installed large park carousels. Customers then could order from an array of menagerie animals, including lions, tigers, frogs, storks and giraffes. The figures had a playful storybook charm and could be ordered with carved or glass eyes.

Herschell-Spillman chariots displayed a wide range of subjects which included Mother Goose figures, bathing beauties, and Uncle Sam emblazoned with an American flag. Decorated with bevelled mirrors and large faceted jewels, scenery panels and rounding boards ranged from lovely landscape scenes to dreamy ladies in summer finery. The overall effect of the Herschell-Spillman park carousels stood up well against competition.

In 1913, Allan retired from the Herschell - Spillman Company; but his retirement was short lived. Two years later, in 1915, he established the Allan Herschell Company.

Concerned citizens of Berkeley, California, succeeded in raising funds to save and restore this fancy Herschell-Spillman carousel at Tilden Park. circa 1914. Restored by the Redbug Workshop

A charming Herschell-Spillman cat from the carousel at Tilden Park, Berkeley, California. The cat is in a similar pose to those produced by the Dentzel Company, but it lacks the deeply carved fur and detailed feline quality of its counterpart.

A sleeping baby, with a bouquet of flowers, nestles in folds of fabric on this Herschell-Spillman stork.

A Herschell-Spillman zebra from a park carousel, circa 1911. Zebras on portable machines are smaller and in a static, less dramatic pose. Herschell-Spillman zebras don't have saddles.

A Herschell-Spillman jumper in a more animated pose than horses found on the company's portable carousels.

The Spillman Engineering Company bought the assets of the Herschell-Spillman Company in 1920 and expanded into the manufacture of other amusement devices. Spillman carousel figures were more elaborate than their predecessors. Jewels were added and intricate relief carvings appeared with more frequency on the trappings. Carousel rounding boards became larger and more elaborate; decorative ceiling panels were added; the overall effect was quite imposing.

After the death of Allan Herschell in 1927, the Allan Herschell Company acquired the Spillman Engineering Company, which continued in business until 1955. Some interesting menagerie figures were produced by the Allan Herschell Company. The most notable included a large elephant, complete with howdah, and a stalking life-like polar bear. Few other menagerie animals were carved as

A perky Herschell-Spellman steed displaying energy and verve on the Tilden Park carousel, Berkeley, California.

A fiery, rare Herschell-Spillman outside row stander. Trappings are elaborate on standing figures carved for the company's park-installed carousels. Note the typical pointed rump of large Herschell-Spillman horses, circa 1911.

A Herschell-Spillman lion from the carousel at Tilden Park, Berkeley, California.

A typical Herschell-Spillman deer from a park carousel, with the usual dog's head carved on the trappings.

Although Herschell-Spillman animals are not as detailed or deeply carved as those of other companies, they are, nonetheless, well-proportioned and appealing.

Chariot on Herschell-Spillman park
carousel at Greenfield Village, Henry Ford
Museum, Dearborn, Michigan. Note the
giraffe and original scenery panels and
Herschell-Spillman Company sign.
Photo-Gloria King

Herschell-Spillman permanently-installed
park carousel with large, elaborately
decorated figures. *Photo-Allan Herschell*

Spillman horses differ from those produced by the Herschell-Spillman Company. This Spillman jumper shows a less attractive head but more elaborate trappings, including figures in relief. circa 1922.

A high-stepping Spillman horse covered in elaborate armour. circa 1922.

An original Spillman Engineering Company signature panel. circa 1922.

Varied figures in relief decorated large, fancy Spillman horses of this period. circa 1922.

This fancy jumper's body is prettier than its rather large, unattractive head. The sweet, perky look of the Herschell-Spillman park horses was ignored by Spillman, whose horses had long, flat noses, high-set eyes and less pleasant expressions, circa 1922.

Allan Herschell carousel from the company catalog. *Courtesy of Allan Herschell*

Aggressive expressions, elongated heads, Roman noses, short legs and high-set eyes mark these as Allan Herschell horses, circa 1928.

the company concentrated its efforts on horses. The appealing Herschell-Spillman ponies were replaced by aggressive jumpers with disproportionately small legs drawn up close to the body. Heads were oversized, eyes were set high; and noses became long and Romanesque.

Around 1930, the easily breakable wooden legs and tails were molded of aluminum and attached to the wooden bodies for extra strength and durability. Molds of complete figures were eventually made, and the aluminum carousel animal was born.

The many carvers of the North Tonawanda Company are, for the most part, unknown; but Allan Herschell will be remembered for his vision and perseverance in bringing happiness to millions of people throughout the world.

Allan Herschell carving shop, circa 1922. Figures on the left, with thick, roached manes and oversized heads, are decorated with fancy trappings. *Photo-courtesy Allan Herschell*

A fancy lead horse in the Trojan style by Allan Herschell. *From the Edwin Ferren III Collection*

A rare Allan Herschell camel. circa 1928. While Allan Herschell horses are poorly proportioned and quite unattractive, some menagerie figures produced by the firm rank well with animals produced by Coney Island Style carvers. *From the Edwin Ferren III Collection*

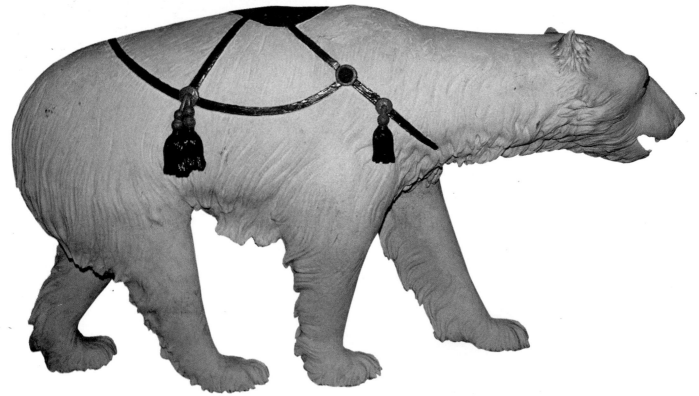

A wonderfully realistic figure—the Allan Herschell Polar Bear, circa 1928. This figure is an exceptionally fine carving. *From the Edwin Ferren III Collection*

A rare, large Allan Herschell elephant, complete with a basket howdah to seat its riders. This figure is one of Allan Herschell's finest. *From the Albert Ricci Collection*

Carvers, Gene Drisco (far left) and Loren White (second from right), pose with large, fancy horses in the Parker factory yard in Abilene, Kansas, in 1908. Very few horses of this style were produced. Note the stack of carving planks in the background. *Photo-Nancy Alley*

Chapter 8
Charles W. Parker

"Colonel" Charles Wallace Parker, the
self-proclaimed "Amusement King."
Photo - Nancy Alley

Charles Wallace Parker, the self-proclaimed "Colonel" and "Amusement King" was born on April 26,
1864, in Griggsville, Illinois. When he was five, his family
moved to a farming community in Dickinson County,
Kansas, where he spent his formative years. With no interest in earning his livelihood from the soil, Parker
worked at a number of menial jobs. Dissatisfied with his
meagre income, the shrewd, ambitious young man looked
to the growing amusement industry to turn his fortune.
In 1882, at the age of 18, Parker invested his scant sav-
ings in shooting gallery equipment; and a legendary
career was born.

Carousels, particularly those produced by the Armitage Herschell Company, later the Herschell-Spillman
Company, were being shipped to the Midwest in increas-
ing numbers. In 1892, the enterprising Parker purchased

a second-hand portable carousel, formed the C.W.
Parker Company, and became part of the nomadic carnival life which he found exciting. For three years Parker
and his two partners toured with the carousel charging a
nickel per ride. Convinced that he was capable of
building bigger and better carousels for the Midwest
trade, Parker bought out his partners and invested his
profits in the first of many carousels bearing the Parker
name.

Parker's first horses were copies of the early Armitage Herschell carousel figures found on the machine
he owned and operated for three years. Although Parker
was not a carver, the showman was involved in every
other detail of his burgeoning business. Orders poured in
for his *Carry-us-alls*; and Parker's factory, situated near
his home in Abilene, Kansas, expanded into the produc-

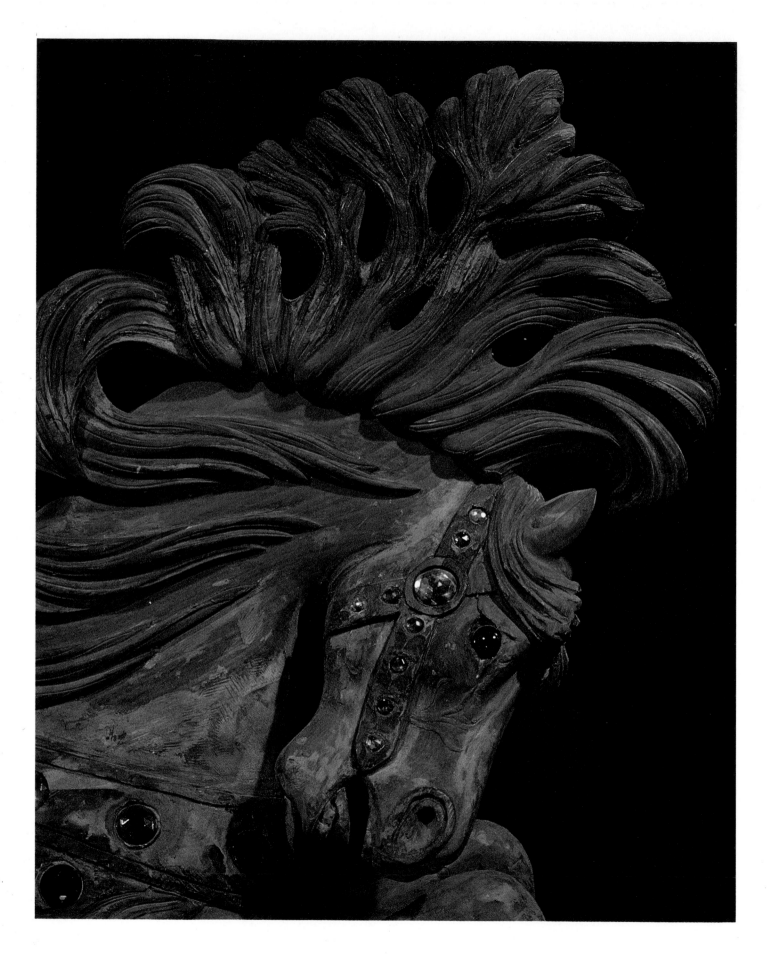

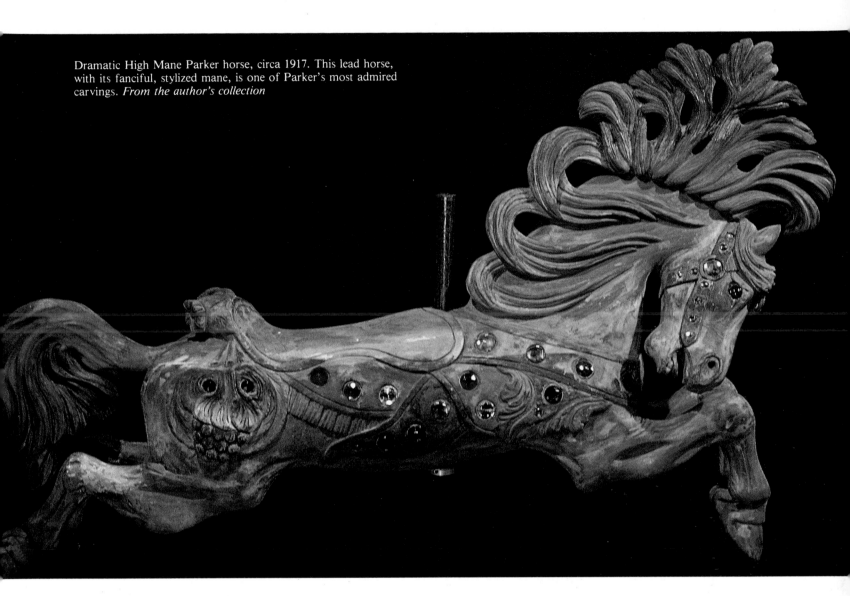

Dramatic High Mane Parker horse, circa 1917. This lead horse, with its fanciful, stylized mane, is one of Parker's most admired carvings. *From the author's collection*

tion of mechanical shooting galleries, military band organs, cylinder pianos, carved wagon showfronts, mechanical and electrical shows, circus banners, and railroad cars.

In 1911, the wealthy Parker moved his family and business to Leavenworth, Kansas. Although he always stressed the cleanliness and purity of his enterprises, the showy flamboyant Parker and his *carny* folk were not embraced by the people of Abilene. Parker's plans to build a six-story factory never materialized — although the building was never more than two stories high, advertisements always showed it as having six stories. Parker's carny background permitted him to exaggerate the truth in order to impress potential customers. Everything the Colonel did had to be represented as the biggest, the best, and always morally clean and pure.

The successful entrepreneur, C.W. Parker, moved his family to this grand home in Leavenworth, Kansas, in 1911. *Photo-Nancy Alley*

105

Above: Early, portable Parker carousel manufactured in Abilene, Kansas. Note the strong similarity to Armitage Herschell horses. *Photo-Don Rand and Ed Openshaw*

Below: An early portable Parker carousel with a grasshopper mechanism that allowed the horses to ride up and down, circa 1900. *Photo-Don Rand and Ed Openshaw*

Carvers, Gene Drisco (far left) and Loren White (second from right), with other Parker factory employees astride early Parker horses that closely resemble Armitage Herschell horses. The men are holding carved heads used on other Parker amusement devices.
Photo - Nancy Alley

Up until the move to Leavenworth, Parker horses assumed the upright position of early Armitage Herschell models. Horses with fancy trappings, large faceted and cabochon jewels, prettier heads and more naturally flowing manes were found on a few large Parker carousels. The overall effect of these fine figures ranked well with many Coney Island style horses.

When Parker moved his business to Leavenworth, his horses underwent a drastic change. The highly stylized figures assumed aggressive, stretched-out positions with all four legs drawn close to the body, allowing for easier stacking and transportation. This feature was a prime consideration in the design of portable traveling merry-go-rounds which had to be dismantled and rebuilt in record time. The Leavenworth horses, ornately decorated and bursting with speed, excited the imagination of children in rural areas throughout the Midwest. The always jumping, flamboyantly American horses, were adorned with flags, ears of corn, Indians and Wild West shooters.

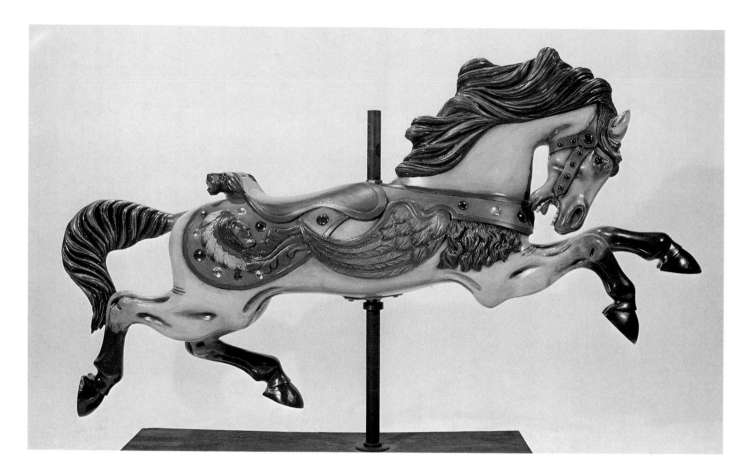

Large, jeweled Indian pony, circa 1917. This graceful horse carries an Indian head in a war bonnet on its blanket and two dog heads at its saddle cantle. *From the author's collection*

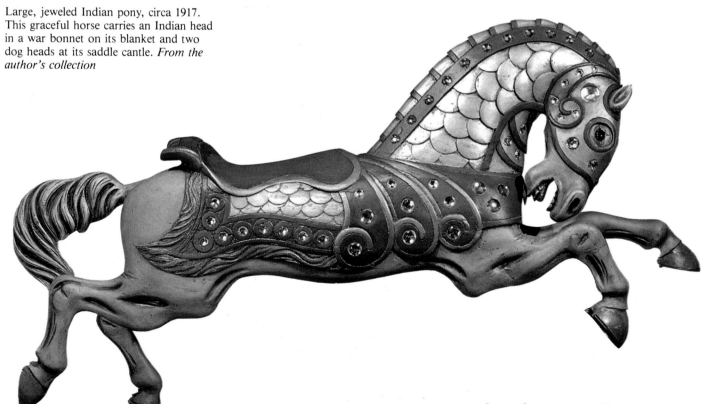

Large, fancy, armoured horse with legs extended in a graceful pose. circa 1918. *From the author's collection*

Fish decorate this fancy Parker horse from the Leavenworth period, circa 1915. *From the author's collection*

Ornate Parker horse, with full intricate mane, in flamboyant pink "park paint." This elaborately decorated horse is on the four-abreast carousel at Jantzen Beach, Portland, Oregon. *Photo - Elizabeth Dewar*

The few menagerie figures found on Parker merry-go-rounds bear little resemblance to the company's attractively stylized horses. Strangely primitive bears, lions, leopards, rabbits, camels, zebras and giraffes have been spotted in Parker factory photos, but it's not known if they were carved at the Parker factory or imported by the Colonel from one of the many countries he visited. Menagerie animals were such a small part of Parker's business that few have survived.

Parker's house organ, *The Bedouin,* stressed the virtuous character and morality of Colonel Parker and his shows. Family photos of his wife and children helped

Carousel companies often filled special orders. This Parker barber chair horse, with a leather seat and tail, is set on a porcelain base, circa 1912. *From the author's collection*

Parker Wooden Horse Ranch in Abilene. Perhaps this was the day of the move to Leavenworth, explaining the herd of wooden animals gathered outside the Parker factory. *Photo-Nancy Alley*

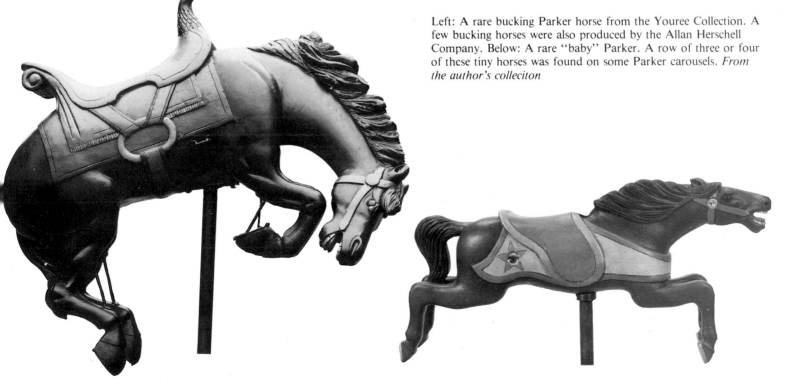

Left: A rare bucking Parker horse from the Youree Collection. A few bucking horses were also produced by the Allan Herschell Company. Below: A rare "baby" Parker. A row of three or four of these tiny horses was found on some Parker carousels. *From the author's colleciton*

111

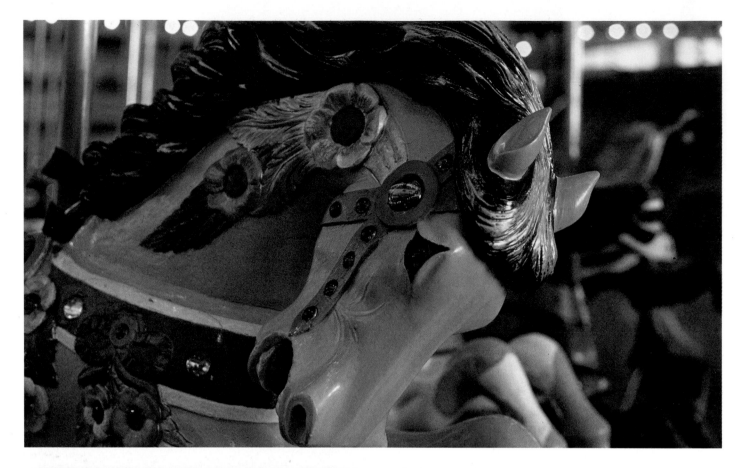

The tucked head is considered by many to be the most attractive head position assumed by Parker horses. This "American Beauty Rose" is on the fancy four-abreast carousel at Jantzen Beach, Portland, Oregon. *Photo - Elizabeth Dewar*

portray the showman as a pure, saintly man who deplored the immoral carnivals with their "con men, freaks and hoochy koochy dancers."

Although business slowed down in the twenties, the factory remained open with Parker's son assuming the reins. Charles Wallace Parker died on October 28, 1932. The Colonel will long be remembered for his energy, creativity and showmanship which brought the hardworking people in rural communities so much entertainment and fun.

Exciting high mane Parker, in gaudy "park paint," on the large carousel at Jantzen Beach, Portland, Oregon. *Photo - Elizabeth Dewar*

Above: Parker catalogs listed this horse as the "American Beauty Rose." It is one of Parker's most admired figures, circa 1915. *Photo-Nancy Alley*

Below: After the move to Leavenworth, Parker horses were highly stylized with a feeling of bursting speed. *Photo - Nancy Alley*

A magnificent, armoured standing horse by Daniel Muller, revered as one of the most beautiful of all carousel figures, at Cedar Point. Sandusky, Ohio. *Photo-Joe Leonard*

Chapter 9

Daniel C. Muller

Daniel Muller with his prize-winning sculpture of a young girl rising from a seashell.

Daniel Carl Muller was born in Hamburg, Germany, in 1872. Carl Müller, a prominent carousel manufacturer, was one of the early German carvers; and it is likely that Daniel was part of the same family.

John Henry Muller, Daniel's father, was also a wood-carver/craftsman and a close friend of carousel builder, Michael Dentzel. Encouraged by the success of Gustav Dentzel, John Henry Muller moved his family to America in 1882. They settled in the Gravesend section of Brooklyn near Coney Island, where it is believed he carved carousel figures for Charles Looff.

In 1888, the Muller family moved to Sunnytown, Pennsylvania, which was close to Germantown, the site of the Dentzel carousel factory. It appears that, at this time, John Henry Muller and his two sons, Daniel and Alfred, who had both attended art school, were hired by

their friend Gustav Dentzel to carve carousel figures for his expanding firm. When John Henry Muller died in 1890, Gustav Dentzel provided fatherly guidance to the Muller sons as they continued carving in his shop.

In 1895, Daniel married Elizabeth Muhe, an innkeeper's daughter. He continued to study art and entered competitions with his outstanding sculptural work. Sensitive female nude figures, as well as a magnificent rendition of a young girl rising from a seashell, were among Daniel's award-winning achievements.

Daniel and Alfred Muller grew tired of working for the strict and demanding Gustav Dentzel. Around 1899, they left his firm to carve figures for the newly formed Philadelphia Toboggan Company. Gustav Dentzel never forgave them for their *lack of loyalty* as their beautiful, sensitively carved horses and menagerie figures launched the Philadelphia Toboggan Company as a major force in the carousel business.

The Muller brothers established the D.C. Muller & Brother Company around 1902. They continued supplying the Philadelphia Toboggan Company with horses and menagerie figures until around 1906. Both Daniel and Alfred Muller were carvers of exceptional talent; but Daniel's sensitive, realistic cavalry horses were a tour de force, reflecting a deep interest in historical accuracy and detail. Daniel's style resembled sculptures by Augustus Saint-Gaudens, whose beautiful statues were revered throughout the world. The D.C. Muller and Brother Company produced carousel figures for machines constructed by a number of firms, including T.M. Harton, Louis Bopp, and T. Long. In addition, the talented brothers owned and operated a number of carousels themselves.

Daniel's energy was boundless. He carved in the carousel shop by day and attended sculptural classes at night. He studied under Charles Grafly, a widely acclaimed portrait-bust sculptor. The two men began a close friendship that continued through twelve years of their student - teacher relationship at the Pennsylvania Academy of Fine Arts.

In 1917, as materials became scarce due to war needs, the D.C. Muller and Brother Carousel Company closed its doors. Daniel and Alfred rejoined the Dentzel firm, then under the helm of Gustav Dentzel's son, William, and continued carving until the demise of the Dentzel factory in 1928. Daniel retired to the New Jersey shore where he enjoyed fishing, his favorite pastime. Daniel Muller died at the age of 79, never knowing that he would become one of the most respected of all carousel artists.

Beasts of the jungle by D.C. Muller and Brother Company, circa 1910. The tiger (below) is from the Summit Collection.

Above: A Muller carousel with a giraffe in an unusual loping position, Below: An exotic sea horse by Daniel Muller, both circa 1912. *Photos-Joe Leonard*

A striding zebra produced by D.C. Muller and Brother Company, circa 1912. *Photo-Joe Leonard*

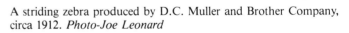

An expressive standing Muller deer with a large rack of real antlers. circa 1910. *Photo-Joe Leonard*

A magnificent Muller goat in an unusual "butting" position. *Photo-Joe Leonard*

Stripped of paint, this outside row stander shows the quality of Daniel Muller's work. circa 1910. *From the author's collection*

The elaborately draped and embellished armoured stander at Cedar Point, Sandusky, Ohio, is one of the rarest of all carousel horses.

Muller's award-winning sculptural talent is evidenced by the detailed carvings on this lifelike Indian pony. *From the author's collection*

A windblown, layered mane creates a feeling of excitement and motion on this large Muller jumper, circa 1912. *From the author's collection*

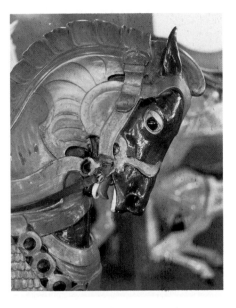

Muller set glass eyes in varying positions to achieve a variety of expressions. Some of his figures looked back at the riders, others appeared startled or frightened. This steed with a roached mane has a doleful look, circa 1910. *Photo-Joe Leonard*

Daniel Muller's attention to detail is evident on this exquisite armoured horse. circa 1912. *Photo-Joe Leonard*

A delicate floral bouquet decorates a lovely Muller jumper on the carousel at Cedar Point, Sandusky, Ohio. circa 1912 *Photo-Joe Leonard*

A delicate standing horse, sensitively portrayed by Daniel Muller, circa 1912. *Photo - Joe Leonard*

This standing Muller horse, seemingly frozen in motion, has an expression of fear in its eyes. *Photo-Joe Leonard*

A large Muller jumper, from an all-jumping carousel, carrying a decorative little cherub on its trappings. circa 1910. *Photo-Joe Leonard*

The coveted "Military" Muller. Muller's interest in historical accuracy and detail is reflected in his impressive cavalry horses, circa 1914. *From the author's collection*

Sensitive, exquisite stander with the Muller trademark of a rippled ribbon and bow. *From the Summit Collection*

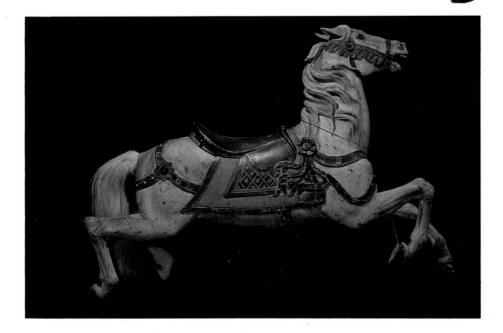

Elongated bodies, slim, bony legs, expressive eyes and intricate manes are typical features of large Muller jumpers, circa 1912. This horse is unusual, as its head turns in toward the centerpole. *From the author's collection*

Illions shop photo, circa 1912. Flanked by his sons, Phillip (third from left) and Rudy (far right), is carver M.C. Illions (second from right). Notice the various stages of construction of carousel figures, from patterns on the wall to finished parts. *Courtesy of Barney Illions and Rose Crane Sokolow*

Chapter 10
Marcus Charles Illions

Master Coney Island Style carver, Marcus Charles Illions.

Born in Russia in 1865, Marcus Charles Illions began his apprenticeship as a woodcarver at the age of seven. The restless, independent spirit that pervaded Illions' life led the accomplished craftsman to run away from his family and homeland seven years later at the tender age of fourteen.

Following a brief stay in Germany, the young Illions settled in England and worked for the Frederick Savage Company as a carver of show wagons, circus carvings, and figures for fairground roundabouts. At the age of twenty-three, Illions was hired by English showman, Frank Bostock, to complete an unfinished order of Savage-built show wagons which he planned to use as part of his first American show. Bostock and Illions, along with the partially carved wagons and an assortment of rare animals, sailed for the New World. As they landed in Boston, they were greeted by the legendary, paralyzing blizzard of '88, making their trip to their final destination, Coney Island, an agonizing adventure.

Undaunted by an unfortunate introduction to the New World, Bostock achieved great success with his exotic menagerie show. By 1894, he added rides and formed the first American traveling carnival. The showman imported a number of Savage amusement devices, including a large gondola carousel and the Chanticleer, a carousel comprised of double-seater roosters which became a trademark of Coney Island's famous Steeplechase Park. Bostock's interest in creating lighter, more portable rides, led him to an association with William Mangels, the ride genius who invented such favorite American amusement devices as the Whip, the Tickler, and the third rail system used on roller coasters and scenic railways.

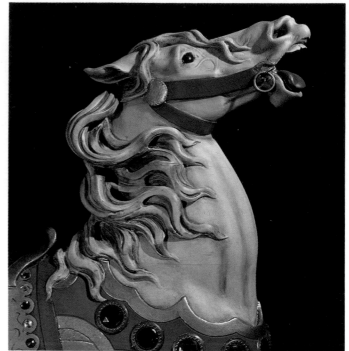

Marcus Charles Illions on his horse "Bob." Illions owned and rode horses most of his life. *Courtesy of Barney Illions and Ruth Crane Sokolow*

Illions parted company with Bostock in 1892 and opened a shop on Dean Street in Brooklyn as a free lance circus and carousel carver. Illions' energy and enthusiasm flowed into his designs and carvings while business details were neglected, resulting in the failure of his company.

Around the turn of the century, Illions was hired by William Mangels to carve horses for the carousels he was constructing. Their alliance produced a number of magnificent machines, including one of the most famous rides in the country, the dazzling Feltman carousel. The original Feltman carousel, carved by Charles Looff in 1880, was a major attraction of the famous landmark restaurant. By 1890, the Feltman complex, which included thrill rides in addition to the popular carousel, was drawing hundreds of thousands of people a year.

In its heyday, Coney Island attracted many celebrities as it became the horse-racing and amusement capital of America. Entertainers Lillian Russell and Lily Langtry, millionaire sportsman August Belmont, William C. Whitney, William K. Vanderbilt and the legendary Diamond Jim Brady were frequent visitors to Coney Island. Brady, a playboy with a fondness for ostentatious, expensive jewelry and beautiful women, so enjoyed the Feltman complex that he maintained an apartment there with his own private entrance to the carousel.

At the turn of the century, the Feltman carousel was partially destroyed by fire. Mangels and his master carver, Marcus Charles Illions, were hired to rebuild the damaged ride. Together, they created one of the most beautiful and revered of all carousels. The replacement horses were outstanding in design and execution — poses were boldly dramatic, and trappings were lavishly adorned with jewels and carvings in relief. Sensitive, expressive faces were set off by thick billowing manes cascading to the saddle.

Many of the original Looff figures were salvaged from the burned machine. While they were simpler in design than the exciting, spirited horses of Marcus Charles Illions, a number of animals were unique. The outside row horses were bedecked with large colored glass jewels set in embossed metal escutcheons. Porcelain light sockets were placed inside the figures through a concealed trap door on the plain side of the animal. The faceted jewels were set over holes drilled through to the hollow interior creating a sparkling illuminated effect. For the sake of uniformity, Illions placed similarly lighted jewels on the replacement horses he carved. While the idea was exciting, the impracticalities of operation must have been overwhelming; the glittering horses lit from the inside never appeared on another carousel. In its heyday, there were twenty-four lavishly decorated carousels operating on Coney Island — the Mangels-Illions alliance was responsible for a large number of them.

Photo above and previous page right showing an exquisite outside stander carved by M.C. Illions from the historic Feltman's carousel of Coney Island. Outside row figures on this carousel had porcelain light fixtures concealed in the hollow interiors of their bodies. Faceted jewels, set over holes drilled to the inside, sparkled as the light shone through, lending a dazzling effect as the carousel turned. *From the author's collection*

One of the master's finest horses. This lovely figure by M.C. Illions carries the carver's name followed by the initials C.I., for Coney Island. Illions only signed his most outstanding carvings, circa 1905. *From the author's collection*

Steeplechase Park in Coney Island was a fun-seeker's heaven. There were huge tumbling barrels to climb through, a mirror maze, sky-high slides, and spinning disks that propelled riders from one disk to another. When exiting the Steeplechase ride, riders found themselves on a stage in front of an audience. As the seated crowd roared, a clown poked the startled participants with an electric shock stick while wind machines, submerged in the floor, blew billowing skirts into the air.

A few of the many rides at Coney Island. The Whip (in the foreground), invented by William Mangels, became one of the most popular of all amusement rides.

A crowd of thrill seekers enjoying the wild Steeplechase ride. Steeplechase horses, carved by M.C. Illions, rode on clacking rails at frightening speeds.

Illions factory photo, circa 1912, with an inventory of animals from various periods. The variety of Illions' head styles are evident in this photograph. *Courtesy of Barney Illions and Rose Crane Sokolow.*

In 1909, Illions formed the M.C. Illions and Sons Carousell Works and included his daughter and four sons in the business. More and more Illions carousels appeared on the Eastern seaboard. With family members carving, painting, and attending to business details, his company prospered.

In the late twenties, as the use of mass-produced figures increased and the demand for handcrafted carousels diminished, the proud, often tyrannical, Marcus Charles Illions closed his shop.

Financially devasted by the crash of '29, the master Coney Island carver died in 1949 at the age of eighty-four.

The diverse moods of Marcus Charles Illions were reflected in his work. At his best, the temperamental, innovative artist was often imitated, but seldom equalled.

Three jeweled outside row jumpers, circa 1908, by M.C. Illions. A wolf-like gargoyle decorates the horse on the left. *From the author's collection.*

A sensitive angel graces the saddle of a Feltman period horse carved by M.C. Illions, circa 1906.

A roaring lion with a harness of chains by M.C. Illions, circa 1908

A standing deer that is one of the few surviving menagerie figures carved by M.C. Illions, circa 1908.

A rare goat by M.C. Illions, in an unusual running pose, circa 1908.

Above left: A fine armoured horse with a huge latticed drape encrusted with multi-colored jewels. This elaborately ornamented horse was worthy of the master's signature which appears on its breast plate. Illions only signed his finest work, circa 1912. Above right: Illions was a master at carving varied and exciting manes. This "Arabian Knight" horse, lavishly decorated with fancy lattice work, appears to be straining against the wind, circa 1912. *Photo-Gloria and George King*

An Illions outside row stander with an exciting tossed mane. Jeweled straps and lattice work decorate the well-proportioned horse. circa 1914. *Photo-Gloria and George King*

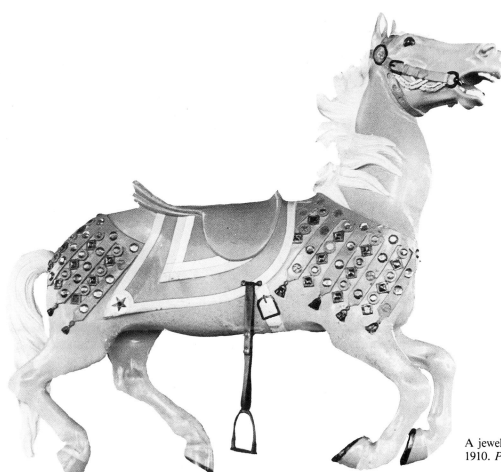

A jeweled jumper by M.C. Illions, circa 1910. *Photo-Gloria and George King*

This photograph is an original from the Illions and Mangels catalogs. The horse is painted in a subtle dapple with a gold leaf mane. *Photo-Barney Illions and Rose Crane Sokolow*

This lovely outside stander, festooned with delicate flowers, is Illions' "American Beauty." *Photo-Barney Illions and Rose Crane Sokolow*

A row of Illions' standers graduating in size from the largest on the outside row to the smallest nearest the centerpole.

Illions' figures had varied shaped heads. This figure has a long, slender, tapering head and a typically exciting mane, circa 1920.

This ornately decorated armoured jumper carries Abraham Lincoln's portrait on its trappings. Carved by M.C. Illions, circa 1916.

An Illions "tour de force"—a magnificent standing horse
blanketed with flowers on one of the last carousels carved by
M.C. Illions and Sons. circa 1925. *Photo-David Roar, courtesy of
Circus World, Orlando, Florida*

A lovely centerpole housing by M.C. Illions and Sons. *Photo-James Gayle*

A firebreathing dragon and lion with the tail of a serpent are part of this fanciful Illions chariot. *Photo-James Gayle*

This lovely carousel was one of the last carved by M.C. Illions, circa 1927. *Photo-Barney Illions and Ruth Crane Sokolow*

A rococo style organ facade carved by M.C. Illions. Illions' talent was not limited to carousel figures as evidenced by this masterful carving now at Geauga Lake Park, Aurora, Ohio. *Photo-Barney Illions and Rose Crane Sokolow*

138

Chapter II

Philadelphia Toboggan Company

Henry B. Auchy, founder of the Philadelphia Toboggan Company, *Photo-Sam High III*

As the demand for carousels increased, Philadelphia entrepreneur, Henry Auchy, decided it was time to enter the carousel business. By the age of thirty-eight, Auchy was a successful liquor and produce distributor and owner/operator of a large sprawling picnic area, Chestnut Hill Park. In 1899, in partnership with Louis Berni, an importer of carousel band organs, he formed the Philadelphia Carousel Company. Auchy hired former Dentzel employees, Daniel and Alfred Muller, to carve for his fledgling company. The company's first carousel, installed in a building surrounded by lush lawns and tall trees in Auchy's park in Philadelphia, was a huge success.

In 1903, Auchy and Chester Albright formed the Philadelphia Toboggan Company, which not only produced carousels, but roller coasters as well. In their first

year, the company produced five beautifully crafted carousels which carried an outstanding assortment of horses and menagerie animals. Around 1907, Daniel and Alfred Muller ceased carving for the Philadelphia Toboggan Company to produce carousels of their own. With the loss of the talented Muller brothers, Philadelphia Toboggan Company carvings changed dramatically. The company ceased production of menagerie animals and never resumed carving them again. Horses of this period were awkwardly posed and poorly proportioned - heads were elongated, eyes set too high; the overall effect was disappointing.

The master carver at this time is unknown, but it appears that a number of craftsmen tried their hand without much success. Orders for Philadelphia Toboggan Company carousels dropped drastically. Until the

Above: Early PTC carousel with two strangers aboard—a Herschell-Spillman stork and frog. It is not uncommon for animals from various companies to appear on the same carousel. As replacements were needed, owners chose figures from a variety of sources. This carousel was sent back to the PTC factory to be rebuilt.

Below: A lovely PTC carousel at Chestnut Hill Park in Philadelphia. This park was the setting for the first carousel produced by the PTC company, founded by Henry Auchy.

PTC sea monster with green glass eyes and a seaweed mane. Few of these creatures were carved as they were frightening to young children. *From the author's collection.*

Above: A snake coils around the neck of this magnificant giraffe. At seven feet, the PTC giraffe is the tallest of all carousel figures, circa 1905. Below: Rare outside row PTC dog in original paint, circa 1905. The realistic animal is on the carousel at Burlington, Colorado.

Above: Adorned with a cluster of flowers, this PTC sea horse, in original paint, is on the carousel at Burlington, Colorado, circa 1905. Below: On the same carousel, an elaborately stenciled blanket and a pensive cherub decorate an early PTC stander.

PTC menagerie figures were carved from 1902-1907. This rare tiger is in original body paint, circa 1905. *Photo-George King*

Early PTC shop photo showing an array of menagerie figures. Menagerie animals carved by PTC are rare. After 1907, the company produced only horses. *Photo-Sam High III*

hiring of Frank Carretta in 1912, the firm produced only one carousel a year. Born in Milan, Italy, Carretta came to America as a boy to apprentice as a furniture carver. Under Carretta's direction, carousels were adorned with massive ornate horses, exquisite chariots and illuminated mirrors surrounded by plump little cherubs. Carretta's exciting designs and carvings revitalized the Philadelphia Toboggan Company; and, once again, their carousels were in great demand. Carretta, a small meticulous man, was married and had one daughter. To better support his family, he worked for the Philadelphia Toboggan Company by day and traveled at night to students' homes to give carving lessons.

By 1915, most carousel figures were roughed out by carving machines. All of the fine finish work was hand done, but the fanciest horses were usually the work of the head carver. Payroll books from 1913 show that the

A 1905 PTC Indian Pony on the carousel at Burlington, Colorado. In original paint, the spirited stander carries a tomahawk, peacepipe, feathers and a wolfskin blanket.

A majestic PTC lion in factory paint, circa 1905. PTC lions were carved in a variety of poses and designs.

This PTC lion, circa 1906, weathered the devastating hurricane of 1938 on the boardwalk at Long Branch, New Jersey. *From the author's collection*

Large, realistic camel with lovely drapery and tassels, carved in the elegant Philadelphia Style. *From the author's collection*

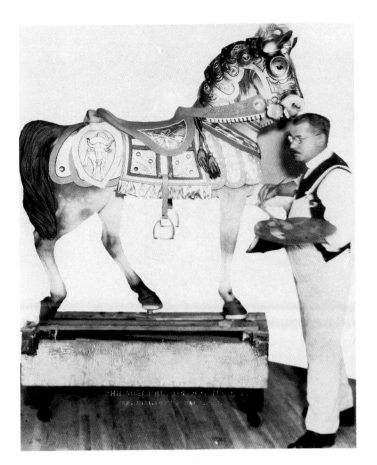

Fastidious Gustav Weiss, painter for the Philadelphia Toboggan Company for many years, always wore a shirt and tie when he worked. In 1915, he prepared and painted fifty-six horses for $94.50.

Above and Below: A 1915 Carretta stander, sporting a delightful leering monkey on its trappings. *From the author's collection*

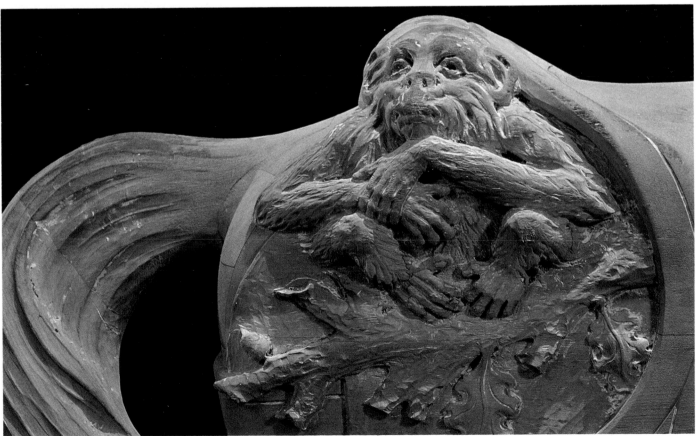

Henry Auchy (far right) proudly poses on a fancy PTC carousel. While the chariots and facade carvings were magnificent, PTC horses of this period were disappointing, circa 1910.

Awkwardly posed, oddly proportioned PTC horses, circa 1909. During the period after Muller and before Carretta, horses' legs were bony and abnormally long, eyes were set high, and necks were short.

company paid $1.00 to have a horse sanded. Gustav Weiss, the company's painter for many years, was paid $95 for retouching and varnishing an entire carousel. In 1915, Weiss prepared and painted fifty-six horses for a total of $94.50. Records from the following year reveal that he was paid $4.50 to paint a king horse and $8.00 to paint each chariot. In 1914, the forty-six animals carved for the Philadelphia Toboggan Company's #29 carousel cost a total of $1,715.99.

In 1919, Samuel High became associated with the company as a stockholder/officer and eventually bought out his partners. In the twenties, some of the finest carvers ever to wield a chisel worked for the Philadelphia Toboggan Company. In addition to Frank Carretta, the artists included Salvatore Cernigliaro, Charles Carmel, and John Zalar.

Under the leadership of Sam High III, the Philadelphia Toboggan Company is still successful in the game and ride business today. The firm ceased producing carousels in 1933, but Carretta remained with the Philadelphia Toboggan Company doing carpentry work until the forties. Perhaps the greatest tribute to the finely crafted carousels produced by this notable company comes from carousel owners themselves who dream of one day owning the very best, a Philadelphia Toboggan Company carousel.

Carretta's beautiful carousels revitalized the Philadelphia Toboggan Company. In 1936, this PTC #44 machine (built in 1917) was sold to Roger Williams Park in Providence, Rhode Island, for $7,500.

PTC employee banquet, 1922. Founder Henry Auchy is seated at the head of the table in the center. At his right is PTC artist, Gustav Weiss.

An Indian and an American flag symbolize the history of America on this PTC chariot at Elitch Gardens, Denver, Colorado, circa 1920. *Photo-Bill Manns*

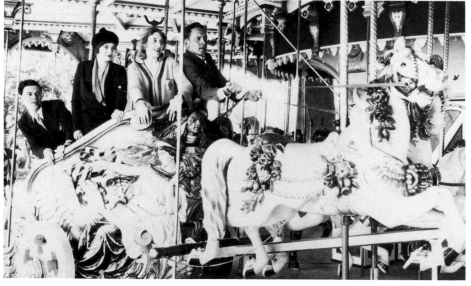

Popular movie stars of the thirties, Sylvia Sydney (second from left) and Frederick March (far right), take a ride on the Columbia chariot aboard the elaborate PTC carousel at Denver's Elitch Gardens, circa 1930.

Closeup of a splendid angel from a Philadelphia Toboggan Company chariot at Denver's Elitch Gardens, circa 1920. *Photo-Bill Manns*

Columbia, a symbol of the virtuous aspirations of America, was glorified on the exquisite PTC chariot at Denver's Elitch Gardens, circa 1920. *Photo-Bill Manns*

Bedecked with flowers, these horses are pulling a magnificent chariot (photo left) at Denver's Elitch Gardens, circa 1920. *Photo-Bill Manns*

An exquisite, armoured signed PTC stander carrying the company initials on a large shield, circa 1920. *Photo-Bill Manns*

One of the last horses carved by the Philadelphia Toboggan Company at Asbury Park, New Jersey, circa 1932. Note the fancy PTC signature carved on the outside row stander.

Strong, powerful PTC outside row jumper. The cut-through mane adds to the attractiveness of this large figure, circa 1917. *From the author's collection*

A similar horse won PTC carver, Frank Carretta, a carving award at the Amusement Park Convention in 1927. *From the author's collection*

After World War I, the Philadelphia Toboggan Company produced three or four carousels a year. Horses like this resplendent stander graced late period PTC carousels.

A layered, flying mane, a sensitive expression, and multiple jewels add to the grandeur of this Carmel stander, circa 1908. *From the author's collection*

Chapter 12
Charles Carmel

Charles Carmel and his family: (left to right) son Benjamin, wife Hannah, sons Matthew and Samuel. *Courtesy of Carol Holden*

Charles Carmel, born in Russia in 1865, immigrated to the United States in 1883, after marrying at the age of seventeen. Charles and his young Russian bride, sixteen year-old Hannah, settled in Brooklyn, a short distance away from the fabled amusement capital, Coney Island.

Although little is known about the early career of Charles Carmel, it is believed that he learned the carving trade as a youth in Russia. Just after the turn of the century, Charles Looff hired Carmel as a carver of carousel figures in his Brooklyn factory. After Looff moved his business to Rhode Island in 1905, Carmel opened his own shop where he carved animals to order for a number of companies that manufactured carousel machinery and frames. Carmel's most notable customers included Mangels, Dolle, Murphy and Borelli. The carver's dra-

matically posed horses, implying a strong aggressive quality, were tempered by gentle, sweet expressions. His creations, often ablaze with jewels, armour and figures in relief, were found on many of the twenty-four carousels which dotted Coney Island.

M.D. Borelli, a poor Italian immigrant who came to America as a young child was one of Carmel's best customers. In his youth, Borelli was employed as a *ring boy,* a job that put him in charge of the brass ring mechanism of the carousel. Befriended and inspired by his employers, the young boy dreamed of owning and operating a carousel one day. Borelli's childhood fantasy became a reality as he went into business as a manufacturer of carousel machinery and frames. The stocky, pleasant man fussed over the Carmel carousel figures as if they were his children. During the off-season, Borelli

A very early Carmel jumper with a "trumpet" style nose, large head, intricate full mane and parallel rear legs. The saddle was originally upholstered in mohair, which was fastened to the wood by decorative brass nails. circa 1900. *From the author's collection*

Early Carmel standers appeared somewhat squarish and had oversized heads compared to later carvings, circa 1902.

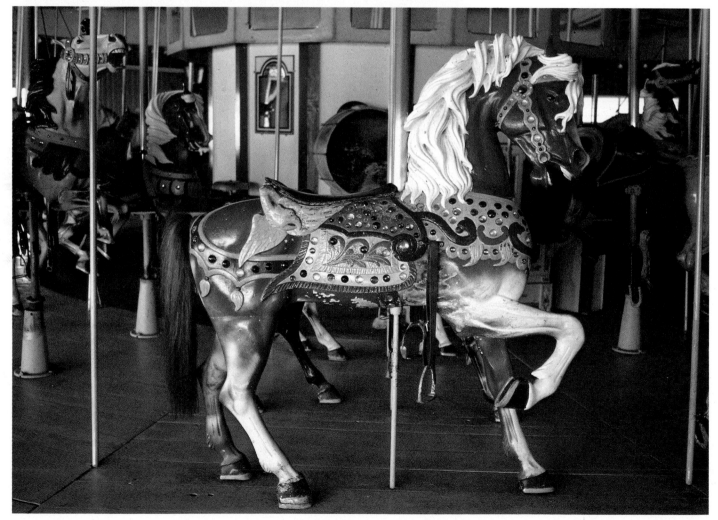

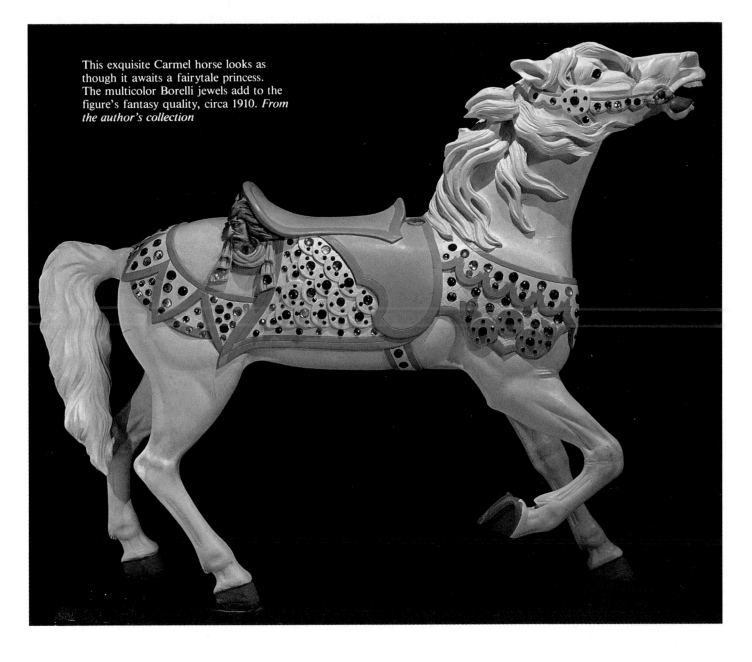

This exquisite Carmel horse looks as though it awaits a fairytale princess. The multicolor Borelli jewels add to the figure's fantasy quality, circa 1910. *From the author's collection*

painted each animal with loving care. Fascinated by glitter and flash, he spent hour after hour adding faceted jewels of all sizes to Carmel's creations. Some Borelli figures have over 300 multicolored gems on their trappings. Occasionally, he became carried away as he glued jewels, not only on the trappings, but all over the animals' heads and bodies!

Charles and Hannah Carmel raised a family of four. The children assisted Charles in the shop by sanding and undercoating the wooden animals. The industrious Carmel worked hard to ensure his children a proper education—and he was not disappointed. Matthew graduated from law school; Ben became a doctor; Elsie, a teacher; and Sam, a businessman.

Carmel was a perfectionist who had little patience with those who didn't meet his high standards as a craftsman. He was described by family members as "strict and demanding but a straightforward, honest and very decent man." Hannah, a warm friendly woman, enjoyed the panorama of life that passed before her home at 202 Ocean Parkway on the way to Coney Island. Ocean Parkway was a bustling thoroughfare with eight individual lanes for strollers, horseback riders, carriages and bicycles. Crossing from one side of the street to another was described as quite an adventure. Their home was close to Prospect Park and its stable of riding horses, which served as models for the carousel carvings of Charles Carmel.

Feathers and fish scales were favorite carved adornments on horses by Charles Carmel. The wolf-like gargoyle at the saddle cantle appeared on a number of his figures, as well as some carved by M.C. Illions. Since both carvers worked for Mangels at the same time, there were some similarities in their work. *Photo-George King*

Instead of merely supplying carved figures to frame manufacturers, more and more carvers turned to owning and operating carousels. In the right location, a carousel could produce a handsome income; $500 a day was not an uncommon amount.

For his first venture as a carousel owner, Carmel selected a site in Coney Island's Dreamland Park. On May 24, 1911, the day before the park was to open, workmen, making last minute repairs, allowed a tar pot to overheat; and the entire park went up in flames. Forty-five fire companies from New York City, Brooklyn and Long Island were unable to bring the blaze under control. Carmel had invested most of his money in the uninsured carousel, and its loss was a devastating blow to the carver and his family.

A grand armoured horse by Charles
Carmel. This elaborate outside row stander
is ready for battle as it awaits a young Sir
Lancelot. It is aboard the four-abreast
carousel at Playland, Rye, New York.
Photo-George King

Dreamland Park in Coney Island, before
the devastating fire of 1911. The song
"Meet Me Tonight in Dreamland"
referred to this park. *Courtesy of George
Siessel*

An outstanding Carmel armoured stander. The rather squarish trappings don't detract from the impact of this majestic horse. *From the author's collection*

A row of dynamic horses by Coney Island Style carver, Charles Carmel.

One of the most beautiful of all carousel jumpers. This exquisite Carmel horse, with its delicate face and dramatic pose, is on the carousel at Playland, Rye, New York, circa 1915.

This boldly posed Carmel jumper, carrying a shield and sword, has a stunning high-flying mane. Like Illions, Carmel carved a variety of exciting manes, many with an interesting reverse flow, others with see-through cuts or layers intricately patterned. *Photo-George King*

This exciting Carmel jumper is a fine example of the Coney Island Style of carving; spirited pose, lavish use of faceted jewels and elaborate ornamentation. The windswept mane creates a feeling of speed and animation. *Photo-George King*

The intricately carved mane, pretty face, bold pose, and fine proportions mark this as a figure from the chisel of Charles Carmel. The fish scale blanket is somewhat flat and squarish, but it does not detract from the harmony of the trappings. *Photo-George King*

In 1913, the Philadelphia Toboggan Company listed Charles Carmel on its payroll as a supplier of carousel horses. Carmel's fee to carve a large jumper or standing horse was $35.00, for a medium jumper or stander, $25.00, and for a small jumper or stander, $20.00. His name appeared as a freelance carver for the Philadelphia Toboggan Company until 1921. As Carmel's health deteriorated, he closed his shop and carved from home a few hours a day, filling orders and repairing animals until about 1925. The carver suffered from diabetes and arthritis and became an invalid until his death from cancer in 1931. Hannah Carmel lived at the home they shared on Ocean Parkway until her death in 1946.

Charles Carmel created what many believe to be the most perfect carousel horse - a harmonious balance of gentleness and drama.

An expressive eye peeks from a cascading forelock on this Carmel stander. The hanging tongue was used quite often by Charles Carmel. *From the author's collection*

The delicate bas-relief roses on this Carmel stander are in sharp contrast to the badger-like creature that adorns the saddle. This stunning horse is on the carousel at Playland in Rye, New York, circa 1915.

A spirited jumper demonstrates the intricate ornamentation on figures carved by Charles Carmel. The huge mane on this horse frames a bouquet of delicate roses.

A Carmel sea dragon that closely resembles those by carver, Charles Looff. The Borelli "touch" is evidenced by the abundance of jewels. *From the Edwin Ferren III Collection*

Very few menagerie figures were carved by Charles Carmel. This massive, heavily jeweled lion shows the many jewels of M.D. Borelli. *From the Edwin Ferren III Collection*

Opposite page: Carmel carousel at Knoebel's Grove, Sunbury, Pennsylvania. *Photo-George Siessel*

166

Cherubs, a favorite subject of carousel carvers, decorated rounding boards, shields, chariots and band organs. This angelic figure embellishes a spirited Carmel jumper on board the carousel at Playland, Rye, New York, circa 1915.

An unusual tilted Mangels carousel with Carmel horses at Euclid Beach, Cleveland, Ohio. *Courtesy of John Caruthers*

Fancy Carmel jumpers on a two abreast Mangels carousel, circa 1905. The photograph was taken in 1920 at Ocean Beach, New London, Connecticut. *Photo-Gail Hall*

A dramatic Carmel-Borelli stander, circa 1910. *From the author's collection*

A pretty stander in the favorite tucked-head position. Its many jewels were the work of M.D. Borelli, who often added over 300 gems to the figures he bought from Charles Carmel. *From the author's collection*

Below and Right: A windswept mane frames a beautiful face on this stunning jumper carved by Charles Carmel, circa 1915. *From the author's collection.*

A Stein and Goldstein outside stander in original body paint. The fearsome look of this roach-maned horse is softened by a profusion of delicate flowers, circa 1912. *From the author's collection*

Chapter 13

Stein and Goldstein

Solomon Stein at the age of twenty-five.

Solomon Stein, born in Russia in 1882, immigrated to America in 1903 at the age of twenty-one and settled in Brooklyn. As a skilled woodworker, he found employment at Wanamakers Department Store as a furniture carver. In addition, the ambitious artist spent his spare time, from dawn until late into the night, filling carving orders on a free lance basis. In 1907, he married Russian-born Annie Goldberg. The couple had three children, Esther, Evelyn, and Sidney.

A year before Solomon Stein came to America, a fellow Russian immigrant, Harry Mandel, settled in the same Brooklyn neighborhood with his wife and son, David. Upon Mandel's arrival, it is believed that immigration officials who assigned any name they wished to non-English speaking arrivals, gave him the name, Harry Goldstein. An accomplished woodworker, Goldstein

worked by day, carving ladies' wooden combs. At night, he attended school to learn the English language. Goldstein, who was in his mid-thirties, became a carver of models for a moldmaker in 1904.

Answering the demand for carousel carvers at nearby Coney Island, Stein and Goldstein met when they joined the William F. Mangels Company Carousel Works in 1905. Mangels employed a number of outstanding craftsmen who eventually formed carousel companies of their own. Such illustrious carvers as Charles Carmel, Marcus Charles Illions, and Stein and Goldstein developed their carving skills under William Mangels' direction.

Impressed with the overwhelming success of Coney Island carousels, Stein and Goldstein decided to strike out on their own. Around 1907, they formed a partner-

These early Stein and Goldstein horses are on the carousel at New York's Central Park. S and G horses of this period are not as attractive as later carvings; eyes are set high, noses are very long and straight, and expressions are mean, circa 1908.

An extremely large, early Stein and Goldstein jumper in an exaggerated pose that is typical of the Coney Island Style of carving, circa 1909. *Photo-George King*

An early standing Stein and Goldstein horse, one of two pulling a large Roman chariot on New York's Central Park carousel, circa 1908.

A dramatic Stein and Goldstein
standing horse, circa 1912.
*Courtesy of the Smithsonian
Institution, Washington, D.C.*

This large stander is a fine example of Stein and Goldstein's use of large buckles, fish scale and flowers. This figure is on the Bushnell Park carousel in Hartford, Connecticut, circa 1914. *Photo-George King*

ship, eventually calling their company Stein and Goldstein, the Artistic Caroussel Manufacturers. A partially converted stable served as their first shop, and huge dray horses, still boarded there, became models for their carvings.

The first Stein and Goldstein carousel was delivered and installed in Virginia Beach. While Stein was traveling to Virginia to check on its installation, the carousel caught fire and burned to the ground. The distraught carver brought a souvenir dish home to his family, calling it his $20,000 plate, a reminder of the cruel loss he suffered. The second Stein and Goldstein carousel, installed at Brockton, Massachusetts, was an immediate success and launched a career that lasted over a decade.

As business prospered, the men moved their families to a quiet residential area in the Ridgewood section of Brooklyn and transferred their business to an abandoned trolley barn. The Stein children recalled the shop as being extremely neat and orderly and filled with a wonderful woody aroma, mixed with the pleasing scent of freshly heated glue. Although their company did not build mechanisms, the two men, working six days a week from dawn to dusk, carved all of the horses themselves.

Stein and Goldstein figures were painted by a professional artist in a variety of bright colors with gold leaf accents (particularly evident on armored horses and chariots). Many outside row standers rivaled real horses in size and scale. In contrast to the angry, aggressive

179

expressions of Stein and Goldstein horses, delicately carved flowers, feathers and tassels were often part of the trappings.

Stein and Goldstein constructed seventeen carousels and owned and operated eleven of them. Their alliance produced the largest carousels ever constructed, carrying five and six rows of horses and seating as many as one hundred people.

In the early twenties, Stein and Goldstein carved circus and carnival figures and supplied wooden horses set on porcelain bases for barber shops. Many a child fearing his first haircut was happily distracted by sitting astride a snarling Stein and Goldstein horse.

As the demand for carousels diminished, the partners branched out into buying, selling and operating other amusement rides. Solomon Stein died of cancer in 1937; he is remembered by his children as "a man who was industrious, intellectually curious, generous in friendship, artistically inventive, loyal and most importantly a man who loved people."

Harry Goldstein operated two parks and an arcade machine business until his death in 1945.

The impressively forceful, yet delicately adorned, carvings of Stein and Goldstein earned them a prominent place in the history of American carousel art.

A typical large Stein and Goldstein jumper on the Bushnell Park carousel, Hartford, Connecticut, circa 1914.

180

A Stein and Goldstein jumper showing typical buckles and straps, flat stringy, windswept mane, oversized saddle and deeply carved flowers, circa 1914. *Photo-George King*

This jumper shows typical Stein and Goldstein features—a fierce expression, short legs drawn close to the body, and bent hoofs. *From the author's collection.*

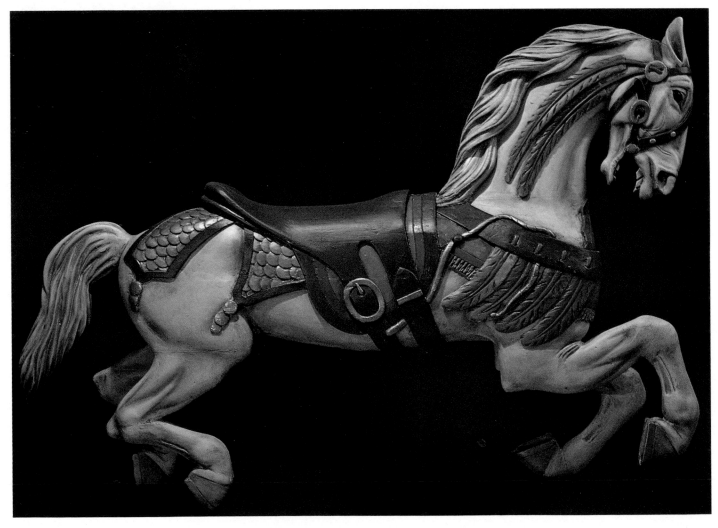

A large standing "King" horse, carved by Stein and Goldstein, in heavy layered armour, circa 1910. *From the author's collection.*

An armoured jumper showing the typical characteristics of Stein and Goldstein horses: elongated body, oversized saddle, and short legs drawn close to the body. The horse has a real horsehair tail which is correct for Stein and Goldstein carvings. Wooden tails were sometimes added to carousel figures through the years as owners replaced the more perishable hair tails, which were always a temptation for children to pull. *From the author's collection*

183

The prominent girth buckle, flowing tassel and bouquet of protruding roses are typical of S & G horses. This stander is on the carousel at Bushnell Park, Hartford, Connecticut, circa 1914. *Photo-George King*

Teeth are bared as this aggressive roach-maned steed strains at the bit. There is nothing soft or sweet about an S & G horse; but there is an exciting impression of nervous energy in their carvings, circa 1908.

A harness of bells decorate the head strap of this large Stein and Goldstein jumper on Nunley's carousel in Baldwin, Long Island, New York, circa 1909. *Photo- George King*

185

Stein and Goldstein jumpers strain at the bit on the Sportland Pier carousel at Wildwood, New Jersey, circa 1910.

The Bushnell Park Carousel was saved for future generations to enjoy by the efforts of concerned citizens of Hartford, Connecticut. This Stein and Goldstein jumper rides the fine four-abreast machine, circa 1914.

Few American carousel carvers could match Stein and Goldstein's armoured horses. This fancy steed rides the Hartford, Connecticut, carousel at Bushnell Park, circa 1914.

187

High set eyes, bared teeth, fish scale armour and cabbage roses mark this as an S & G jumper, circa 1914.

This horse has delicate rose embellishments and an unusually exciting mane for a Stein and Goldstein carving. The large figure is on Nunley's carousel in Baldwin, Long Island, New York, circa 1909. *Photo-George King*

Stein and Goldstein horses of this period have a softer expression than very early figures, but a feeling of aggressiveness is still implied. S & G often decorated the trappings of their horses with deeply carved roses. Most carvers used flowers on their figures, but Stein and Goldstein's large cabbage roses are extremely impressive. This horse is on the carousel at Bushnell Park, Hartford, Connecticut. circa 1914. *Photo-George King*

One of the largest horses ever carved, this Stein and Goldstein lead horse, embellished with ribbons, tassels and roses is Stein and Goldstein at their best. Gold and silver leaf, subdued by the years, blends with the rich patina of the body paint. The exquisite horse, at one time, was on the carousel at Rockaway Beach, New York. *From the author's colleciton.*

Looff figure on display at the North Carolina Museum of History in Raleigh, showing the construction of a carousel horse. *Photo-Neil Fulghum, North Carolina Museum of History*

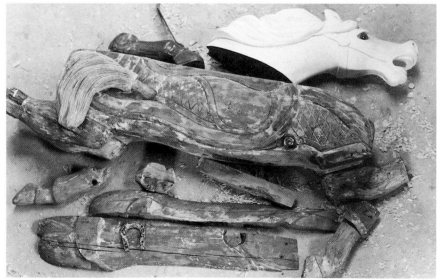

A disassembled Parker horse in need of major repair including replacement of missing parts. *Courtesy of William Zensuis*

190

Chapter 14

Restoration

Artist/craftsman, Leonard Pavia, applies the finishing touches to a tiger he has restored.

Although carousel carvers were given free rein to use their skill and imagination, they often had to follow a limited number of pre-set poses and designs. Working from large patterns drawn on brown paper or cardboard, shop carpenters, using heated hide glue and wooden dowels, laminated two-to-three inch planks of bass, poplar or apple wood into the rough shape of the figure. To reduce the weight of the animal, the inside of the body was a hollow box. Before carving machines were in use, the head, legs and tail were roughed out by shop carpenters and finished by the carver after the parts were joined to the body. The fine finish work created the personality of the figure, and the mark of the individual carver provided each animal with its own unique identity.

Collectors refer to carousel animals that have been stripped, repaired, sanded and repainted (to the original look or to their liking) as being restored. Many, especially those with an antique or museum background, have the traditional attitude that the finish on a relic of the past should not be disturbed. Carousel animals, however, fall into a unique category.

Most certainly, animals, crestings, and scenery in original paint should be left as found. Fine old paint, especially on animals which were returned to the factory for repainting, is also best left alone unless major repairs are necessary. Unfortunately, however, the majority of carousel figures are found in what is known as *park paint*. Park paint on occasion can be attractive; but it is usually a garish finish, carelessly applied, with little sensitivity for the artistry of the figure. Finely detailed carv-

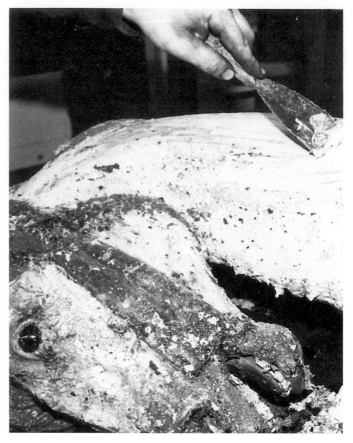

The horse rests on an inverted table top as the stripping compound is brushed on. A pan catches the drippings which may be reapplied. Hand stripping, although tedious and time consuming, is the safest method for removing paint. *Courtesy of Bruce Kneevals*

After the paint softens, a putty knife and fine steel wool are used to remove layers of loose paint. *Courtesy of Bruce Kneevals*

ings are often obliterated by as many as thirty layers of encrusted paint. Objections to the removal of a finish of this quality cannot be justified.

Before beginning the restoration process, it is a good idea to photograph the animal in its pre-restored condition. By using a fine sharp artist's knife, it is sometimes possible through very careful scraping to expose areas of original paint. Entire animals have been painstakingly stripped this way or by a carefully controlled layer by layer removal with a commercial product. If a good deal of original paint is uncovered intact, many collectors choose to display the figure in this partially stripped condition, which can be very attractive. If you decide to proceed with a complete restoration, it is important to photograph and record original colors if at all possible. Some collectors elect to duplicate these colors, while others choose to paint to suit their fancy. If one decides on the latter, a photographic record of original paint is important as a guide to follow if an accurate restoration is attempted at a later date.

Stripping

The first step in the restoration process is to strip the paint to bare wood. Remember - never, under any circumstances, sandblast wood to remove paint. Sandblasting raises the grain and destroys the crispness of the carvings. There are a number of safe procedures to use. Some collectors prefer a hand-held lamp or heat gun which softens the paint for easy removal. As the pigment loosens, it can be peeled, scraped or brushed off. This method and the hand-stripping method using a commerical compound require about ten percent skill and ninety percent patience.

Hand stripping a carousel animal with a commercial paint remover usually takes from ten to fourteen hours, depending on the number of coats of paint and the intricacy of the carvings. If possible, it's a good idea to work outdoors, since fumes can be a problem. If you must work indoors, be sure there is adequate ventilation. Necessary tools include putty knives, wood chisels, paint

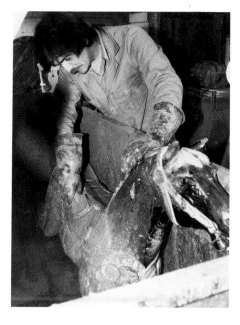

A professional cold dip tank used for stripping wood. *Courtesy of Victor Michaels, Bix Carriage House, Summit, New Jersey*

The horse soaks in a stripping solution. *Courtesy of Victor Michaels*

After the paint softens a bristle brush is used to clean through to the wood. *Courtesy of Victor Michaels*

scrapers, steel wool and scrubbing brushes with natural bristles.

The animal should be laid flat on its side in a pan large enough to catch reusable drippings. An inverted table top and discarded car hood are two imaginative pans that collectors have devised.

A thick layer of stripping compound, with a heavy or gel-like consistency, should be brushed on in one direction. If one application doesn't penetrate in an hour or two, the remover can be reapplied. A putty knife will easily clean through to the wood when the paint has softened properly. A figure with many layers of paint, as well as manes, tails, and other heavily carved areas, usually requires repeated applications; and handpicking with knives or embossing tools is often necessary. A quick *blast* hosing with water or the application of a thin solvent is the final step in removing remaining paint residue from the animal. Hand stripping is messy and unpleasant, and many opt to leave the job to a professional.

Dip Stripping

This method can be satisfactory, if the professional stripper uses a cold dip tank and has a careful appreciation for wood. It's important, however, to stress cold dip since a hot solution can play havoc with wood and glue. Excess soaking in the tank should be avoided, and

brushing to remove paint also must be carefully done to avoid scratching or marring fine details. One advantage of the dip method is its ability to clean tiny crevices in the mane and tail, which often require a great deal of tedious hand picking.

No matter which method you choose, if you remove all of the paint properly, crisp, carved details will be uncovered if the animal is in good condition.

Structural Repair

Unless you're a skilled craftsman with unlimited patience, it's unwise to tackle major structural repair. This may require taking the entire animal apart - repairing, refitting, redowling and regluing all parts for a perfect fit. Large parts of the figure may be missing, requiring the carving talent of an experienced craftsman.

The most common minor problems encountered are joint separations in the legs, nicks and gouges in the wood, and small missing parts (usually from the hoofs or ears). A list of tools necessary for structural repair includes wood dowels, clamps, electric drill, wood chisels, rasps, carving tools, small electric block sander with a thick foam pad attachment, clear silicone caulk, sandpaper, resin filler, epoxy or carpenter's glue and masking tape. The most frustrating part of joint repair is the awkward angles one encounters in attempting to pull the

After gluing and inserting a new dowel into the knee joint, Carver-craftsman, Holger Jensen, hammers in pinch dogs to pull the awkwardly angled parts together. After the glue sets they are removed and fill is applied. *Courtesy of Holger Jensen*

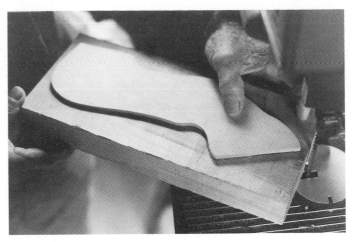

A pattern or template is used to duplicate the proper size and proportion of the missing part. *Courtesy of William Zensuis*

pieces together. Ingenious methods have been devised using pinch dogs, web straps, wood or bar clamps, and even heavy elastic bands. The first step in joint repair is separating the problem parts so that new glue can be applied. Sometimes the dowels, which fasten the parts together, are intact; and after the surfaces are scraped clean, the old dowel just needs to be coated with glue and reinserted. If dowels are broken, they must be removed and replaced.

If glass eyes are cracked or chipped, they should be removed and replaced. If they are just scratched or dull, try a coat of high gloss varnish or clear nail polish to restore their luster. Cover replacement eyes with masking tape to prevent scratching during the restoration process. Cracked or worn jewels should be removed now but not replaced until all painting is finished.

If an entire ear or part of a similar size is missing, a carved wood replacement should be made. If just a portion is missing, it's easier to drill holes to receive dowels smaller than the original contour of the part. Small amounts of fast-drying resin filler can then be built up around the dowels which act as an armature. Through the use of chisels, rasps and sandpaper, the final shape can be formed.

Before proceeding with the filling of small dents and pitted surfaces, there is a decision to be made about how you want the finished animal to look. The extent and amount of fill and sanding required will be determined by your decision. Some collectors prefer an antique or *old* look, achieved by applying a glaze or stain over the painted surfaces, which has a drabbing effect on the colors. This finish is enhanced by leaving small imperfections in the wood, lending an antique look as the glaze is picked up.

Restoration with a high gloss finish involves the complete filling of all imperfections and countless hours of sanding to achieve a consistently flawless surface. An epoxy or polyester resin based filler - available at pattern maker or automotive supply stores - is an ideal fill - it dries very hard, can be carved and sanded and will not shrink. While this product is excellent as a filler, remember never to use it in weight-bearing or stress areas. The resin fill sets very quickly, so it's important to mix small amounts at a time. When the fill dries to a crumbly consistency, a damp cloth wiped over its surface provides a more even finish to sand. When final repairs, fill, and sanding are complete, the animal is ready for a prime coat.

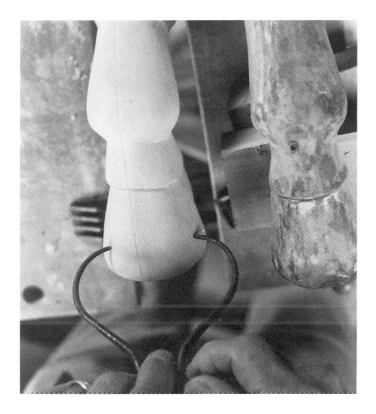

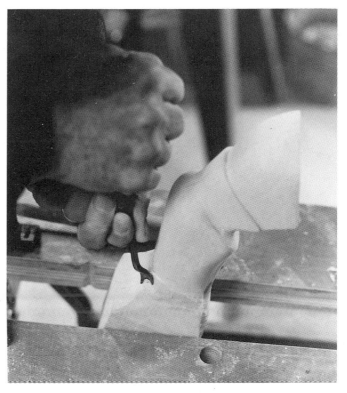

Measuring the legs with calipers is necessary to achieve an exact duplication. *Courtesy of William Zensuis*

The shape of the leg takes form. *Courtesy of William Zensuis*

Carver-craftsman, William Zensuis, puts finishing touches on the horse he has restored. *Courtesy of William Zensuis*

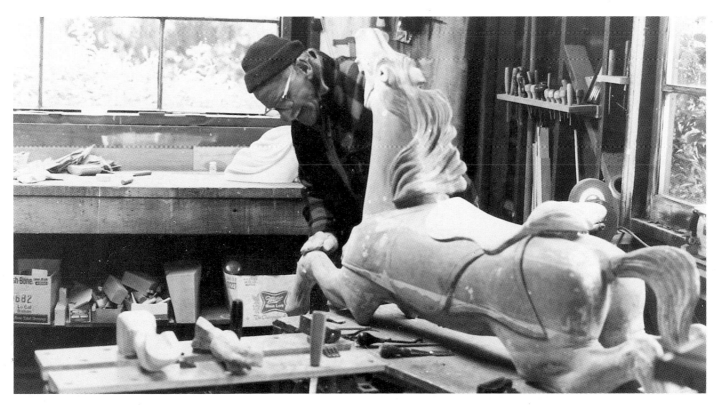

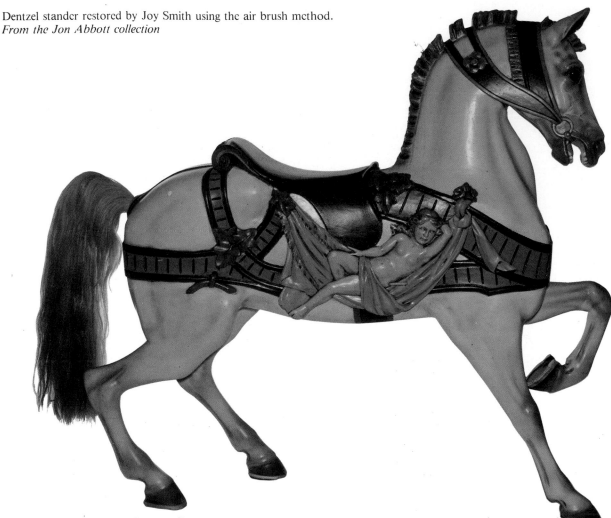

Dentzel stander restored by Joy Smith using the air brush method. *From the Jon Abbott collection*

Prime Coat

Removing paint from glass eyes and faceted jewels is a tiring, frustrating job. Before priming your animal, it is important to coat eyes and jewels with either masking tape, vaseline or rubber cement. The prime coat may be sprayed or brushed on; but, either way, care must be taken not to allow the paint to build up in depressed areas. After the primer is fully dry, the figure is ready for an overall sanding, followed by at least another coat of prime. To achieve a smooth finish, it is important to thoroughly brush or blow loose dust particles away between coats of paint. Sometimes additional sanding and coats of primers are necessary, if overlooked imperfections need additional fill and sanding.

Painting

The steps involved in locating, recording and duplicating original paint can be frustrating and tedious; but there is great satisfaction in doing an authentic restoration on an outstanding figure. However, an exact duplication of colors is not always possible or practical.

In this case, most collectors either paint in the style of the original or use colors that they find harmonious and satisfying. Paint chips from a hardware or paint store are very helpful when deciding on a color combination. Unless you have a trained artist's eye, visualizing the final effect of your color choices can be difficult. Many collectors solve this problem by filling in a variety of color combinations on outlined drawings of the figures until they find one that appeals to them.

The type or brand of paint you select is a matter of personal preference. Oil-based Japan paints, which dry to a flat opaque finish, were used originally; but they've changed over the years and may be difficult to find. It's safe to use either an oil or water-based paint, but it is important to use a compatible primer. Oil glazes and stains may be applied over either type of paint without problems. Those who prefer oil paint feel that the longer drying time allows for fine shading and subtle tonal differences. On the other hand, supporters of the fast drying, water-based paint feel that the quick drying time is

An Illions jumper with a flawless high gloss restoration by Jo and Rol Summit. Note the use of transparent glass paint over silver leaf on the trappings and the exciting mane done in gold leaf. *From the Summit Collection*

an advantage in maintaining a steady work pace, instead of long waiting periods between coats.

A high-gloss paint is not advisable in finishing a carousel horse. A flat or satin finish provides a better base for shading with glazes or toners. Tube oils or acrylics can be used but may appear lumpy or thick compared to the smoother finish of liquid paints.

There are a number of techniques in painting a carousel figure. Again, the choice is a matter of personal preference. Depending on the desired effect, hand-painted figures are usually finished with a stipple brush or sponge (which gives a hairlike, strongly shaded appearance), an antique glaze (which results in a muted, aged feeling) or a smooth high gloss look. While hand painting is the most popular method, some collectors prefer to use an airbrush. Subtle shading and fine pinstriping are advantages to the airbrush method; but becoming adept takes a bit of practice, since problems can occur with spattering paint from clogged lines or incorrect mixtures.

Most collectors paint the body first; two coats usually provide proper coverage. Shading can be achieved through the use of tube oils or acrylics thinned to a transparent consistency. If you're satisfied with the look after the trappings have their final coat, you can then, after the animal is completely dry, apply a flat, satin, or high gloss varnish or polyurethene clear finish as a final coat. If, however, you feel that you would prefer a more aged or antique look, it's time to apply an overall glaze.

Glazing

The glaze, which emphasizes the fine details of the carvings, allows for highlighting and, in effect, brings the wooden animal to life. Glaze, a combination of linseed oil, turpentine, varnish and pigment (usually raw or burnt umber) can be mixed or purchased at a paint store and is the same as the final coat you apply when antiquing furniture. Since the process can be messy, wear

197

your oldest clothes and work out of doors if possible. Glaze is applied with a brush, a section at a time, or over the entire figure, depending upon how fast you work and the setting time of the glaze. There is usually plenty of time to work the glaze before it sets firmly unless it's an unusually hot day. As the dark, runny liquid is applied, you'll feel certain that you're ruining a perfectly good paint job — but don't panic! When the figure is completely coated in every crevice with glaze, fold a soft pad of cheesecloth and, beginning at the head, wipe lightly in one direction. As the cheesecloth picks up the glaze, you'll be able to control the final effect you wish to achieve. The antique look takes hold as surface imperfections and finely detailed carved areas pick up the glaze. Highlights can be emphasized by applying more pressure as you wipe the surface. Important: if you change to a clean pad of cheesecloth, be prepared for additional toner to be removed. When you're satisfied with the final effect, it is very important not to disturb the glaze finish until it's thoroughly dry. Sometimes this can take a week or more, depending on temperature and humidity.

Before handling the animal, test the underside to be sure the glaze is dry. A final protective coat of varnish or polyurethene may now be applied; however, this is not a necessary step if there will be no wear and tear on the figure. New jewels can now be set with a clear silicone caulking compound.

Staining

Stain is best used on an animal that is free of fill and in excellent condition. Every bit of paint must be removed from the figure, and a smoothly sanded surface is essential in achieving the right effect. The stain you select should be applied over the entire animal. Old wood usually absorbs stain thoroughly; but, if any excess remains, wipe it away immediately. After the stain has thoroughly dried, rub fine steel wool over the body of the animal with extra pressure applied to areas of the body that you wish to highlight. After brushing or blowing away dust particles, the trappings should be carefully coated with a satin finish paint in the colors you have selected. It is important to avoid any overlap onto the stained body and to remember that the colors you choose must be of a brighter intensity than the finished look you desire. After the paint has thoroughly dried, a coat of stain is applied to the trappings, wiping with a pad of cheesecloth after every few brush strokes. After the stain is completely dry, a final coat of flat or satin varnish (or polyurethene) must be applied to the entire figure to bring out the beauty of the stained wood.

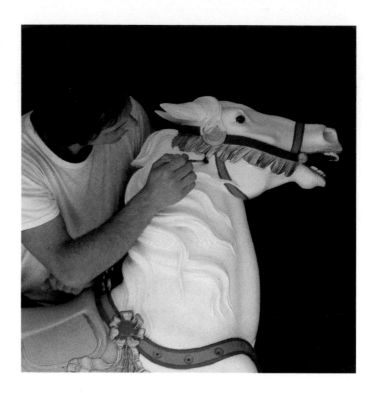

Artist Bill Carlone puts the finishing touches on a Muller jumper he has prepared for glazing.

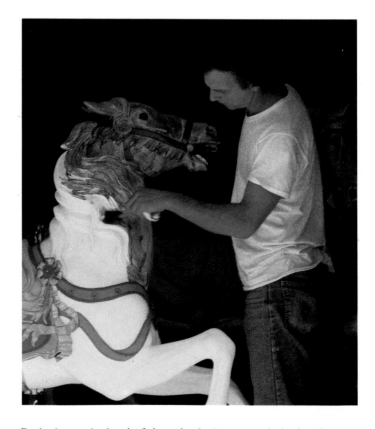

Beginning at the head of the animal, the runny, dark glaze is applied to a thoroughly dry surface.

As the glaze is wiped with a wad of cheesecloth, the detailed features of the horse emerge.

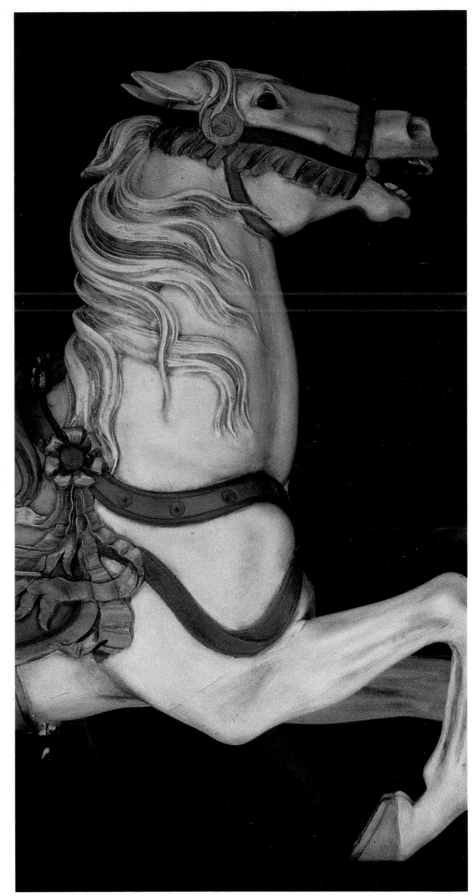

By wiping in places where highlights should be emphasized and leaving more glaze in depressed areas, such as the mane, the figure seems to come alive.

The Dentzel deer, restored by Bill Carlone, and the Dentzel ostrich, restored by Nina Fraley, were both finished in an antique glaze. Notice how the glaze emphasizes the detailed carvings of the fur and feathers. *From the author's collection.*

Paint and stain restoration by Charles Bennett. Dentzel stander is stained except for the mane and trappings, which are painted and then stained. *From the author's collection*

A Muller Indian Pony restored by Charles Bennett with stain applied over painted trappings. Notice how the stain glaze reveals the "tooled leather" bridle and breast strap. *From the author's collection*

Display Stands

There are a number of ways to display a carousel animal. Some figures are mounted on a floor-to-ceiling pipe held by floor flanges, often covered with a turned brass sleeve. Others are mounted on stationary fiberglass or metal bases (available through carousel dealers) which are fine if the animal is to stay in one place. For ease of portability a one-inch piece of plywood mounted on rubber ball coasters works very well. Floor flanges and black pipe threaded on one end can be purchased at plumbing supply stores, and the most satisfactory sizes seem to be ½" pipe and flange for standing figures, and 1¼" pipe and flange for jumpers. This size allows room for a brass sleeve to slide over the pipe if desired. Some collectors use industrial collars with an Allen fitting to hold the animal up on the pole, while others drill a hole through the pole and rest the figure on a half-inch stove bolt or a large industrial cotter pin.

A one inch piece of plywood, 24" wide by 66" long, provides a sturdy stand for this large horse. A 1¼" pipe is screwed into floor flanges that are fastened to the body of the horse and the stand. For ease of movement, six rubber ball casters are attached to the plywood base.

Shipping

If you can't use a truck, van or trailer to transport a carousel figure, a station wagon works well. Most of the largest animals can be carried on top of a mattress tied to a station wagon roof rack. It's important to tie the animal with smooth rope to avoid scratching the wood or painted finish. The figure must be securely tied to all four corners of the roof rack.

If an animal is being shipped to you by common carrier (also listed as motor freight), it must be shipped in a closed crate. The best crates are made using a frame of nailed 2 x 4's, enclosed with sheets of masonite or plywood. Animals must be secured from any movement with well-padded wooden braces secured in front and back, as well as above and below the figure.

Insurance

When you buy a carousel figure, immediately insure it through a fine-arts floater on your homeowners policy. Be sure the policy stipulates that the animal is always covered during shipment and while off your premises.

Illions Factory Paint Procedure

A mixture of white lead, turpentine and boiled oil was used as a prime coat. After the prime was completely

A frame of two by fours and a plywood floor make a sturdy crate. The horse is firmly held by padded supports above and below the body. The crate is ready to be enclosed using sheets of masonite or plywood.

Barney Illions (son of M.C. Illions and painter for many years in Illions' shop) proudly displays his recent restoration of an animated Illions' jumper. Note the gold leaf mane and tail. *From the Cole Collection*

dry, two coats of flat white were applied with additional sanding and filling between each dried coat. The body of the animal was then covered with one coat of a very flat thick Japan paint using white and blends of natural horse colors. A stipple brush blended body colors into a realistic Dapple, Pinto, Palamino, Chestnut, etc.

Subtle blends of pinks or white mixed with raw umber were used to highlight muscles, veins, nostrils, ears, etc. Hoofs were black or white blended with raw umber; and manes, with rare exception, were finished in gold leaf. Rich blended colors were used on the trappings and trim was in aluminum leaf. The mane and trim received a coat of white shellac and then a coat of sizing before the leaf was applied. After the leaf was set, the trim was coated with a thin transparent colored glaze which was applied and blended with small pieces of cotton. English vermillion was used to pinstripe, and two or three coats of spar varnish were applied overall as a final step.

Chapter 15

Operating Carousels in North America

The following is a list of handcrafted operating carousels in the United States and Canada. Some carousels are *pure* machines (unchanged through the years) while others are altered and consist of a mixture of figures by various carvers. Carousels are often relocated and some operate only at fair times, others just on weekends. Check before visiting!

ARIZONA

Tucson, Old Tucson, Spillman

ARKANSAS

Jonesboro, Midway of Mirth, Parker, circa 1925-1927

Judsonia, Lloyd Choate Carnival, Spillman

Little Rock, War Memorial Park, Spillman

CALIFORNIA

Anaheim, Disneyland, Dentzel-Looff-Stein and Goldstein-Carmel

Berkeley, Tilden Park, Herschell-Spillman, circa 1912

Buena Park, Knott's Berry Farm, Dentzel, circa 1907, Dentzel, circa 1902

Castro Valley, Stein and Goldstein-Allan Herschell

Lodi, Micke Grove Park, Allan Herschell, circa 1920

Los Angeles, Griffith Park, Spillman-Looff, circa 1926

Monterey, Capone's Warehouse-Edgewater Packing Co., Herschell-Spillman, circa 1915

Newport Beach, The Fun Zone, Allan Herschell, circa 1928

Riverside, Castle Park, Philadelphia Toboggan Company #31, 1915

San Diego, Seaport Village, Mangels-Looff, circa 1900

San Diego, Balboa Park, Herschell-Spillman, circa 1910

San Francisco, Fleischaker Zoo, Dentzel-Illions, circa 1921-1922

San Francisco, Golden Gate Park, Herschell-Spillman, circa 1914

Santa Clara, Marriott's Great America, Philadelphia Toboggan Company #45, 1918

Santa Cruz, Santa Cruz Beach, Looff, circa 1912

Santa Monica, Santa Monica Pier, Philadelphia Toboggan Company #62, 1922

Valencia, Six Flags' Magic Mountain, Philadelphia Toboggan Company #21, 1912

COLORADO

Burlington, County Fair Grounds, Philadelphia Toboggan Company #6, 1905

Colorado Springs, Cheyenne Mountain Zoo, Allan Herschell

Denver, Elitch's Gardens, Philadelphia Toboggan Company #51, 1920-1928

Denver, Lakeside Park, Parker, circa 1908

Pueblo, Parker-Stein and Goldstein

CONNECTICUT

Bridgeport, Pleasure Beach, Carmel-Dentzel

Bristol, Lake Compounce, Carmel-Looff-Stein and Goldstein

Hartford, Bushnell Memorial Park, Stein and Goldstein, circa 1914

Middlebury, Lake Quassapaug, Philadelphia Toboggan Company circa 1904

New Haven, Lighthouse Point Park, Carmel-Looff

DISTRICT OF COLUMBIA

Mall, Jim Wells, Herschell-Spillman-Spillman

National Cathedral, Dare, circa 1892

Smithsonian Institution, figures on display and Herschell-Spillman on Mall

FLORIDA

Daytona Beach, Forest Park, Allan Herschell-Carmel

Jacksonville Beach, Griffen's Amusement Park, Herschell-Spillman

Orlando, Barnum City Circus World, Illions

Orlando, Disneyworld, Philadelphia Toboggan Company #46, 1918

Orlando, James Strates Shows, Philadelphia Toboggan Company #28, 1914

Panama City, Long Beach Resort, Philadelphia Toboggan Company, #59, 1922

Panama City, Miracle Strip, Spillman

Sarasota, Ringling Bros. and Barnum and Bailey Circus World, Illions, circa 1920

Tampa, Royal American Shows, Philadelphia Toboggan Company #26, 1913, Philadelphia Toboggan Company #34, 1915

GEORGIA

Atlanta, Six Flags over Georgia, Philadelphia Toboggan Company #17 1908

Rossville, Lake Winnepesaukah, Philadelphia Toboggan Company #39, 1916

ILLINOIS

Aurora, Pioneer Park, Herschell-Spillman, circa 1901

Gurnee, Mariott's Great America, Dentzel, circa 1920's

Lyons, Fairyland Amusement Park, Mixture, circa 1920

Melrose, Kiddieland, Philadelphia Toboggan Company #72, 1925

INDIANA

Indianapolis, Children's Museum, Dentzel, circa 1917

Logansport, Riverside Park, Dentzel, circa 1902

Schereville, Sauzer's Kiddieland Amusement Park, Illions-Mangels

IOWA

Mt. Pleasant, Old Thrashers, Herschell-Spillman

Story City, Story City Greater Community Congress, Herschell-Spillman, 1913

KANSAS

Abilene, Dickinson County Historical Society, Parker

Hutchinson, Clown Town Kiddieland, Parker

Leavenworth, Agricultural Hall of Fame, Allan Herschell-Herschell-Spillman

Wichita, Joyland, Allan Herschell, circa 1908

LOUISIANA

New Orleans, City Park, Carmel-Mixture

MAINE

Old Orchard Beach, Palace Playland, Philadelphia Toboggan Company #19, 1910

MARYLAND

Bethesda, Bethesda Square, Herschell-Spillman, circa 1915

Glen Echo, Glen Echo Park, Dentzel, circa 1922

Largo, Watkins Regional Park, Dentzel-Muller, circa 1905

Ocean City, Playland Amusement Park, Herchell

Ocean City, Trimpers Rides and Amusements, Herschell-Spillman

MASSACHUSETTS

Agawam, Riverside Park, Illions-Mangels

Belchertown, Belchertown State School, Stein and Goldstein, circa 1912

Holyoke, Mountain Park, Philadelphia Toboggan Company #80, 1929

Hull, Paragon Park, Philadelphia Toboggan Company #85, 1928

Lunenberg, Whalom Park, Looff-Mixture

Martha's Vineyard, Oak Bluffs, C.W.F. Dare, pre 1884

North Dartmouth, Lincoln Park, Philadelphia Toboggan Company #54, 1920

Sandwich, Heritage Plantation, Looff-Parker

MICHIGAN

East Lansing, Michigan State University Museum, Herschell-Spillman, circa 1910

Dearborn, Greenfield Village, Herschell-Spillman, menagerie

MINNESOTA

Bloomington, Shakopee Valley Park, Philadelphia Toboggan Company #76, 1925

St. Paul, Fair Grounds, Philadelphia Toboggan Company #33, 1914

MISSISSIPPI

Meridian, Highland Park, Dentzel, circa 1894-1909

Tupelo, City Park, Allan Herschell

MISSOURI

Eureka, Six Flags over Mid America, Philadelphia Toboggan Company #35, 1935

St. Louis, Sylvan Spring Park, Dentzel

NEBRASKA

Minden, Harold Warp Pioneer Village, Herschell-Spillman

NEVADA

Henderson, Westworld, Savage Gallopers, 1889

Incline Village, Ponderosa Ranch, Herschell-Spillman-Mixture

NEW HAMPSHIRE

Glen, Storyland, German, circa 1900

Lincoln, Natureland's Fantasy Farm, Spillman

Salem, Canobie Lake Park, Stein and Goldstein-Dentzel, circa 1903

NEW JERSEY

Asbury Park, Casino, Philadelphia Toboggan Company #87 1932

Asbury Park, Palace Amusements, Stein and Goldstein-Illions-Mangels-Dentzel, circa 1910

Clementon, Clementon Lake Park, Philadelphia Toboggan Company #49, 1919

Keansburg, R.A.B. Amusements, Mangels-Looff, circa 1914

Ocean City, Gillians' Fun Deck, Spillman, circa 1925

Ocean City, Wonderland Pier, Philadelphia Toboggan Company #75, 1926

Point Pleasant Beach, Dentzel, circa 1909

Prospertown, Six Flags Great Adventure, English, circa 1890

Seaside Heights, Casino Pier & Pool, Dentzel-Looff

Seaside Heights, Freeman's Amusement Center, Illions-Carmel-Borelli, circa 1916

Seaside Heights, Funtown USA, Illions

Wildwood, Sportland Pier, Stein and Goldstein

NEW MEXICO

Carlsbad, President's Park, Dentzel, circa 1903

Roswell, Spring River Park, Spillman-Mixture

NEW YORK

Albany, New York State Museum, Herschell-Spillman, circa 1915

Baldwin, Nunley's Carousel, Stein and Goldstein

Binghamton, George Johnson Recreational Park, Allan Herschell

Binghamton, Ross Park Zoo, Allan Herschell

Brooklyn, Coney Island, B & B Carousel, Carmel

Brooklyn, Coney Island, Steeplechase Park, Herschell-Spillman

Brooklyn, Prospect Park, Mangels-Carmel

Canandaigua, Roseland Park, Philadelphia Toboggan Company #18, 1909

Charlotte, Ontario Beach Park, Dentzel, circa 1905

Elmira, Eldridge Park, Carmel-Looff

Lake George, Gaslight Village, Parker

Lake George, Storytown USA, Dentzel

Lake George, Charlie Woods, Looff, circa 1895

New York City, Central Park, Stein and Goldstein, circa 1908

Olcott, New Rialto Park, Allan Herschell, circa 1915

Owego, Skyline Park, Spillman

Pine Lake, Lords Amusement Park, Parker #91

Queens, Flushing Meadows, Corona Park, Mangels-Illions, circa 1903-1908

Queens, Forest Park, Dentzel-Muller, circa 1910

Rochester, Sea Breeze Park, Philadelphia Toboggan Company #36, 1915

Rye, Playland, Mangels-Carmel

Schenevus, Schenevus & Maryland Fire Co., Herschell-Spillman track machine #409 circa 1909

Syosset, Nassau County Museum, Primitive, circa 1860

Tonawanda, Dealings Amusement Land, Spillman, circa 1915-1920

Verona, Joel's Steak House, Allan Herschell

Westbury, (East Meadow), Eisenhower Park, Herschell-Spillman, circa 1914

NORTH CAROLINA

Burlington, City Park, Dentzel

Carolina Beach, Seaside Park, Herschell-Spillman

Charlotte, Carrowinds, Philadelphia Toboggan Company #67, 1923

Raleigh, Chavis Park, Allan Herschell, circa 1925

Raleigh, Pullen Park, Dentzel, circa 1911-1912

Rocky Mount, City Park, Herschell

OHIO

Aurora, Geauga Lake Park, Illions

Bascom, Meadowbrook Park, Spillman

Chippewa Lake, Chippewa Lake Park, Herschell, circa 1921

Greenville, Jimmie Chance Shows (carnival), Spillman

Kings Mill, Kings Island, Philadelphia Toboggan Company #79, 1926

Lancaster, Pugh Amusements, Hubner (German)

Middletown, Fantasy Farm, Allan Herschell-Mixture

Middletown, Americana Great American Amusement Park, Philadelphia Toboggan Company #71, 1925-1927

New Philadelphia, Tuscora Park, Herschell-Spillman

Powell, Gooding Zoo Park, Illions-Mangels, circa 1914

Put-In-Bay, Frosty Bar, Spillman, circa 1917

Sandusky, Cedar Point, D.C. Muller & Bros., circa 1912, Dentzel, circa 1920, Dentzel, circa 1921

Youngstown, Idora Park, Philadelphia Toboggan Company #61, 1922

OKLAHOMA

Spring Lake, Parker

OREGON

Portland, Jantzen Beach Shopping Center, Parker, circa 1921

Portland, Oaks Amusement Park, Herschell-Spillman, circa 1907

Portland, Washington Park Forestry Building, Illions-Carmel

PENNSYLVANIA

Allentown, Dorney Park, Dentzel, Philadelphia Toboggan Company #38, 1916

Conneaut Lake, Conneaut Lake Park, D.C. Muller, circa 1905

Easton, Bushkill Park, Mixture, circa 1903

Elysburg, Knoebel's Grove, Carmel, circa 1910, Stein and Goldstein

Gettysburg, Fantasyland Storybook Gardens, Spillman

Harvey's Lake, Hanson's Park, Looff-Stein and Goldstein-Carmel, circa 1909

Hershey, Hershey Park, Philadelphia Toboggan Company #47, 1919

Honesdale, Hillside Park, Herschell-Spillman, circa pre-1922

Ligonier, Idlewild Park, Philadelphia Toboggan Company #183, 1930

Tipton, Bland Park, Spillman

West Mifflin, Kennywood Park, Dentzel, circa 1926

RHODE ISLAND

Misquamicut, Atlantic Beach Casino, Illions

Pawtucket, Slater Rock, Looff

Riverside, Crescent Park, Looff, circa 1895-1905

Warwick, Rocky Point Park, Herschell-Spillman

Watch Hill, Watch Hill Beach, Dare *Flying Horses,* circa 1884

West Greenwich, Lake Mishnock, Looff-Allan Herschell-Stein & Goldstein-Mixture

SOUTH CAROLINA

Myrtle Beach, Grand Stand Amusement Park, Carmel

N. Myrtle Beach, N. Myrtle Beach Amusement Park, Herschell, original paint on scenery

SOUTH DAKOTA

Madison, Prairie Village, Armitage Herschell, circa 1893

Sioux Falls, Joyland Children's Amusement Park, Parker, circa 1917

TENNESSEE

Memphis, Libertyland Amusement Park, Dentzel, circa 1923

TEXAS

Abilene, Nelson Park, Parker

Amarillo, Joyland Park, Parker

Arlington, Six Flags over Texas, Dentzel

Brenham, Fireman's Park, Herschell-Spillman, circa 1910-1914

Dallas, State Fair Park, Dentzel

Fort Worth, Forest Park, Carmel-Parker

Houston, Astroworld, Borelli-Carmel, Dentzel, Philadelphia Toboggan Company #77

Lubbock, MacKenzie Park Playground, Parker

San Angelo, Neff's Amusement Park, Parker

San Antonio, Kiddie Park, Allan Herschell, circa 1920

San Antonio, Playland Park, Parker, circa 1917

UTAH

American Fork, Utah State Training School, Looff, circa 1906-1911

Lehi, Saratoga Springs, Saratoga Fun Park, Parker

Ogden, Lorin Farr Park, Parker-Allan Herschell

Salt Lake City, Lagoon Amusement Park, Herschell-Spillman

VERMONT

Putney, Santa's Land, German, circa 1900

Shelburne, Shelburne Museum, Dentzel, figures on display, circa 1896

VIRGINIA

Buckroe Beach, Buckroe Beach Amusement Park, Philadelphia Toboggan Company #50, 1920

Hampton, Bayshore Park, Parker

Richmond, Kings Dominion, Philadelphia Toboggan Company #44, 1917

Virginia Beach, Seaside Park, Spillman

Williamsburg, Busch Gardens, The Old Country, Allan Herschell, circa 1919

WASHINGTON

Bickleton, City Park, Parker

Long Beach, Double Rides, Herschell-Spillman, circa 1928

Puyallup, Western Washington Fair, Philadelphia Toboggan Company

Seattle, Fun Forest Park, Borelli-Looff-Illions

Spokane, Expo Grounds, Looff, brass ring

Tacoma, Point Defiance Park, Parker, circa 1906

WEST VIRGINIA

Huntington, Camden Park, Spillman

WISCONSIN

Baraboo, Circus World Museum, Allan Herschell, circa 1930

Madison, Vilas Park (zoo), Herschell-Spillman

Waterloo, Fireman's Park, Parker

Wautoma, Christman Amusements, Parker, circa 1911

Wisconsin Dells, Storybook Gardens, Herschell

CANADA

Alberta, Calgary, Pioneer Park, Herschell-Spillman, circa 1904

British Columbia, Vancouver, Playland Park, Parker

Canadian Northland Shows (carnival), Herschell-Spillman, circa 1911

Ontario, Amherstburg, Bob-lo Island, Illions-Mangels, circa 1906-1908

Ontario, Crystal Beach Amusement Park, Philadelphia Toboggan Company #12, 1906

Ontario, Grand Bend, Herschell-Spillman

Ontario, Niagara Falls, Skylon Tower, Philadelphia Toboggan Company, circa 1900

Ontario, Niagara Falls, Maple Leaf Village, Allan Herschell

Ontario, St. Catherine, City Park, Looff, circa 1903

Ontario, Toronto, Centerville, Dentzel, circa 1920

Quebec, Montreal, Expo, La Ronde Park, Belgian, circa 1870

Saskatchewan, Saskatoon, Western Development Museum, Herschell-Spillman

Carousels with Fiberglass Animals

CALIFORNIA

Santa Clara, Marriotts Great America, circa 1976, double decker

ILLINOIS

Gurnee, Marriotts Great America, circa 1976, double decker

WISCONSIN

Spring Green, House on the Rock Museum, wooden and unique fiberglass carousel animals on the world's largest seven abreast machine created by Alex Jordan.

Identifiable Features of Carousel Animals

HERSCHELL-SPILLMAN CAROUSEL CARVINGS

ARMITAGE HERSCHELL COMPANY

Menagerie Animals

Camel, elephant.

Horses circa 1884—1899

Rigid poses; upright ears; parallel legs; mortise joints at rear legs; simple trappings; occasional jewels; hair tails; carved horseshoes; protruding rigid manes; perky expressions; carved wood or glass eyes; flat saddles.

HERSCHELL-SPILLMAN COMPANY

Menagerie Animals

Camel, cat, chicken, deer, dog, frog, giraffe, goat, kangaroo, lion, mule, ostrich, pig, rooster, stork, tiger, zebra.

Traveling Style Horses circa 1903—1920

Same as Armitage Herschell except for softer expressions; short flowing manes; carved and glass eyes; long flat saddles.

Park Style Horses circa 1910—1920

Pretty heads; alert expressions; noses swooped up; pointed rumps; little vein or muscle delineations; hair tails; animated poses; carved and glass eyes; elaborate ornamentations; jewels; intricate flowing manes; small hoofs.

SPILLMAN ENGINEERING COMPANY

Menagerie Animals

Camel, cat, chicken, deer, dog, frog, giraffe, goat, kangaroo, lion, mule, ostrich, pig, rooster, stork, tiger, zebra.

Horses circa 1920—1945

Long heads; small high set eyes; pointed rumps; full wavy manes; intricate ornamentations; high cantles; high pommels; large nostrils; jewels; figures in relief e.g. angels, lions, flowers; animated poses; hair tails.

ALLAN HERSCHELL COMPANY

Menagerie Animals

Camel, deer, elephant, giraffe, lion, polar bear, tiger.

Horses circa 1915—1955

Poor proportions; short legs drawn tight to bodies; oversized heads; round dish saddles; long Romanesque noses; small high set eyes; short manes; short necks; large mouths; slight muscle delineations; unpleasant expressions; carved and glass eyes; simple trappings; short flowing or thick roached manes; carved tails.
  1930—1950 horse's bodies were wooden, legs and tails were aluminum.
  1950—1955 all aluminum horse.

DENTZEL CAROUSEL CARVINGS

Menagerie Animals

Bear, cat, deer, dog, donkey, giraffe, goat, hippocampus, kangaroo, lion, ostrich, pig, rabbit, rooster.

Horses circa 1867—1900

Proud stately heads; long noses; large nostrils; very long curving manes; flipped forelocks; fine proportions; erect regal poses; barrel chests; large glass eyes; large prominent teeth; simple trappings; short saddles; low pommels; high curved cantles; hair tails; detailed muscles; carved horseshoes; no set-in jewels; occasional jewels fastened with brass escutcheons; alert forward ears.

Horses circa 1900—1928

Understated elegance; pretty sweet faces; graceful poses; slim legs; realistic proportions; intricate flowing or cropped manes; eagles' heads with glass eyes often carved at the back of saddles; elaborate wood tails doweled to legs; fancier trappings of clowns, Indians, flags, cherubs; low pommels; high and low cantles; no jewels; carved horseshoes; fine muscle delineations.

Horses added in the twenties were more aggressive and boldly posed—manes were tossed, eyes more wild.

LOOFF CAROUSEL CARVINGS

Menagerie Animals

Buffalo, camel, deer, dog, donkey, dragon, elephant, giraffe, goat, lion, panther, stork, teddy bear, zebra.

Horses circa 1876—1890

Perky faces; often pug noses; short necks; long slim legs; full intricate manes; gentle smiling faces; forelocks; plaid blankets; plaster rosettes holding round etched starburst beveled mirrors; jewels; tassels; long low saddles; glass eyes; long bodies; hair tails; detailed muscles; carved horseshoes; cantles sometimes in shape of bird's head.

Horses circa 1891—1918

Pretty heads; arched wooden or hair tails; full flowing intricate or thick roached manes; exciting animated exaggerated poses; flaring nostrils; large prominent teeth; lavish decorations; intricate trappings in relief e.g. cherubs, rabbits, birds, flowers, guns; long saddles; high cantles; flat pommels; jewels, heavy round cheek bones; large prominent muscles; carved horseshoes; glass eyes; some peekaboo manes; some with pouting closed mouths.

PARKER CAROUSEL CARVINGS

Menagerie Animals

Supplied by factory, origin unknown. Small primitive: bear, buffalo, camel, elephant, giraffe, goat, lion, rabbit, zebra.

Horses—Abilene circa 1895—1911

All jumpers; small horses are copies of Armitage Herschell figures; perky expressions; rigid static protruding manes; large nostrils; parallel legs; simple trappings; wide breast collars; forward upright ears; long saddles; flat pommels; high cantles.

Large, ornately jeweled jumpers (similar to Coney Island style horses) added around 1900 with cabuchon and faceted jewels; lovely flowing intricate manes; varied leg positions; pretty faces; ornate trappings; hair tails; good proportions; alert eyes; slight muscle delineations.

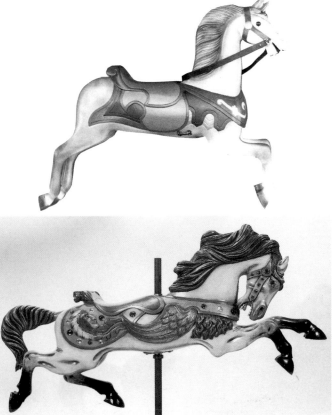

Horses—Leavenworth circa 1911—1932

Stretched out running positions; legs close to bodies; stylized manes; long narrow heads; parted forelocks; metal horseshoes embossed C.W. Parker; aggressive expressions; fancy trappings; cabuchon and faceted jewels; long saddles; flat pommels; high cantles; small hoofs; figures in relief e.g. flowers, ears of corn, fish, flags, six-shooters; short carved tails with high arch and parallel ridges; legs often parallel; flat rounded nostrils; tails doweled to legs; crude construction.

MULLER CAROUSEL CARVINGS

Menagerie Animals

Camel, deer, donkey, giraffe, goat, lion, sea horses, tiger, zebra.

Horses circa 1902—1917

Muller trademark-rippled ribbon and knot or bow; realistic; very animated; fine crisp detailed trappings; standing figures often have military motif; expressive glass eyes set in varied positions; carved eyelids; elevated tongue tips; good proportions; detailed bridles and bits; fine buckles and straps; some twitching ears; prominent neck muscles; hair tails; no jewels; heads sometimes turned in; slim legs; intricate manes; forelocks; curved saddle; some with metal horseshoes.

Horses circa 1912—1917

Large jumpers—stretched out bodies; rear legs at sharp angles; thin bony legs; wild layered manes; intricate straps; jewels.

PHILADELPHIA TOBOGGAN COMPANY CAROUSEL CARVINGS

Menagerie Animals

Burro, deer, dog, giraffe, goat, hippocampus, leopard, lion, sea monster, tiger, wolf.

Horses circa 1899—1906

Pretty, sensitive faces; large bodies; short necks; large nostrils; varied animated poses; short full manes; finely detailed figures in relief; e.g., cherubs, devils, wolves; large glass eyes; sensitive expressions; no jewels; hair and wood tails; curved saddles; low pommels; high cantles.

Horses circa 1906—1912

Overall odd look; long heads; high set eyes; large lumpy bodies; standers—very long skinny legs; roses in relief on lead horses; jumpers—short legs close to bodies; poor proportions; usually plain trappings; no jewels; awkward poses.

Horses circa 1912—1918

Attractive faces; strong somewhat boxy bodies; prominent muscles; active poses; expressive eyes; curved saddles; low pommels; high cantles; full intricate manes; occasional jewels; fancy trappings; carved tails; large hoofs; powerful feelings, well constructed.

Horses circa 1919—1932

Pretty faces; fine proportions; large powerful bodies; sensitive expressions; doleful eyes; heavy muscles.

ILLIONS CAROUSEL CARVINGS

Menagerie Animals

Camel, deer, giraffe, goat, hippocampus, lion, tiger.

Horses circa 1892—1909

Pretty faces; small deep set glass eyes; proud strong poses; lovely intricate flowing manes; thin heads; long noses; long rounded bodies; long saddles; high pommels; high cantles; strong muscles; elaborate trappings; many jewels; scrollwork; hair tails; tongues sometimes out; long ears.

Horses circa 1905—1920

Very animated; aggressive; sometimes nasty looking; varied manes sometimes skimpy; large high set protruding glass eyes; some with frightened expressions; rounded long bodies; some quite unattractive with short heads and underslung jaws; fancy trappings; many jewels; exaggerated poses; inner row horses quite plain.

Horses circa 1920—1927

Pretty faces; good proportions; wild exciting full manes; great animation; pretty wooden tails; jumpers have straight rumps from tail to knee; windswept manes (forward flow); jewels; lattice work trappings; figures in relief e.g. cherubs, eagles, lions; graceful poses; large glass eyes.

CARMEL CAROUSEL CARVINGS

Menagerie Animals

Camel, dragon, goat, lion.

Horses circa 1900—1905

Large heads; very full billowing manes; large nostrils; swoop noses; small eyes; small saddles (usually upholstered in mohair); stiff poses; short legs; hair tails; large teeth; simple trappings; some with jewels.

Horses circa 1905—1925

Sweet beautiful faces; squarish cheek bones; good proportions; animated dramatic poses; tongues often out; intricate full-flowing manes; short saddles; high pommels; high cantles; figures in relief; trappings include fish scales, feathers, heavy armour; trappings sometimes squarish; hair tails; small expressive deep-set glass eyes; long flowing forelocks; layered trappings; jewels (sometimes over 300 on Borelli animals); narrow carved hoofs; arched necks; some bat-wing saddles.

STEIN AND GOLDSTEIN CAROUSEL CARVINGS

Menagerie Animals

None.

Horses circa 1907—1918

Huge outside standers; aggressive nasty expressions; exaggerated poses; large prominent straps and buckles; eyes set at slant and high; large nostrils; some tossed manes; large prominent teeth; fancy trappings e.g. fish scale, feathers, tassels, roses, heavy elaborate armour; long curved saddles set far back; high pommels; high cantles; no jewels; hair tails; cropped or most often "C" curved manes usually stringy and flat to bodies; no forelocks; long bodies; hoofs bent back; jumpers have short legs.

Carousel Terminology

Pronunciation of carvers' names:

Carmel	Car´mêl´	**Looff**	Lōoff
Cernigliaro	Chêr´nig li ar o	**Stein and Goldstein**	Stīn and Gold´stīn´
Dentzel	Den´sûl	**Zalar**	Zâ´lar
Illions	Ill´ē ûns		

Abreast   Rows of animals arranged side by side on a carousel; e.g., 1, 2, 3, 4 or 5 abreast carousel.

All Jumping Machine   All animals move up and down, no stationary figures.

Band Organ   Musical instrument accompanying carousel—loud rhythmic sounds; e.g., drums, cymbals, often incorrectly called calliope.

Band Organ Figures   Decorative carved figures of people on band organ facade which often move or *play* instruments or *lead* in time to music.

Baroque   Style of art characterized by much ornamentation and curved rather than straight lines.

Bedroll   Blanket rolled under rear of saddle—often used as decoration on carousel horses.

Brass Ring   Mechanism with arm that dispenses silver rings and an occasional brass ring which allows the rider who *catches* it a free ride.

Brass Sleeve   Decorative pole cover either smooth or turned, lending a roped effect.

Cabochon Jewel   Stone cut in convex shape—polished but not faceted; often found on Parker horses.

Carousel   Carroussel, caroussel, carousell, carrousele, carroussel, merry-go-round, flying horses, carry-us-all, gallopers, roundabout, flying or spinning jenny, steam riding gallery, hobby horses, whirligig, steam circus.

Centerpole   Wood or metal center support of the carousel.

Chariots   Stationary benches between painted or carved facades for the more timid riders.

Dry Rot   An invasive deterioration of wood due to excessive dampness.

Factory Paint   The finish on carousel figures sent back to the maker for repainting.

Fiberglass or Aluminum Figure   Reproductions made from molds of carved animals.

Flying Horses   Horses hung by rods or chains that swung out as the carousel revolved.

Gallopers   English name for jumping horses.

Hippocampus   Figure with the head of a horse and the tail of a fish.

Inner Rows   Rows of animals other than the outside row graduating in size from largest on outside row to smallest on row closest to the centerpole.

Jumper   Horse that goes up and down with no feet touching the platform.

King Horse   Large, fancy horse often heavily laden with armour.

Lead Horse   Large, most elaborately decorated horse on the carousel.

Menagerie Figure   Any carousel animal other than a horse.

Mixed Carousel   Machine with animals on board carved by two or more carving shops.

Monogrammed Figure   On special order, some companies carved or painted initials of customer on trappings.

Muller-Dentzel   Two carvers' names used to describe animal carved by Muller while he was employed by Dentzel.

Original Paint   The finish on an animal when it first came from the factory.

Outside Row   Row of animals closest to viewers—usually the most elaborately decorated carousel figures.

Park Carousel   A nonportable carousel that was designed for permanent installation.

Park Paint   Paint applied to animals while carousel was in operation, often over many other layers of paint.

Peek-A-Boo Mane   Elaborate manes with openings cut to the other side.

Period Paint   Old paint but not factory finish.

Pin Striping   A fine line of paint applied as a decoration on the trappings of a carousel figure.

Portable Carousel   A traveling carousel that could be dismantled and erected in a few hours.

Prancer   Stationary horse with rear feet on platform, front legs raised.

Primitive Figure   Early, simply carved animal.

PTC   Shortened version of Philadelphia Toboggan Company.

Pure Carousel   Figures on board were carved by the company that produced the carousel.

Rein Ring   Round metal ring fastened to horse at either side of mouth for attaching reins.

Relief Carvings   The projection of figures and forms from a flat surface.

Restored Carousel Animal   One that has been stripped, repaired and repainted.

Roached or Cropped Mane   Short, cut mane.

Rococo   Style of decoration developed from the baroque characterized by profuse ornamentation imitating foliage, rockwork, shellwork, scrolls, etc., often done with delicacy and refinement.

Romance Side   The fancier side of a carousel figure - side facing outside.

Rounding Board or Rim   Long narrow carved or painted decorated board on upper outer facade of the carousel.

Saddle Blanket   Folded fabric carved under the saddle.

S & G   Shortened version of Stein and Goldstein.

Scenery or Carved Panels   Boards decorated by carvings, paintings or mirrors on the centerpole housing.

Shields   Decorative carved mirrored or painted plaques covering place where rounding boards meet.

Signature or Signed Figure   Carousel animal with name or initials of carver or company carved into trappings.

Stander   Stationary horse with three or four feet on the platform.

Stationary Machine   Carousels with no moving animals.

Stripped Animal   Figure with paint completely removed to bare wood.

Track Machine   Early carousel with the platform set on wheels that ran on a circular track.

Trappings   Carved decorations on a carousel animal.

Tucked Head   Popular pose of carousel horse—head down, chin in, close to neck.

Bibliography

Braithwaite, David
Fairground Architecture
Hugh Evely, Limited, London, 1968

Braithwaite, David
Savage of King's Lynn
Patrick Stevens Limited, 1975

Carousel Art Magazine
Issue #6 (1979) #8, #10 (1980)
Marge Swenson, Garden Grove, California

Fraley, Nina
The American Carousel
Redbug Workshop, Berkeley, California, 1979

Fried, Frederick
A Pictorial History of the Carousel
A.S. Barnes & Co., Inc., New York 1964

Fried, Frederick
Daniel Carl Muller
National Carousel Association, Merry-Go-Roundup
Volume 5 Number 3, July 1978

Gianoli, Luigi
Horses & Horsemanship Through the Ages
Crown Publishers, Inc., New York, 1969

Gottkenker, Tina Cristiani
Carvers and Their Merry-Go-Rounds
Second Annual Conference Committee
National Carousel Roundtable, 1974

Huddleston, James
The Magic Merry-Go-Round
Pageant 1957

Kyriazi, Gary
The Great American Amusement Park
Castle Books, a division of Book Sales, Inc.
Secaucus, New Jersey, 1978

Mangels, William F.
The Outdoor Amusement Industry
Vantage Press, Inc., New York, 1952

McCullough, Edo.
Good Old Coney Island
Charles Scribner's Sons, New York, 1957

Smollar, David
Carousels: Joy Going 'Round
The Miami Herald, Miami, Florida, January 25, 1980

Summit, Roland
Flying Horses Catalogue #1, The Carousels of Coney Island
Rolling Hills, California, 1970

Williams, Barbara
John Zalar, The Master Carver
The Merry Go Round Up, National Carousel Association, Inc., 1979

Census of Operating Carousels
American Carousel Society Census
National Carousel Association Census

Index